United States Department of Agriculture

A Nursery Guide for the Production of Bareroot Hardwood Seedlings

Forest Service

Agriculture Handbook 733

November 2019

The use of trade or firm names in this publication is for reader information and does not imply endorsement by the U.S. Department of Agriculture, Forest Service of any product or service.

Pesticides used improperly can be injurious to humans, animals, and plants. Follow the directions and heed all precautions on the labels. Store pesticides in original containers under lock and key—out of the reach of children and animals—and away from food and feed. Apply pesticides so that they do not endanger humans, livestock, crops, beneficial insects, fish, and wildlife. Do not apply pesticides when there is danger of drift, when honey bees or other pollinating insects are visiting plants, or in ways that may contaminate water or leave illegal residues. Avoid prolonged inhalation of pesticide sprays or dusts; wear protective clothing and equipment if specified on the container. If your hands become contaminated with a pesticide, do not eat or drink until you have washed. In case a pesticide is swallowed or gets in the eyes, follow the first-aid treatment given on the label, and get prompt medical attention. If a pesticide is spilled on your skin or clothing, remove clothing immediately and wash skin thoroughly. Do not clean spray equipment or dump excess spray material near ponds, streams, or wells. Because it is difficult to remove all traces of herbicides from equipment, do not use the same equipment for insecticides or fungicides that you use for herbicides. Dispose of empty pesticide containers promptly. Have them buried at a sanitary landfill dump, or crush and bury them in a level, isolated place. NOTE: Some States have restrictions on the use of certain pesticides. Check your State and local regulations. Also, because registrations of pesticides are under constant review by the Federal Environmental Protection Agency, consult your county agricultural agent or State extension specialist to be sure the intended use is still registered.

Nomenclature for scientific names follows the U.S. Department of Agriculture, Natural Resources Conservation Service PLANTS (Plant List of Accepted Nomenclature, Taxonomy, and Symbols) database (2008). http://plants.usda.gov.

An Orchard Innovations Reprint Edition
November 2020

ISBN: 978-1-951682-49-1

Printed in the United States of America

Cover photo credit: Photo by ***Chase Weatherly.***

Back cover photo credits (left to right and bottom):
Greg Hoss, Doug Gillett, Randy Rentz, Ron Overton, and Greg Hoss.

A Nursery Guide for the Production of Bareroot Hardwood Seedlings

U.S. Department of Agriculture, Forest Service

Agriculture Handbook 733
November 2019

Editor

Ken McNabb

Coordinating Editor

Carolyn C. Pike

CONTENTS

CONTENTS (continued)

Oaks growing at the Wilson State Nursery in Wisconsin. (Photo by C. Pike, USDA Forest Service.)

About the Authors

Dan Bremer served as the district director of the U.S. Department of Labor, Wage and Hour Division, for 6 years in Atlanta, GA, and for 2 years in Little Rock, AR, and as an instructor at numerous compliance officer training classes. Since retirement from the Department of Labor, Bremer has been a consultant to many business entities who wish to bring workers to the United States on short-term visas. He has advised many business entities on issues of compliance with various State and Federal labor laws and maintenance of proper records and procedures. Bremmer has testified as an expert witness on numerous Fair Labor Standards Act lawsuits. He formed AgWorks 20 years ago to help farmers, foresters and other seasonal employers to find legal workers and to comply with complex labor laws. He served on the Lake Park, GA, City Council and served two terms as the chairman of the Lake Park Area Chamber of Commerce. He has a B.S. degree in Business Management from Missouri State University and attended the Masters of Public Administration Program at Florida International University in Miami, FL. He served in the United States Marine Corps in 1968, 1969, and 1970.

Robert E. Cross, Jr., recently retired from the forest industry after 43 years, and during that time helped produce 2.3 billion seedlings, bareroot and containerized, 40 million of which were hardwoods, representing over 80 different species. Upon retirement, he had reporting responsibility of the ArborGen bareroot nurseries. Earlier in his career, he managed two International Paper logging jobs and cruised and marked timber. He was a member of the Southern Nursery Association and sold horticultural plants to this industry for over 5 years. He has been involved with installing, collecting and compiling data on several white papers and research studies. Cross has made more than 200 presentations to customers and businesses on the importance of proper seedling production, handling and outplanting and the importance of genetic improvement. He also helped develop software that is used to determine seedling deployment by State and county using soil and temperature information.

Charles Bingham Davey (1928–2015). "Chuck" Davey was one of the most widely known and respected forest soil scientists in the United States. Raised in upstate New York, he received a forestry degree from the New York State College of Forestry in Syracuse, NY, and went on to receive M.S. and Ph.D. degrees in forest soils from the University of Wisconsin-Madison, Madison, WI. After brief employment in the U.S. Army and the USDA Experiment Station in Beltsville, MD, Davey joined the faculty at North Carolina State University in 1962 where he remained active for the rest of his life. His early research work in tree nutrition was instrumental in the creation of the NC State Forest Fertilization Cooperative, and his work with nurseries lead to the development of a Forest Nursery Management Program, which helped establish nurseries and train nursery managers. For decades, he provided nursery fertility recommendations and problem diagnosis services to nurseries in the United States and other countries. He produced more than 100 publications in national and international scientific journals and supervised or co-supervised more than 100 Ph.D. and 50 M.S. students. Winner of numerous recognitions and awards including the Barrington Moore Award for Biological Research from the Society of American Foresters, Davey is considered by many as one of the "founders of forest soil science in North America."

Scott Enebak is a professor of forest pathology, the director of the Southern Forest Nursery Management Cooperative in the School of Forestry and Wildlife Sciences at Auburn University, Auburn University, AL. Enebak has been a faculty member at Auburn University since 1995 and is responsible for undergraduate courses, forest biology at the Summer Practicum and forest health to graduating seniors. His areas of research expertise include the identification of soil fumigants—research conducted by the Southern Forest Nursery Management Cooperative at Auburn University. Other research interests include using biological and alternative disease control treatments for fungal diseases of nursery, forest, and landscape trees. His research projects have included the identification of a canker disease on hardwoods, a biological control treatment for chestnut blight, and the identification of resistance to hypoxylon canker in aspen. Enebak earned his B.S. in Silviculture from the University of Minnesota, St. Paul, MN, with the College of Forestry, his M.S. at University of Minnesota, Department of Plant Pathology, and his Ph.D. in Plant Pathology from West Virginia University, Morgantown, WV.

Richard Garrett graduated from Virginia Tech, Blacksburg, VA, with a B.S. in Forestry. He has worked in the nursery program for the Maryland Department of Natural Resources since 1984.

Bob Hawkins is the Nursery Section supervisor for Indiana's State Nursery program. Upon graduating from Purdue University with a Forestry degree, he joined forces with the Indiana Department of Natural Resources in 1987. He started at the nursery in the Tree Improvement section and later became the Nursery Section supervisor, where he has spent 30 years in nursery management. His work with Indiana's seedling program at the Vallonia State Nursery emphasizes growing fine-quality hardwoods. He is active in the Northeast Area Nurserymen Association and has held offices within the organization at various times over his career. Hawkins has hosted several joint Northeast/Southern Nurserymen conferences where nurserymen from across the country come together to discuss common nursery concerns and various nursery cultural practices. He has written several articles for Native Plants Journal and Tree Planters' Notes. He was an essential part in the development of Indiana's mechanical seeders used to sow their 50+ tree and shrub species.

Gregory A. Hoss, retired as Forest Nursery supervisor, George O. White State Forest Nursery. He graduated from the University of Missouri, School of Forestry, Columbia, MO, with a B.S. in Forest Management in May 1975. For about 18 months, he worked for the USDA Forest Service in Wyoming, and in 1977 began a 35-year career with the Missouri Department of Conservation, first as resource forester in Poplar Bluff for 11 years, then as an assistant district forester out of the Kansas City Forestry Office for 7 years. In 1995, he was transferred to the George O. White State Forest Nursery as assistant nursery superintendent and promoted to forest nursery supervisor in June 1997, a position he held for 15 years until his retirement in 2012. Hoss has written articles on trees, seed, and nursery management for the Native Plants Journal, Tree Planters' Notes and Missouri Conservationist magazines. He has been very active in the Society of American Foresters (SAF), serving on the board of directors and elected an SAF fellow in 2001. In retirement, he wrote a nursery manual for the Missouri Department of Conservation describing the management of the George O. White State Forest Nursery. He still keeps in touch with the nursery business, and on his farm, he maintains seed orchards and collects native tree and shrub seed for sale to nurseries and seed companies.

Robert P. Karrfalt, is an emeritus scientist, USDA Forest Service. He most recently served as the director of the USDA Forest Service National Seed Laboratory, a position he held from 1986 until retirement at the end of 2017. He was first hired as assistant director of the Eastern Tree Seed Lab in 1975 and served as manager for the international seed exchange program at the lab from 1980 until 1986, during which time the lab evolved into the National Tree Seed Laboratory. In 2005, the lab became the USDA Forest Service National Seed Laboratory and Karrfalt was charged with being the Forest Service strategic resource for seed science and technology with all native plants. During his 34+ years of assisting conservation workers with seed problems, he has worked in every region of the United States and numerous countries. He has authored dozens of technical articles, co-edited the recent revision of The Woody Plant Seed Manual, and presented more than 40 seed workshops at various domestic locations as well as in the Caribbean and in China. He represented the U.S. Government at the International Seed Testing Association and the Forest Reproductive Materials Certification Scheme in the Organization for Economic Cooperation and Development, both of which facilitate the international trade of seeds.

Ken McNabb is the W. Kelly Mosley Professor Emeritus in the School of Forestry and Wildlife Sciences at Auburn University, AL, where he served for 26 years as extension specialist and professor in the area of plantation regeneration. During that period, he contributed 12 book chapters, 12 refereed journal articles, 54 nonrefereed articles, 7 videos, organized 68 professional meetings, and delivered over 100 State/county presentations, 44 regional presentations, and 16 international presentations. McNabb has received numerous Extension awards including the Society of American Foresters National Technology Transfer Award (2010). He served 10 years as director of the Auburn University Southern Forest Nursery Management Cooperative, 4 years as State coordinator for the Forestry and Wildlife Extension Team, and 3 years as special assistant to the provost and director of the Office of International Education. Prior to working at Auburn, he spent 3 years as the Farm Forestry Research Advisor with the United States Agency for International Development in Peshawar, Pakistan, and for 6 years coordinated regeneration research at Jari Forest Products in northern Brazil, including responsibilities for the annual production of more than 25 million seedlings. He is a fellow in the Society of American Foresters with past service to the Society as chair of the Alabama Division, the War Eagle Chapter, and the International Forestry Working Group, as well as a member of the World Forestry Committee and the Forest Science and Technology Board.

Lawrence A. Morris is a professor of Forest Soils in the Daniel B. Warnell School of Forestry and Natural Resources at the University of Georgia, Athens, GA. He has over 35 years of experience in soil management, seedling establishment, and root-soil interaction research. He is the author or coauthor of 10 book chapters, 20 outreach publications, and more than 100 scientific articles or conference proceedings on topics ranging from nutrient management in forests, soil compaction effects on root and tree growth, plant competition, use of soil amendments in plantation forests, and phytoremediation of contaminated sites. He regularly teaches courses in forest soil management, urban tree management, waste utilization in forests, pedology, and the natural history of Georgia. He has served as the chair of the Forest and Range Soils Division of the Soil Science Society of America and as president of the Soil Science Society of Georgia. Currently, he serves as vice-chair of the Georgia Soil Classifiers Advisory Board. Morris is a Fulbright scholar and recently received the Southeastern Society of American Foresters Award of Excellence in Research and Development.

Carolyn (Carrie) Pike, has served as the area regeneration specialist for the USDA Forest Service, State and Private Forestry, based at Purdue University, Lafayette, IN, since 2015. Previously, she worked at the University of Minnesota, where she spent over 15 years running the daily operations of the Minnesota Tree Improvement Cooperative from the Cloquet Forestry Center, Cloquet, MN, and earned her Ph.D. in Natural Resources at the University of Minnesota in 2013.

Randy Rentz retired as nursery manager for the Louisiana Department of Agriculture and Forestry. He received a forestry degree from Louisiana Tech University, Ruston, LA, in 1980 and began his nursery career soon thereafter with the Louisiana Office of Forestry as assistant nursery manager for the Beauregard Nursery from 1981 to 1986. After a brief period of working as a consultant and container nursery owner, Rentz moved on to be the nursery superintendent of the Louisiana Department of Agriculture and Forestry (LDAF) Columbia nursery from 1990 to 2000. He became the assistant reforestation chief for the LDAF from 2000 to 2010, moving up to the State reforestation chief from 2010 to 2015. He is currently an operating partner with WR Environmental LLC, Columbia, LA.

Jackie W.D. Robbins, earned his B.S. and M.S. from Clemson University, Clemson, SC, and his Ph.D. from North Carolina State University, Raleigh, NC, in Biological and Agricultural Engineering. He received specialized training, such as the 1965 National Science Foundation Princeton University Hydrology Institute, a 1968 Environmental Protection Agency Water Quality Studies, and a 1978 National Science Foundation Science Faculty Professional Development Grant for a sabbatical leave to study/research micro-irrigation as a visiting professor at the University of Hawaii, Honolulu, HI. He retired from academic teaching, research, and administration in 1989. Robbins has been an active member of American Society of Agricultural and Biological Engineers (ASABE) and the Irrigation Association (IA) for 50+ years, serving on committees and boards and in elected positions. He is an ASABE life member and an IA Pioneer of Irrigation. He coauthored the chapters "Overview of Irrigation Systems" and "Agricultural Sprinkler Systems" of IA's sixth edition of *Irrigation*. He has published and consulted domestically and internationally on animal waste management, nonpoint pollution, and irrigation, and he holds U.S. Patent #4430020, Drip Irrigation Hose. He is the founder of Robbins Association/Irrigation-Mart Inc., a full-service Agricultural and Forestry Irrigation Distributor/Dealership established in 1978, now with 50+ employees and multiple locations.

Jeff Sibley serves as the Bohmann Endowed Professor in the Department of Horticulture at Auburn University, Auburn University, AL. Before joining the Horticulture Department in 1994 as a research associate, he owned and operated Grassland Nursery in Muscle Shoals, AL, for 8 years, a family business he grew up being a part of. Over the past 25 years, most of Sibley's research and teaching has focused on horticultural crop production and business management practices affecting the "green" industry. He is noted for research in the area of waste management, particularly focused on utilization of agricultural, industrial, municipal, and waterway wastes in various horticultural applications. To date, Sibley has taught more than 3,000 undergraduates and written over 200 publications. He finished high school in Mt. Hope, AL, and earned a B.S. and M.S. at Auburn University and a Ph.D. from the University of Georgia, Athens, GA.

David B. South is an emeritus professor at the School of Forestry and Wildlife Sciences at Auburn University, Auburn University, AL, where in 1977 he helped establish the Southern Forest Nursery Management Cooperative. His research on weed control was useful in registering several herbicides for use on pine and hardwood seedlings. Through publications, presentations, short courses, nursery visits, and consulting, he has helped nursery managers refine and improve management practices. He published numerous scientific articles, was elected to the Alabama Foresters Hall of Fame, and received the Society of American Foresters' Barrington Moore Award for excellence in research. He exposed various myths related to chilling hours, seedbed density, top-pruning, soil pH, terminal buds, planting depth, nursery fertilization, and relative growth rates. He also developed a root-bound index (RBI) for container seedlings and a transplant-stress index (TSI) for outplanted seedlings. He conducted research in Scotland, South Africa, and New Zealand, and he visited nurseries in Australia, Brazil, Canada, China, England, Finland, France, Guatemala, India, Spain, and Sweden.

Tom Starkey earned his B.S. from North Carolina State University, Raleigh, NC, in Forestry and Conservation, and his M.S. and Ph.D. in Plant Pathology from Penn State University, State College, PA. From 1977 to 1984, he was an assistant professor in Plant Pathology at the University of Georgia, Athens, GA. From 1984 to 1994, he was an agricultural missionary in Haiti, where he was responsible for nursery production, reforestation, and agricultural self-help projects. From 1994 to 2006, he worked with International Forest Company in Odenville, AL, and Moultrie, GA, where his focus was nursery management, production, and development assigned to projects in the Southern United States and also in Mexico and Dominican Republic. In 2006, Starkey became a research fellow with the Southern Forest Nursery Management Cooperative in the School of Forestry and Wildlife Sciences at Auburn University, Auburn, AL. Starkey continued research in the area of seedling quality and nursery production until he retired in August 2016. Since that time, he has continued his consulting efforts in reforestation within the Southern United States and resides in Opelika, AL.

Joseph M. Vande Hey is the reforestation team leader and nursery superintendent for the Wisconsin Department of Natural Resources F.G. Wilson State Nursery in Boscobel, WI, having been the reforestation leader for the past 3 years and the nursery superintendent for the past 20 years. The Reforestation Program comprises nursery operations, forest genetics and tree improvement, and reforestation monitoring. The nursery produces 3 to 9 million seedlings annually and about 35 different native species of conifers, hardwoods, and shrubs for reforestation, conservation, and wildlife habitat. Vande Hey's philosophy on nursery production is to produce the best seedlings possible using the most effective and efficient techniques. He served as president of the Northeastern Association of State and Federal Conservation Nurseries for 6 years. He has coordinated research programs with university and Federal personnel with studies related to the use of fertilizers, *Diplodia* spp. infection on red pine, the production of root cuttings from bigtooth aspen, and nursery fumigation. He has authored or coauthored several research papers and articles. Prior to his current position, Vande Hey worked for 3 years as tree improvement technician and for 6 years as tree improvement superintendent for the Oklahoma Division of Forestry, working primarily with the genetic improvement of loblolly pine and the operation of a containerized nursery program. He received a B.S. degree in Forest Management from the University of Wisconsin, Stevens Point, WI, in 1989.

Chase Weatherly is the production coordinator for ArborGen's Arkansas Nursery in Bluff City, AR. He has been the chief grower at this nursery since 1997 and has overseen the planting and production of more than 850 million bareroot pine seedlings as well as more than 55 million bareroot hardwood seedlings. Weatherly has given many talks and presentations to various groups concerning bareroot nursery production. During his 20 years as a grower, his focus has been on process and quality improvement in all aspects of pine and hardwood seedling production.

Jim Wichman earned an A.S. in Agriculture from Vincennes University, B.S. in Forestry, and M.S. and Ph.D. in Forestry and Weed Science from Purdue University, Lafayette, IN. He has served as a district forester, nursery manager, and nursery program supervisor for Indiana Division of Forestry from 1973 to 2005. Wichman received the Richard Leiber Award of Excellence from the Indiana Department of Natural Resources in 1985. Retired in 2005, he chaired the Political Action Committee for Indiana Forestry and Woodland Owners from 2014 to 2018.

Foreword

Temperate hardwoods are cultured across the United States, with most production occurring in the eastern half of the country. Most chapters within this manual cover one topic for the entire area. Other topics exhibit geographic variation such as seedbed preparation and sowing, weed management, and practices related to lifting and packing. These chapters provide a range of content to give a full perspective. Other topics, such as fertilizer and soils, can be applied more generally regardless of location. The seed chapter highlights topics related to hardwood seed, but readers may also want to refer to *The Woody Plant Seed Manual*, which is available online (Bonner and Karrfalt 2008). Protocols for handling many commercially valuable species are fairly well established because of extensive research and decades of production. Research on the culture of most hardwood species is far from complete, and many questions remain. This paucity of research is not unique to hardwood—other species (tree and plant) favored for restoration plantings are not as well studied and pose unique challenges to nurseries. Our goal is to provide practical, up-to-date science-based information on hardwood seedling culture. We recognize that each nursery is unique, and these recommendations may need to be adjusted to meet local conditions.

A cadre of professional nursery workers, many with decades of experience working in nurseries across the Eastern United States, wrote this guide. The audience for this guide is nursery managers who grow temperate hardwood trees in a bareroot nursery in the Eastern United States. Beginners who wish to construct a new nursery or have no experience growing hardwoods will find greater detail in other manuals devoted to culture of bareroot stock, such as the *Tropical Nursery Manual* (Wilkinson et al. 2014), *The Woody Plant Seed Manual* (Bonner and Karrfalt 2008), and the *Forest Nursery Manual* (Duryea and Landis 1984). Also, while hardwood trees can be grown successfully in containers, their copious root systems require large containers; the management of these is beyond the scope of this manual.

– Carolyn (Carrie) Pike

References

Bonner, F.T.; Karrfalt, R.P., eds. 2008. The woody plant seed manual. Agric. Handb.727. Washington, DC: U.S. Department of Agriculture, Forest Service: 274–280.

Duryea, M.L.; Landis, T.D., eds. 1984. Forest nursery manual: production of bareroot seedlings. The Hague/Boston/Lancaster: Martinus Nijhoff / Dr. W. Junk Publishers, for Forest Research Laboratory, Oregon State University, Corvallis. 386 p.

Wilkinson, K.W.; Landis, T.D.; Haase, D.L. [et al.]. eds. 2014. Tropical nursery manual: a guide to starting and operating a nursery for native and traditional plants. Agric. Handb. 732. Washington, DC: U.S. Department of Agriculture, Forest Service. 376 p.

This oak tree and me,
we're made of the same stuff.
– Carl Sagan –

Introduction

1

K. McNabb
Ken McNabb is W. Kelly Mosley Professor Emeritus, School of Forestry and Wildlife Sciences, Auburn University, AL

Outline

Facing Page: *Nursery worker in tall hardwoods. (Photo by Greg Hoss.)*

The Importance of Hardwood Seedling Production

It's easy to get the wrong idea about hardwoods. Recent surveys indicate that hardwood seedlings make up less than 5 percent of the total number of seedlings produced in the Eastern United States (Hernández et al. 2017). Of the approximately 1 billion tree seedlings produced in the Eastern United States in calendar year 2016, a little over 42 million were hardwoods. For many reasons, however, that relatively small number does not accurately reflect the true importance of hardwood seedlings to the forest economy or ecology of the region. First, for some States, particularly Ohio, Indiana, Illinois, Iowa, and Missouri, hardwoods are 75 percent of their total nursery production and the foundation of their seedling production and reforestation programs. Second, hardwood prices across the region are about three times higher than conifer prices, and hardwood sales can represent a significant amount of revenue for those nurseries producing them. The sale price of a premium graded hardwood, for example, can be as much as 10 times that of an ungraded loblolly pine. The relatively small production numbers for hardwoods do not necessarily indicate their economic importance to nursery sales.

The number of hardwood seedlings produced also does not indicate their ecological importance. Many species of hardwoods are planted as much to produce wildlife food as to provide an economic return. Landowners have been interested in hardwoods to improve wildlife habitat for a variety of reasons. Whether mast-producing oaks or fruit-producing cherries, the benefits to wildlife from hardwood seedling sales is hard to quantify. In addition, landowners have often been interested in planting hardwoods for purposes related to environmental improvement such as wetland conservation, species diversity, and any number of environmental quality issues. The impact of these efforts can be significant in terms of seedling sales and service to an environmental quality mission.

Finally, many hardwood sales are for a small number of seedlings for programs such as Arbor Day celebrations, Boy Scout troop activities, and city landscaping projects. These activities reach a large number of people involved in improving their homes and communities. It is hard to determine how this might affect the public's perception of forestry and its understanding of the contribution of forest tree nurseries to environmental management and the quality of their lives. So, while forest tree nurseries in the Eastern United States may produce over a billion seedlings, much of the public relates to the sale and utilization of only a small portion of that production because it directly impacts the public's lives.

The Challenge of Hardwood Seedling Production

Although hardwood seedling production serves a variety of very important functions, they are not always easy to grow. More than a few nursery managers may have felt that the headaches are not worth either the sales or the public relations benefits that hardwood production may provide. The list of disadvantages to growing hardwoods is long.

- **Species diversity.** A single nursery may grow anywhere from 10 to 40 hardwood species, each with their own characteristics and challenges. This diversity is perhaps the most challenging aspect of growing hardwoods. One need only contemplate trying to accurately sow walnut (Juglans nigra L.) with an average of 40 seed per pound, followed by green ash (*Fraxinus pennsylvanica* Marsh.) with 20,000 seed per pound. This challenge is to be followed by differing stratification characteristics, growth rates, pests, and other characteristics that may differ among species.
- **Genetic improvement.** The seed for virtually all hardwoods come from open pollinated natural stands. There are few seed orchards that might provide some genetic improvement and consistency. Using seed from natural stands increases seedling variability in the nursery bed.
- **Seed production.** There are few commercial producers of high-quality hardwood seed. Much of the seed used in hardwood seedling production must be gathered and processed locally. Some species have fleshy fruit, some have wings, dormancy and stratification requirements vary greatly, and seed crops are highly irregular.
- **Bed spacing.** While pine seedlings may be produced at 20 to 25 seedlings per square foot of nursery bed, hardwoods usually are grown at somewhere between 5 and 15 seedlings per square foot. This means increased nursery bed space that must be fumigated, tilled, bedded, maintained, and harvested.
- **Cultural treatment.** Hardwoods consume more water and fertilizer than do pine. Species react differently to top pruning. Information on weed control is more limited than for conifers.
- **Lifting.** Their size and root structure make hardwoods much harder to lift as compared to conifers. The process typically requires significant hand labor and increased handling and sorting. The mechanization of hardwood lifting is not well developed and fewer seedlings can be carried on a trailer or in an individual container.

- **Grading.** Because there is considerable morphological diversity in most hardwood crops, grading and/or culling is often required, which increases labor and supervisory inputs.
- **Storage.** Hardwoods require a significant amount of cooler space due to their larger size. Packaging is sometimes more problematic because of hardwood root morphology. Some species of hardwood store well, others do not.
- **Research support.** One of the most serious drawbacks to hardwood seedling culture is the nearly total lack of active research looking at seedling production improvement. While there have been past studies related to seedling quality and outplanting performance, other issues like weed control, nutrition, genetic improvement, and harvest mechanization have not received the concentrated effort or funding that has been afforded the culture of conifers.

The Objectives of This Guide

Fortunately, even with all the serious challenges faced by hardwood nursery managers, a cadre of dedicated professionals is meeting these challenges. Much of what is known about hardwood seedling culture is scattered throughout the various nursery managers, university personnel, and Federal researchers who have worked with hardwood seedlings. Much has been learned over the past 40 years since Robert Williams and Sidney Hanks of the U.S. Department of Agriculture, Forest Service, prepared the first *Hardwood Nursery Guide* in 1976. It is well past time that the state of knowledge for hardwood seedling culture be redefined and documented. That is the primary objective of this guide.

Geography is one of the more difficult challenges faced by the organizers of this guide. A wide variety of climate and topography may be found in the "Eastern United States" (USDA Forest Service, Regions 8 and 9). The average low and high temperatures, number of frost-free days, and other basic climatic characteristics vary greatly when comparing Pennsylvania to Mississippi. Frozen soil is unlikely in South Carolina, but it is an annual event in Wisconsin. Topography in the Eastern United States varies from the heights of the Appalachian Mountains of Vermont and New Hampshire (upwards of 5,000 feet [ft]; 1,500 [meters] m), to the Mississippi River Delta of Arkansas (as low as 100 ft; 30 m). All these factors impact sowing dates, timing of cultural activities, lifting, and planting dates. Nevertheless, many of the same hardwood genera are spread across the region, and in some cases the same species might have a very wide distribution. More importantly, the problems faced by nursery managers in one part of the region are not all that different from the problems in another part. Seedbed preparation, weed control, and lifting operations are similar wherever the nursery may be located, although the timing may be different. The important consideration when organizing this guide was to gain and incorporate the perspective of experienced managers and researchers from across the region.

This guide is the result of contributions from a large number of individuals who either have direct field experience in the cultivation of hardwoods or considerable research experience with hardwood culture. It is hoped the guide will be a useful and practical source of information and that both the inexperienced and the experienced nursery manager find it beneficial.

Reference

Hernández, G; Haase, D.L.; Pike, C. [et al.]. 2017. Forest nursery seedling production in the United States – fiscal year 2016. Tree Planters' Notes. 60(2): 21–28.

Seed Acquisition, Conditioning, and Storage

R.P. Karrfalt and C. Pike

Robert P. Karrfalt is emeritus scientist, USDA Forest Service, West Lafayette, IN

Carolyn (Carrie) Pike is regeneration specialist, USDA Forest Service Eastern Region, State and Private Forestry, West Lafayette, IN

2

Outline

Facing Page: *Acorns. (Photo by C. Pike, USDA Forest Service.)*

Introduction

The production of most hardwood seedlings begins with acquisition of seeds, exceptions being stem cuttings (cottonwoods, willows, and hybrid poplars), or grafted stock (high-value hardwoods such as black walnut (*Juglans nigra* L.). This chapter discusses the various technologies involved in producing and wisely managing high-quality seedlots. Some nurseries collect and process their seed requirements completely in house. Other nurseries, either by choice or obligation, contract part or all of this process. In either case, knowledge of the entire process is important to assess the qualifications of contractors and suppliers, as well as to judge the quality of their product.

Readers should become familiar with the *The Woody Plant Seed Manual* (Bonner and Karrfalt 2008), which discusses a full range of seed topics. That book features both general material on the topics and species- or genera-specific information such as seed collection dates, numbers of seeds per pound, and germination requirements. This chapter covers those latter topics in more detail and some seed-related topics that have emerged since the publication of *The Woody Plant Seed Manual.* (See the glossary in Appendix 2-1 of this chapter.)

Seed Development

Hardwood trees are phylogenetically classified as angiosperms—plants that produce their seeds in fruits that develop from flowers. Seed development starts with flowering and ends with seeds (formed from ovules in the ovaries of the flowers) and fruit (formed from the ripening of the ovaries). By observing the flowering, seed collectors can gain information about the quality and quantity of a future seed crop. The number of flowers will be a good predictor of the seed crop unless flower structures are damaged by frost or herbivory before the seeds fully develop.

Flowers occur in a diverse array of structures and habits. Perfect flowers contain both male and female parts (such as those of tulip poplar, *Liriodendron tulipifera* L.), while imperfect flowers are either male or female (such as those of oaks, *Quercus* spp.). Generally, if flowers are imperfect, both the male and female flower will still occur on the same tree, a condition named monoecious, although some species (for example ashes, *Fraxinus* spp.) will produce male flowers exclusively on one tree and the female flowers exclusively on another tree, a condition named dioecious. There is a third habit, polygamous, in which both perfect and imperfect flowers occur on the same tree (such as red maple, *Acer rubrum* L.). Knowing the type of flowers and how they occur on the parent facilitates assessing the presence and abundance of a flower crop and provides the earliest information on when and how many seeds might be available. Trees with no or few flowers will produce low- seed crops. *The Woody Plant Seed Manual* describes the flower type for a large number of genera.

Seed Bearing Age

The age at which trees first produce seed varies among and within species. Some species produce large quantities of seed within a few years of planting (European alder, *Alnus glutinosa* L., for example), but generally seed production is highest for middle-aged trees, 15 to 20 years after planting. Seed production in other species takes decades: bur oak (*Quercus macrocarpa* Michx.) for example, does not bear commercial quantities of seed until 35 years or older.

Seed collectors generally favor open-grown trees with large full crowns because such trees have a high number of branches capable of flower production and often produce seed prolifically. In contrast, trees growing within the tight confines of the forest often have limited crowns and produce fewer seeds, so are not as sought after by seed collectors. Trees with full crowns may also produce seed sooner than a similar-aged tree growing in a natural forest with restricted light. Lastly, open grown trees may produce flowers closer to the ground and on different sides of the crown facilitating collection. However, convenience should not override the need to have a sufficiently broad genetic makeup represented in a collection of seeds. A bulked seedlot ideally has an even proportion of seeds from at least 10 unrelated mother trees. Trees with poor form or that are diseased should not be used as seed trees.

Frequency of Seed Crops

Seed production is highly cyclical in hardwood trees, although some species, such as silver maple (*Acer saccharinum* L.), produce at least a small crop every year. Bumper seed-crops occur periodically, typically at intervals of 2 to 5 years, as exemplified with sugar maple (*Acer saccharum* Marsh.). Seed quality is usually the highest during bumper seed years because the number of seeds is usually sufficient to compensate for predation and infestation by insects. Abundant seed crops also lead to lower seed costs because more seeds can be collected per hour in the field and higher amounts of seeds can be extracted per unit weight of fruits. Therefore, seed collections should be focused on bumper years and poor seed years passed over when possible. Such a strategy can only be followed, however, if the seeds can be stored for several years. When long-term storage is not possible, seeds must be collected as needed. Refer to *The Woody Plant Seed Manual* to learn if the seed of a specific species can be stored.

Determining When to Collect Seeds

For most trees, seed should be picked when the fruit is ripe or physiologically mature. At this stage, seeds will have maximum viability and vigor (fig. 2.1). Seed collectors and buyers should become knowledgeable of physical cues that indicate maturity because most hardwood seed cannot mature after separation from the mother plant. Seed maturity is frequently indicated by a change of the fruit color from green to yellow, greenish yellow, or red and purple. The softening of fleshy fruits is another indicator. Note that the color changes may not be the same with every individual or population of plants. Seasoned collectors learn to recognize the physical signs of maturity for species they collect. Novices should seek out seed maturity indices from the appropriate genus chapter in *The Woody Plant Seed Manual.*

Most hardwood seeds ripen in the fall, but notable exceptions include seeds of red maple and elms (*Ulmus* spp.), which ripen in the spring, and mulberry (*Morus* spp.), which ripens in the summer. Maturity can vary spatially within the crown of a single tree with seeds on a southern aspect possibly maturing sooner than those on a northern aspect. A stand of trees with a southerly aspect may mature sooner than a stand with a northerly aspect, or a stand at a different elevation. Lastly, maturity can vary by genotype, as observed in common garden studies and seed orchards.

Seed quality is a critical consideration for collectors and encompasses both maturity and absence of insects or pathogens. Quality must be assessed in the field by cutting (known as a cut test) or tearing open a sample of seeds to observe the embryo and food storage tissues (endosperm and/or perisperm) if present (fig. 2.2). The internal parts in an immature seed are soft and milky, whereas in a mature seed, they are firm, white or cream-colored, and the embryo generally fills the seed or the embryonic cavity. Seeds that lack mature internal structures or ones that are damaged by disease or insects should not be collected. Signs of insect damage include the presence of frass, larvae, or feeding galleries or holes. Refer to the drawing of the internal seed anatomy in the appropriate genus chapter in *The Woody Plant Seed Manual.*

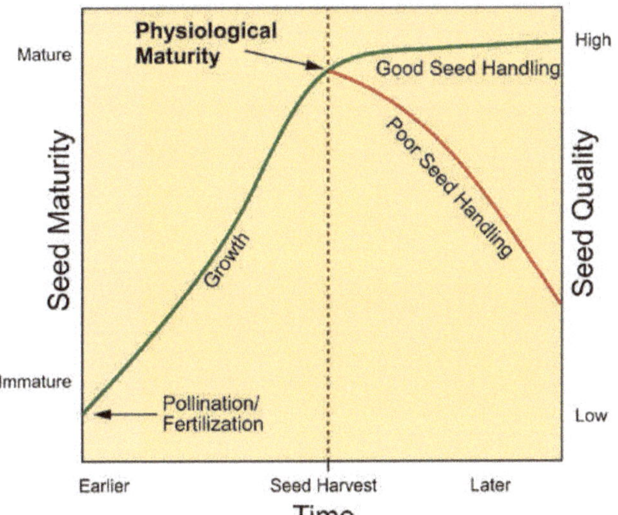

Figure 2.1—Seed quality and maturity changes over time.

Figure 2.2—A longitudinal cut of this ash seed shows it has a fully developed seed and embryo. (Photo by R. Karrfalt, USDA Forest Service.)

Several factors must be considered when scheduling the seed collection. Seeds that disseminate quickly after ripening, such as cottonwood (*Populus deltoides* Bartr.), require diligent forecasting. The seeds of blue (*Fraxinus quadrangulata* Michx.) and black (*Fraxinus nigra* Marsh.) ash shed shortly after maturity, while green ash (*Fraxinus pennsylvanica* Marsh.) and sycamore (*Platanus occidentalis* L.) can retain the seeds for months after reaching maturity. Predation from squirrels, deer, and birds can rapidly deplete a seed crop, especially crops of nuts or fleshy fruits that are rich food sources for the predator. Seed drop can indicate seed maturity, but caution needs to be exercised because the earliest seeds to fall can often be aborted or insect damaged and not an indicator of seed maturity. A cut test can assess quality. Strong winds or warm, dry conditions can accelerate seed dispersal and end seed collection efforts. Monitor weather forecasts and consider their possible effect on planned seed collections. *The Woody Plant Seed Manual* lists approximate maturity dates for most genera as a baseline, but is not a substitute for a field assessment.

Calculating Seed Requirements

Nursery managers must figure out the amount of seed needed to produce a certain number of seedlings for sale. Given the periodicity of good seed years, calculations of seed requirements should be projected across multiple years. However, for recalcitrant species that cannot be stored long-term, projections are usually based on annual needs. Appendix 2-1 provides definitions for these terms: pure live seed, seed purity, seed weight, germination, and viability. Chapter 5 of *The Woody Plant Seed Manual* gives a thorough discussion of these terms and how their values are determined. Table 2.1 describes the steps to calculate the amount of seeds needed. Pure seed has a specific definition in official testing rules (AOSA, Association of Official Seed Analysts). Pure seeds are the seeds that appear undamaged to the naked eye and may or may not be viable (or have the potential to germinate). Seed weight is expressed as the number of seeds per pound, ounce, gram, or kilogram. A hypothetical seedlot might have a seed weight of 48,000 seeds per pound. However, because it has a purity of 75 percent, a pound of this seedlot will only contain 36,000 pure seeds for sowing. A test of viability does not involve any attempt to germinate the intact seed. Instead, viability is estimated when germination is difficult or takes a long time to complete because the seeds are highly dormant. Tests of viability include tetrazolium staining, embryo excision, and x-ray tests. Refer to chapter 5 in *The Woody Plant Seed Manual* for a complete explanation of the viability test. Pure live seed (PLS) is the product of seed weight, purity, and germination, expressed as a number of pure live seeds by a given weight (pound, ounce, gram, or kilogram). This allows estimating the value of a seedlot for reforestation because it gives the likely maximum number of plants that can be obtained from the given weight. The PLS is the actual number of seed to prepare for sowing to reach a specific number of seedlings.

Seed Purity X Seed Weight X Germination = PLS

or

Seed Purity X Seed Weight X Viability = PLS

Every seedlot will have specific values for the above factors and, therefore, a specific pure live seed value. The nursery manager should keep a record of these values for each seedlot of each species and calculate average values to plan seed requirements. When lacking historical data from the nursery, a manager can refer to the average values for any specific genus as listed in *The Woody Plant Seed Manual.*

With the number of pure live seeds (PLS) per unit weight determined, the next step is to divide the number of seedlings needed by the PLS to arrive at the weight of seeds required. This seedling production target can be on either an annual or multiyear basis. The initial estimate of needed pounds of seed must, however, be further adjusted for losses in the nursery that can occur from imperfect germination rates, premature death of seedlings, or seedlings that grow slowly and fail to meet grade standards. These losses in the nursery are collectively represented by the nursery survival factor (table 2.1), which is the percentage of pure live seeds that germinate and grow into plantable seedlings, calculated as the number of plantable seedlings divided by the number of pure live seeds:

Number of plantable seedlings = (PLS)/(survival factor)

Permanent sample plots, sometimes called history plots (Landis and Karrfalt 1987), located within nursery beds can be used to estimate the survival factor. For example,

***Table 2.1**—Stepwise assessment questions to compute the amount of seeds to collect for a known production number.*

Question	Value	Calculated quantity of seeds needed
How many plants are to be produced?	200,000/yr	
How many years of production will this collection provide?	3	200,000 x 3 = 600,000
What is the ratio of seedlings to viable seeds? [1]	80%	600,000 / 0.8 = 750,000
What is the viability of the seeds?	80%	750,000 / 0.8 = 937,500
How many seeds are there per unit weight?	99,000	937,500 / 99,000 = 9.5 lbs
What is the purity?	95%	9.5 / 0.95 = 10 lbs
What volume of the "raw" collection unit? [2, 3]	0.8 lbs/bu	10 lbs / 0.8 lbs/bu = 12.5 bu

bu = bushels. lbs = pounds. yr = year.

* This is the nursery survival factor.

** That is, how many seeds, fruits, or cones must be collected to obtain the desired weight of pure seeds?

*** Is there sufficient capacity for postharvest storage and timely conditioning for the desired volume of seeds?

1,250 pure live seeds are needed to produce 1,000 plantable seedlings if the nursery survival factor is 80 percent.

The formula to calculate the number of plantable seedlings, as shown in chapter 4b of this guide, is equivalent to this formula, but factors nursery density into the calculation.

The history plot also provides information on how the crop is progressing through the growing season. This information informs the manager whether production targets will be met and whether any corrections to cultural practices, pest control, or the number of trees available for distribution are necessary. History plots are covered in greater detail in chapter 10 of this guide.

Seed Acquisition

Seed Collection

The first four sections of this chapter laid the ground-work for seed collection by describing the biology needed for predicting the occurrence of seed crops, determining when they are ready to collect, assessing their likely quality, and estimating how much seed should be collected. With that information, the work can be scheduled and appropriate resources acquired and prepared.

Nurseries or their parent organizations that have the personnel and equipment for seed collection can potentially exercise the necessary control over the process by directly supervising operations. When the collections are not made by nursery staff, seed can be acquired with formal contracts or by local collectors, provided there is good communication between nursery and collectors. This communication can be in the form of a formal contract or simple information sharing, stating clearly the species to collect, collection sites, timing, criteria for seed quality, amount of reimbursement, and the method of reimbursement. Nurseries that purchase raw fruits and seeds need to assess seed quality at the point of arrival, or may find they have acquired poor-quality seeds or an inordinate quantity of trash. Long-term relationships with experienced collectors are beneficial for nursery operations to meet their seed needs with locally sourced material.

Methods of Seed Collection

The actual gathering of the seed or fruit from the plant takes many forms, depending on the botanical characteristics of the mother plant. The seed-bearing structure can portend the effort required. Fruits that are persistent and/or tightly bound to the tree, such as sweet gum (*Liquidambar styraciflua* L.) and sycamore, require more effort to collect. Persistent fruits may require hand twisting or a sharp cutting tool, such as pruning shears, to sever the connection. Fruits that are not persistent can be easily picked by hand or pulled off with rakes, hooks, or vacuum. Some fruits fall naturally upon ripening and can be collected from the ground, or the tree can be shaken to release fruits. Acorns and walnuts are actually not ripe until they drop naturally and should only be taken from the ground. Yard tools such as rakes, leaf blowers/vacuums, forks, and shovels can be useful in gathering seeds from the ground or off low plants (fig. 2.3). Persistent fruits that are high in the crown require some other means of reaching them, such as climbing or bucket trucks. Climbing requires adequate training and equipment to be done safely; bucket trucks allow quick access to the crown with a high degree of worker safety. Another method for obtaining seeds from tall trees is to collect them from trees felled for harvest or fallen over from storm damage (Bonner, 1970), but make certain that the seeds are sufficiently mature at the time the tree fell. The fruits may appear mature, but the appearance could be due to the general drying of the whole treetop rather than a true maturation. Collect promptly after felling to forestall losses to birds or mammals. Collecting from felled trees may not be cost-effective because fruits or cones may shatter or become deeply covered by limbs, tops, and foliage. Sometimes destructive sampling, such as cutting a seed-laden branch with a pole pruner, is effective but future seed may be limited. Striking limbs with long poles or shaking them with ropes can cause seeds to drop into a tarp or netting below. Ropes can be thrown over limbs by hand if the limbs are not too high, or a large slingshot can be used to shoot a weight and draw string over the limb. (Knight, Karrfalt, and Mason, 2010) (fig. 2.4).

Postharvest Storage

Raw seed and fruit that arrive at a nursery must be stored properly until seed is cleaned. Proper postharvest storage is

***Figure 2.3**—Fruits such as acorns can be gathered from the ground after natural seed drop. (Photo by R. Karrfalt, USDA Forest Service.)*

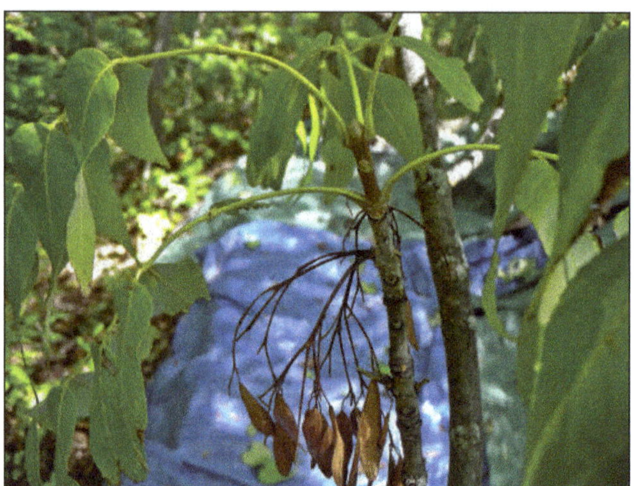

Figure 2.4*—Tarps are sometimes necessary to catch small seeds that are shaken from the tree. ((Photo by R. Karrfalt, USDA Forest Service.)*

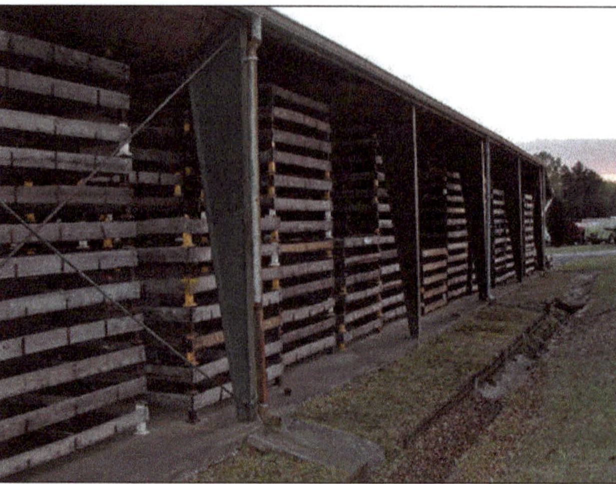

Figure 2.5*—Screen-bottomed racks for postharvest drying of seeds. Spacers allow natural air flow around each rack in the stack. (Photo by R. Karrfalt, USDA Forest Service.)*

critical to avoid reduced seed quality and expensive losses in viability. The seed or fruit type dictates the method of handling. Three types of hardwood seeds and postharvest storage recommendations are described below. See page 66 in *The Woody Plant Seed Manual* for a more complete discussion of postharvest seed storage.

Desiccation-tolerant seeds with dry fruits. Seeds in this group, also called orthodox seeds, maintain high viability when dried to low moisture content. In general, desiccation-tolerant seeds are dried in ambient conditions and sheltered from precipitation. Examples include tulip poplar and elms. Seeds are stored postharvest in layers only a few inches deep on screen or mesh-bottomed trays (fig. 2.5). This allows moisture in the seed to diffuse into the air.

Desiccation-tolerant seeds with a fleshy fruit. Orthodox seed with a fleshy fruit must be kept moist until the seed is separated from the fruit; examples include cherries (*Prunus* spp.) and dogwoods (*Cornus* spp.). If the fruit is allowed to dry, it can become very difficult to remove later. The consequences of not removing the fruit include a substantial increase in the bulk of the seedlot, greater difficulty in removing empty seeds, and, upon rehydration, the pulp will serve as a source of trash and microbial contamination. Postharvest, fleshy fruit can be watered or placed in high humidity until the seed is extracted. Seeds are often held in tubs, trays, or plastic bags. Storing seed in a cooler offsets heat that builds from fermentation that could damage seeds. Aeration can prevent excessive fermentation and mold growth. Once the seed is extracted, it should be dried in the same way as desiccation-tolerant seeds from dry fruits (see section on seed storage).

Desiccation-intolerant or recalcitrant seed. Drying these types of seeds to a low-moisture content kills them. As a general rule, moisture content must be kept at above 25 percent. Examples include oaks and buckeyes (*Aesculus* spp.). Recalcitrant seeds are typically held in trays, tubs, or plastic bags (Bonner 1973; Bonner and Vozzo 1987; Tylkowski 1984) in a cooler or occasionally in a root cellar or other cool location but usually cannot be stored for extended periods of time.

The length of time seeds are held in postharvest storage is as important as the method for storing them because quality declines over time in storage. Species vary in how quickly a measurable loss in seed quality will occur. Species that are dormant can be held longer in postharvest storage than species that are not dormant. For example, desiccation-intolerant white oak (*Quercus alba* L) or live oak (*Quercus virginiana* Mill.), which do not go dormant, must be processed within a few days of collection to ensure germination does not commence or proceed too far (Bonner and Vozzo 1987; McDonald 1969). In these cases, germination can be retarded by storing the acorns in plastic bags in a cold room as close to 34 °F (1 °C) as possible and in layers only a few inches thick. Germination may commence rapidly in the white oak group when acorns are stored in deep layers.

Seed Extraction, Hulling, and Singularizing

Seed must be separated from its hull, fruit, and impurities to prevent spoilage, prepare for sowing, and to reduce the bulk for storage. The primary objective in all fruit handling and extraction is to obtain as much viable seed as possible and to maintain a high extraction factor, which is the yield of clean seed expressed as a percent of rough fruit. Seed may be cleaned in-house or contracted to a seed-cleaning facility. Any contract with an external cleaner should include specifications on seed purity, percentage of full seed, and moisture content, along with expected completion date. Most contractors process seed for a variety of customers simultaneously, which can occasionally lead to processing delays. Removing pulp, pods, husks, twigs, and other debris substantially reduces the weight.

Desiccation-tolerant dry fruits have a variety of fruit types: globose heads of achenes, pods, capsules, clusters of samaras, or single fruits. Many species have an appendage (wing, a pappus, or bract) to remove before the seed can be cleaned or sown mechanically. Hullers or scarifiers used to remove these appendages must be operated carefully. Hulling and scarifying applies force to the seeds to separate the appendage, which may be tightly bound to the fruit, like the wing on tulip poplar fruits, for example. Excessive force can damage seeds, while too little force may fail to remove the appendage. Some level of mechanical damage generally occurs. The seed for some species may be too delicate for these machines and require hand rubbing (for example, red maple). The brush machine (Karrfalt 1992) is an alternative hulling device that imparts minimal damage on a variety of species (figs. 2.6 and 2.7). Hammermills are sometimes used but can cause higher levels of mechanical injury to the seeds (Young et al. 1983). Note that hulling operations generate high amounts of dust, and machine operators need to use a mask or respirator. The macerators used for dry fruits also generate copious amounts of fine dust.

Desiccation-tolerant species with fleshy fruits are often cleaned with macerators, which use water to wash away pulp as it is forced off the seed (fig. 2.8). Blenders with rubber tubing over the blades can serve as macerators for small seeds or small seed-lots. In some cases, the fruits can be simply crushed and the pulp rinsed away. Generally, a presoak of 1 to several days softens the pulp and makes for an easier separation from the seed. This accelerates the cleaning process and reduces the chances for mechanically injuring the seeds. Water must be changed daily to prevent fermentation and to control mold.

Figure 2.7—*Tulip tree and green ash seeds after treatment with the brush machine. (Photo by R. Karrfalt, USDA Forest Service.)*

Desiccation-intolerant seeds can have a fruit with either a dry (oaks) or a fleshy exterior (redbay, *Persea borbonia* L. Sprang.). These fruits are handled just like the fruits of dessication-tolerant species, but the seed must be kept from drying.

Cleaning Seed

One goal of hulling/extraction is to produce a seedlot that flows freely, allowing individual seeds to be separated. Once in a flowable state, seeds are cleaned further to remove

Figure 2.6—*Brush machine for hulling indehiscent fruits, dewinging and singularizing seeds. (Photo by R. Karrfalt, USDA Forest Service.)*

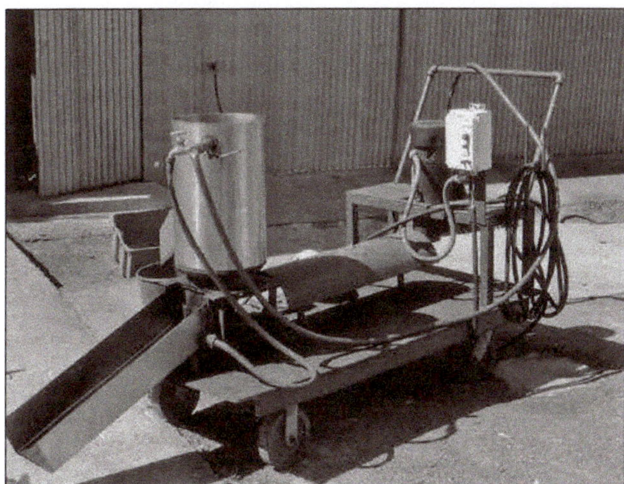

Figure 2.8—*A macerator for de-pulping fleshy fruited seeds. (Photo by R. Karrfalt, USDA Forest Service.)*

Figure 2.9*—This small blower removes trash with positive pressure. (Photo by R. Karrfalt, USDA Forest Service.)*

Figure 2.10*—A small aspirator removes trash with vacuum. (Photo by R. Karrfalt, USDA Forest Service.)*

trash and empty seeds using a variety of machines, mainly with forced air. A blower applies air as a positive pressure (fig. 2.9), essentially blowing away the unwanted trash. An aspirator applies negative pressure (fig. 2.10), sucking away the trash. Screens (fig. 2.11) can separate the seeds from trash that is both larger and smaller than the seed. A machine can be equipped only with screens, or combined with forced air in an air-screen machine, sometimes called a fanning mill (fig. 2.12). The seed-cleaning discussion in *The Woody Plant Seed Manual* focuses on the use of expensive machinery. Brandenburg (1977) and Brandenburg and Park (1977) discuss the mechanical methods and principles of seed cleaning in detail. Efficient nursery operation often requires investment in this type of equipment to obtain the needed quantities of high-quality seed. But it is also possible to adequately clean smaller amounts of seed with low-cost tools such as the aspirator (fig. 2.10) and hand-held screens (fig. 2.11).

For mechanical cleaning to be effective, there must be some physical difference between the seed and the trash, and between the good seed and empty seed. Physical differences include width, thickness, length, weight or density, shape, surface texture, or color. Round-hole screens separate differences of width, while oblong-hole screens separate differences in thickness. Seed of different length may be separated using indent cylinders (fig. 2.13). The aspirator, blower, or air-screen machine use forced air to separate seeds by weight separations. Density separations can occasionally be made with water (fig. 2.14) or on a specific-gravity table (fig. 2.15), that uses forced air to make a gentle stratification of the light and heavier particles (e.g., seeds). A shake of the table pulls the strata apart. Inclined drapers (fig. 2.16) and spiral separators rely on particle shape and the ability to roll downhill to make a separation. If one particle has a surface texture with more friction than another particle, a vibratory separator (fig. 2.17) can separate the two. Color separation has had no application in forestry.

Seed Purchase

Many nurseries prefer the convenience of purchasing clean seed from reputable seed suppliers, when the quality and

Figure 2.11*—Hand screens showing the three main types of screens used to clean seedlots (counter-clockwise from left): perforated metal round hole, perforated metal oblong holes, and woven wire. (Photo by R. Karrfalt, USDA Forest Service.)*

Figure 2.12—Air-screen machines come in many sizes and are used for basic seed cleaning; a small cleaner is in front of a very large cleaner. (Photo by R. Karrfalt, USDA Forest Service.)

quantity desired is available on the open market. Ideally, the genetic source (describing the origin) and the quality of the seed (germination rate) are third-party verified at an accredited laboratory 6 to 9 months before the purchase. All requests or contracts for purchase should state the desired genetic source, germination, purity, and moisture content. In some cases, the seed should be tested for potential diseases. Each State generally has its own crop improvement association that certifies genetic origin, but sometimes interstate agreements apply.

Seed Testing

Seedlot Sampling

Seed that is extracted and cleaned is referred to as "finished seed." This seed should be evaluated in a seed-testing laboratory for its reproductive potential, economic value, and quality. As stated above, the reproductive potential is calculated by the pure live seed or PLS. Seed testing—the process to determine seed quality—begins by drawing a sample of seeds from the seedlot in a manner that will accurately represent the entire seedlot as a whole. A poorly drawn seed

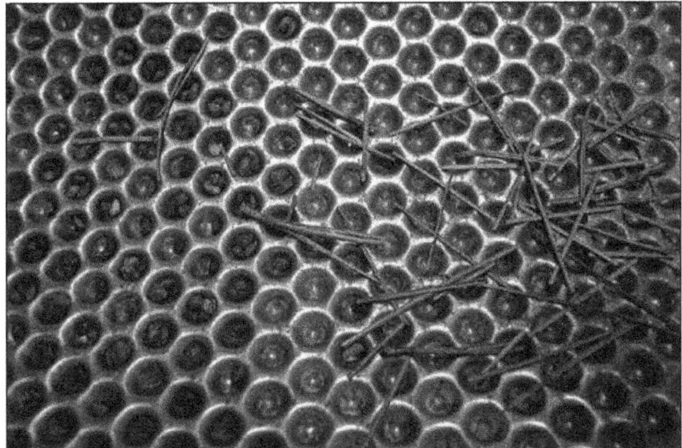

Figure 2.13—Seeds are caught in the indents of the cylinder, while long objects slide away. (Photo by R. Karrfalt, USDA Forest Service.)

sample may result in serious failures in seedling culture months later. Appendix 2-2 provides a detailed procedure for sampling seedlots for testing.

The timing of seed testing is critical in managing seed supplies. An initial test needs to be made on the entire seedlot once it is in the final finished state, including a full test of purity, 1,000 seed weight (number of seeds per unit weight), and germination or viability. From this data, the manager will know if the seed collection succeeded in producing the desired quantity of pure live seeds. High-quality seedlots of desiccation-tolerant species will maintain germination for decades when properly stored. However, periodic retests of germination are necessary during storage. As long as moisture content does not change in storage (and it should not if the seed is stored correctly), purity and 1,000 seed weight do not need to be retested after the initial test. In general, viability is retested at 3- to 5-year intervals to monitor changes

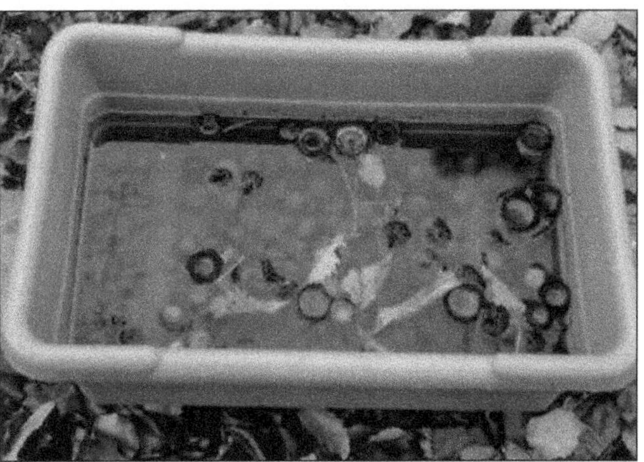

Figure 2.14—Floating acorns in water separates good seeds (sinkers) from damaged seeds (floaters) and trash. (Photo by R. Karrfalt, USDA Forest Service.)

Figure 2.15—A specific gravity table for separating seeds from trash using weight differences. (Photo by R. Karrfalt, USDA Forest Service.)

Figure 2.17—The vibratory separator removes trash from seeds by differences in surface texture. (Photo by R. Karrfalt, USDA Forest Service.)

in germination that would require additional collections. The actual interval depends on projections of seed requirements to meet seedling production goals.

Seed should be tested for germination sometime within the 6 months before sowing in the nursery. Managers using seed without a current season germination test risk a costly crop failure. Schedule seed tests well in advance of sowing or shipping because a full test on a seedlot can take up to 3 months or more to complete, depending on the germination requirements of the species. Other tests may be done in 1 week or less. Coordination with the seed laboratory on scheduling tests is helpful for both the laboratory and the nursery.

Testing Seed Moisture

Seed moisture has traditionally been tested using a constant-temperature oven or electronic moisture testers that have been calibrated using the oven method. Chapter 5 of *The Woody Plant Seed Manual* describes both methods. However, the most appropriate and uniformly applicable way to assess seed moisture is the equilibrium relative humidity test (eRH) (Karrfalt 2014). As seeds dry, they will eventually come into equilibrium with the air around them as long as that air is held relatively constant at one relative humidity. Figure 2.18 shows the relationship of the range of relative humidities and the moisture content of green ash. At 30-percent relative humidity, seed moisture content is approximately 7 percent, a safe moisture content at which this species can be stored (Bonner 2008). A seed equilibrium relative humidity of 30 percent would be a good general target to dry seed for long-term storage and is usually achievable with dehumidifiers or heating the air.

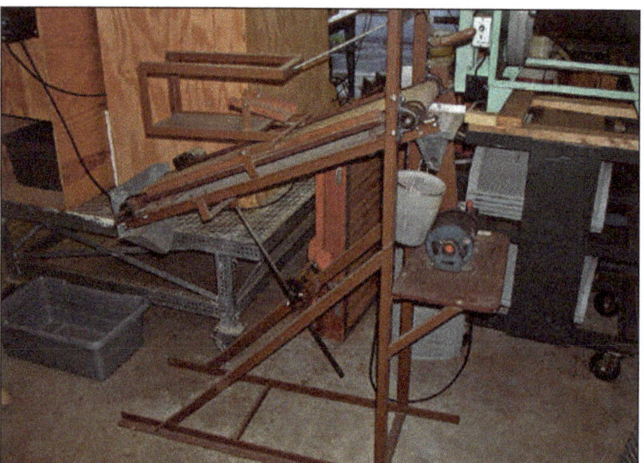

Figure 2.16—The inclined draper separates particles on their ability to roll or slide down an inclined belt. (Photo by R. Karrfalt, USDA Forest Service.)

Tests of eRH are conducted using any quality hygrometer with a probe that can be isolated with the tested seed in a sealed chamber (see examples in figs. 2.19 and 2.20). Seeds usually equilibrate to the relative humidity of the air around them. In the closed test chamber, the air is no longer the dominant factor and the relative humidity of the chamber equilibrates to that of the seed. If a seed had been equilibrated at 30-percent relative humidity, the air in the test chamber would adjust to 30-percent relative humidity. If the relative humidity of the ambient air in the chamber was 25 percent, the seed would lose moisture to the jar air until jar air was also at 30-percent relative humidity. If the ambient air was 35-percent relative humidity, then the seed would absorb moisture until the jar air was at 30-percent relative humidity. The amount of moisture lost or gained during the test is negligible. This test can be run on seed at any level of purity, full seed percentage, or viability. This makes it useful in evaluating the condition of seed in postharvest storage.

Several important facts must be recognized in testing eRH. First, the eRH of seed just off the seed dryer will usually be

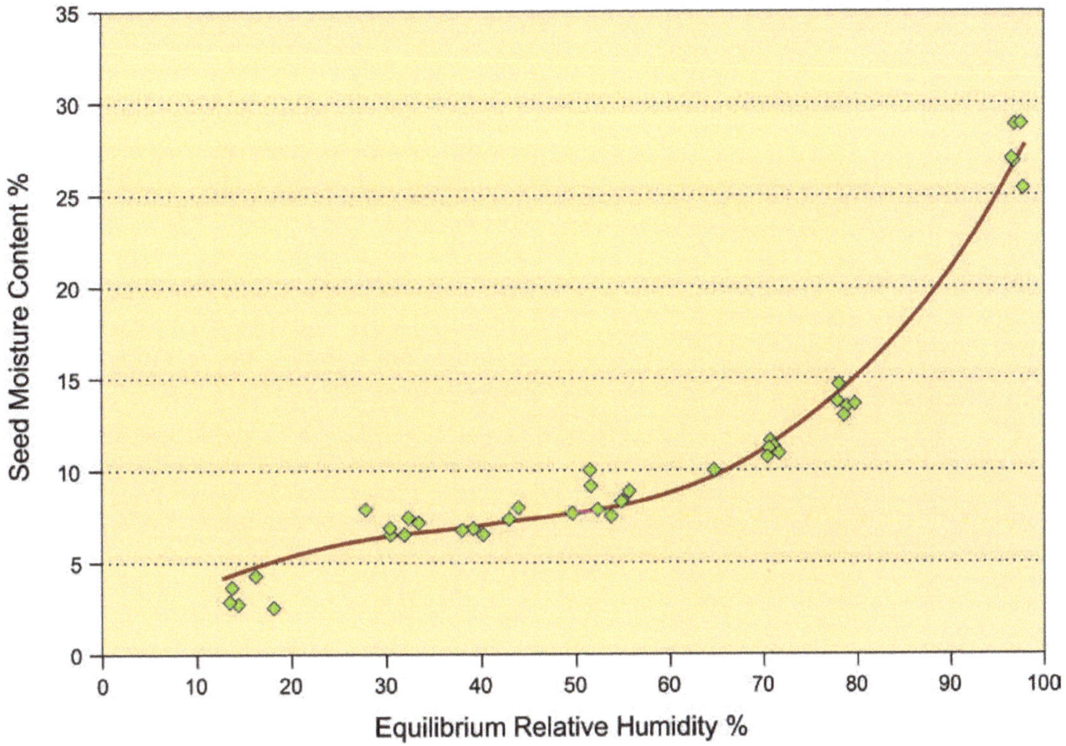

Figure 2.18*—Green ash moisture content graphed against relative humidity.*

lower than the inner seed because the surface of the seed dries faster than the seeds' interior. Larger seed, for example walnuts (*Juglans* spp.), persimmons (*Diospyros* spp.), and plums (*Prunus* spp.) will often also require time to reach internal equilibrium. In these cases, seed should be held in the test jar overnight to achieve equilibrium, improving the accuracy of the eRH. The hygrometer need not be attached to the test jar as the sample equilibrates overnight. If test chambers are inexpensive, it is possible to have many samples equilibrating at one time. The hygrometer can be attached at the end of the overnight equilibration period and a reading taken after 10 minutes. If the seed is at a higher-than-desired eRH, it can be returned to the dryer immediately. In this case, an overnight equilibration period is not needed. When the eRH is found to be acceptable, then an overnight equilibration is recommended to be sure the seed is at internal equilibrium and the true eRH is not too high.

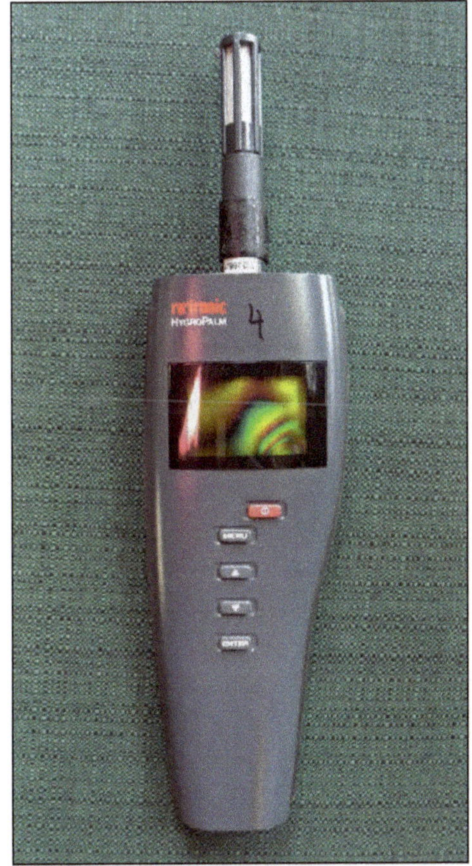

Figure 2.19*—Handheld hygrometer for measuring equilibrium relative humidity of a seed lot. (Photo by R. Karrfalt, USDA Forest Service.)*

Dormancy and Preparation for Sowing

Operational Timing

Dormancy is an adaptive trait with different seeds following different maturation paths, depending on the strategies that result in successful reproduction. Seed that is shed in the fall

Figure 2.20—*A recycled peanut butter jar used as a test chamber for measuring equilibrium relative humidity (eRH) to test if the seed is dry for storage. A 30-percent eRH is good for all seeds that should be dried. (Photo by R. Karrfalt, USDA Forest Service.)*

is usually unable to germinate immediately and is considered dormant. Seed dispersed in the spring lacks dormancy and requires timely handling to place them into storage and/or sown in the nursery. This is especially true for the small seed of *Populus* spp. and *Salix* spp., which must be sown within a few weeks or placed into dry freezer storage. Some species, such as those in the genus *Quercus*, maintain high moisture at maturity and must find conditions favorable for germination and seedling establishment soon after falling from the mother plant. In contrast, seeds with deep dormancy, such as *Prunus* spp. and tulip poplar, can live for years in the soil and forest litter until conditions are good for seedling establishment, when germination commences.

From a nursery standpoint, species with no dormancy require little handling to get complete germination and a full stand of seedlings, provided that seed is handled properly and timely. Most species in temperate climates develop "desiccation tolerance," or the ability to dry to low-moisture content, and dormancy accompanies this tolerance. Dormant seed can be stored because the desiccation suspends respiration, putting the seed into stasis. A few desiccation-tolerant species are shed from the mother in spring or early summer, including cottonwoods and aspens (*Populus* spp.) and red maple. Because these seed are shed early in the growing season, they can germinate easily upon rehydration and produce a seedling in the same growing season in which they were formed.

The seed coats of legumes are impermeable to water and can remain dormant for extremely long periods. Once the seed coat is ruptured, even slightly, the seed will take up water and swell. The condition of not being able to absorb water is referred to as "hard-seeded." Many hardwoods have a very hard seed coat but are not "hard-seeded" because they can absorb water. Therefore, a simple test to tell if a species is hard-seeded is to soak the seed. If the weight of the seed increases after soaking, it is not hard-seeded. Methods for dealing with impermeable seed coats are discussed in *The Woody Plant Seed Manual.*

Dormancy

Seed dormancy is common among hardwood species, but with a few exceptions, seed can be treated to stimulate germination. Dormancy has two main causes:

- Seed coat dormancy caused by an impermeable or hard seed coat that prevents water or oxygen from reaching the embryo or prevents the embryo from breaking out of the seed coat even if water and oxygen pass in.
- Internal physiological dormancy or a morphologically undeveloped immature embryo.

Usually only one type of dormancy is present, but some seeds exhibit double dormancy, a combination of seedcoat and internal dormancy, such as redbud (*Cercis canadensis* L).

Stratification is the most common technique to break internal dormancy. During stratification, seed is subjected to cold, moist conditions that release the germinative capacity of the seed. Although it is traditional to think of dormancy as a barrier to germination, it is perhaps more appropriate to think of it simply as arrested development and growth necessary for various regeneration strategies in the wild. Biochemical-level studies of the germination process have found that germination occurs once there is the proper amount and proportion of growth-promoting and growth-regulating hormones at the meristematic regions of the embryo. Seeds that shed naturally with immature embryos, such as black and blue ash, will mature under moist conditions at temperatures between 59 to 68 °F (15 to 20 °C).

Stratification Procedures

A dry seed goes through two major periods of water uptake in order to germinate. The first is when the seed first comes into contact with water. The second is when the radicle emerges and germination commences. Between these two periods of water uptake, the moisture content of the seed is relatively constant (see fig. 2.21). The first period of water uptake needs to be complete for stratification to occur. Trees are typically prepared for stratification by soaking in water overnight or for 1 to 2 days. After draining the water, seed is placed into plastic bags and stored in a cold room for a specified period. This process, used for at least 50 years, has produced workable results for many species but had two faults. First, the surplus water tended to pool on the bottom of the bag and submerge some seeds, depriving them of oxygen and causing anaerobic respiration, evidenced by the foul odor when the bag was opened. The second fault was that excess water could result in radicles emerging from some or all the seeds once the dormancy was overcome. Seeds with emerging radicles are not desired because they are difficult to sow and may be killed or weakened when the radicle breaks off during sowing.

One approach to controlling radicle emergence was to use shorter stratification periods. This approach, however, forfeits the benefit of faster germination and increased seed vigor that can be obtained with longer periods of stratification. Seeds with higher vigor can germinate under less-than-optimal conditions, such as temperatures that are lower or higher than optimal. This is an advantage when weather conditions are abnormally warm or cold during germination. Also, faster germination shortens the establishment period of seedling development, when seedlings are most vulnerable to damping off or to being washed out of the soil with heavy rains. For species that require stratification longer than 60 days, the extra water can be an issue in breaking dormancy because of the wide range of time required to break dormancy among individual seeds in these more-dormant species. The period to break dormancy in the most-dormant individual seeds can be so long that the least-dormant seeds will germinate before the full seedlot is ready to grow. Trials over the last 20 years have shown that removing the capillary water from around the seeds will keep them from germinating, regardless of how long the stratification period is. Therefore, the objective in preparing seeds for stratification is to have them fully imbibed but denied the water needed for germination to commence.

Once seed is fully imbibed, the seeds' surface must be dried. The seed must be exposed to air that is dry enough to remove the water. This is generally at 60-percent relative humidity or less. When this step is completed the seed will no longer have a shine from capillary water or a surface water film. Seed will appear to be damp and not as they were when dry. As only the surface water is to be removed, the seed must be constantly rotated so they are uniformly dried. The dryer used to dry seed for storage can be used if the seed in the drying basket are continually turned in some way so that no drying front develops. The ancient method of spreading the seed out in thin layers will also work but is labor-intensive and requires a good bit of space, as well as generally favorable weather. A more mechanized method is to place the seed in a tumbler, such as a small concrete mixer, and blow air across the seed as they are turned in the tumbler. A pedestal fan makes a convenient tool to blow air over the seed, as it can be adjusted to the height of the drum. The drying must be closely observed and stopped immediately upon the disappearance of the surface film of water.

The final step for stratification is to place the seed into a 4-mil (1 mil = 1000th of an inch) poly bag, weigh the bag of seed, and place it in the cold room at temperatures between 32 and 40 °F (between 0 and 4.5 °C). The bags should be weighed at weekly intervals to be sure they are not drying as would be indicated by a decrease in weight. Should the weight decrease, add just enough water to the bag to bring the weight back to the original value. Seed are kept in the cooler for as long as dictated by experience, a reliable reference, or a laboratory germination report. The last point to be made on seed stratification is to count back from the desired sowing date to determine when to start seed preparation.

Fall Sowing

Many nurseries will plant hardwood seed in the fall to take advantage of natural conditions, as an alternative to stratifying seed in a cooler. Fall sowing requires that seed be available before the ground freezes. The beds must also be protected from predation through the winter. Over the last decade, this practice has failed in some cases because the winters are too mild or there is a mild period in between two

> Seeds soaked in water for a sufficient length of time will become fully imbibed, unless they have impermeable seed coats. The question then is what steps can determine a sufficient length of time for the soak. Step one is to take some seeds and weigh them. Step two is to place them in a water soak for 24 hours. Then take them out of the water, surface dry them, weigh them again, and return them to the water for another 24-hour soak. These steps are repeated until the weight gain between 2 days is essentially 0. There may be some fluctuation at the later weighings with different amounts of water drained from the seed on different days. Once the number of days of water soak to full imbibition is determined, it can be used operationally. Time to full imbibition for specific species may sometimes be found in the literature. Assistance may also be available from a seed laboratory such as the National Seed Laboratory.

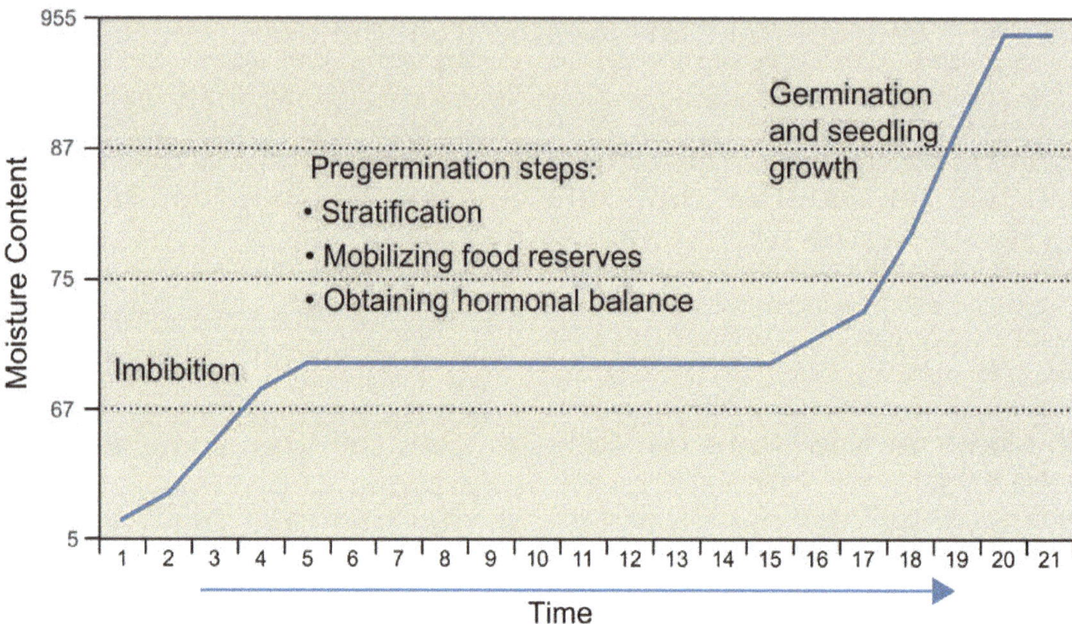

Figure 2.21*—A generalized curve of water uptake during different phases of germination. The actual timing, in terms of days, will vary by species.*

extended freezing periods. In the first case, stratification is incomplete and in the second, germination occurs during the winter instead of in the spring and the seedlings are killed in the second period of freezing weather. Fall sowing does have the advantage of not requiring a cooler for stratifying seed.

Seed Storage

Managing Seed Moisture

Seed moisture is the single most important factor in maintaining seed vigor in storage (Justice and Bass 1978). A nursery with any significant amount of seed in storage must be able to manage seed moisture to prevent spoilage. Therefore, whether seeds are produced in-house or purchased, the nursery needs the capacity to dry seeds and to test their moisture status. When buying fully finished seed, the seed should be dry as specified in the purchase contract but should be checked once the containers are opened. Test the moisture any time a seedlot is opened for any reason. As seedlots are repeatedly sampled for testing or withdrawing seeds to sow, moisture from the outside can enter the bag. The preceding section on seed storage has information on storage containers, as well as chapter 5 in *The Woody Plant Seed Manual.*

The ancient method of drying seed is to spread it in thin layers and continually turn it as it is exposed to dry air. Often that means spreading the seed in a warm, dry building or out in the sun on tarps. The faster and vastly more efficient method is to place the seed in a pressurized dryer (fig. 2.22). Pressurizing the air in the dryer causes the air to spread uniformly through the seed. The seed at the bottom of the seed tray will dry first and the upper layers in succession. There is no need to turn the seed; in fact, it is counterproductive.

Storage Length

Seeds that are desiccation-tolerant can be stored for extended periods of time; in some cases for decades, provided they

Figure 2.22*—A small pressurized seed drier. (Photo by R. Karrfalt, USDA Forest Service.)*

are equilibrated at a relative humidity of approximately 30 percent, sealed in a moisture-proof container, and stored between 0 and 20 °F (between -18 and -7 °C). A 6-mil thick poly bag can usually serve as the moisture-proof container, but plastic, glass, or metal cans or bottles also work. Keep the container as full as possible to minimize the amount of moisture carried in the air that will be absorbed by the seed as the container cools in the freezer. Although 0 °F (-18 °C) is optimal for long-term storage, its benefits might not be realized, as operational seedlots are normally consumed before the advantage of the lower temperature can be observed.

Several exceptions are worth noting. For one, red oak (*Quercus rubra* L.) is desiccation-intolerant but can be stored just below freezing or slightly above freezing for up to 3 years. Seed will perish over time and usually be completely dead by the end of the fourth year. Not all seedlots or species will respond the same. Hickories (*Carya* spp.) are desiccation-tolerant but are damaged by freezing temperature and should be stored at temperatures slightly above freezing. They should be prepared for storage the same as other desiccation-tolerant species—dried and placed in moisture-proof containers. The appropriate genus chapter in *The Woody Plant Seed Manual* provides known storage conditions for a given species.

References

Bonner, F.T. 1970. Hardwood seed collection and handling. In: Silviculture and management of southern hardwoods. Louisiana State University 19th Annual Forestry Symposium: 53–63.

Bonner, F.T. 1973. Storing red oak acorns. Tree Planters' Notes. 24(3): 12–13.

Bonner, F.T. 2008. *Fraxinus*. In: Bonner F.T.; Karrfalt R.P., eds. 2008. The woody plant seed manual. Agric. Handb. 727. Washington, DC: U.S. Department of Agriculture, Forest Service: 537–543.

Bonner, F.T.; Karrfalt, R.P., eds. 2008. The woody plant seed manual. Agric. Handb. 727. Washington, DC: U.S. Department of Agriculture, Forest Service: 274–280.

Bonner, F.T.; Vozzo, J.A. 1987. Seed biology and technology of *Quercus*. Gen. Tech. Rep. SO-66. New Orleans, LA: U.S. Department of Agriculture, Forest Service, Southern Forest Experiment Station. 21 p.

Brandenburg, N.R. 1977. The principles and practice of seed cleaning: separation with equipment that senses dimensions, shape, density, and terminal velocity of seeds. Seed Science and Technology. 5(2): 173–186.

Brandenburg, N.R.; Park, J.K. 1977. The principles and practice of seed cleaning: separation with equipment that senses surface texture, colour, resilience and electrical properties of seeds. Seed Science and Technology. 5(2): 187–198.

Justice, O.L.; Bass, L.N. 1978. Principles and practice of seed storage. Agric. Handb. 506. Washington, DC: U.S. Department of Agriculture, Forest Service.

Karrfalt, R.P. 1992. Increasing hardwood seed quality with brush machines. Tree Planters' Notes. 43(2): 33–35.

Karrfalt, R.P. 2014. Assembling seed moisture testers, seed dryers, and cone dryers from repurposed components. Tree Planters' Notes. 57(2): 11–17.

Knight K.S.; Karrfalt, R.P.; Mason, M.E. 2010. Methods for collecting ash (*Fraxinus* spp.) seeds. Gen. Tech. Rep. NRS-55. Newtown Square, PA: U.S. Department of Agriculture, Forest Service, Northern Research Station. 14 p.

Landis, T.D.; Karrfalt, R.P. 1987. Improving seed-use efficiency and seedling quality through the use of history plots. Tree Planters' Notes. 38(3): 9–15.

McDonald, P.M. 1969. Silvical characteristics of California black oak (*Quercus kellogii* Newb.). Res. Pap. PSW-53. Berkeley, CA: U.S. Department of Agriculture, Forest Service, Pacific Southwest Forest and Range Experiment Station. 20 p.

Tylkowski T. 1984. The effect of storing silver maple (*Acer saccharinum* L.) samaras on the germinative capacity of seeds and seedling growth. Arboretum Kornikie Rocznik. 29: 131–141.

Young, J.A.; Budy, J.D.; Evans, R. 1983. Germination of seeds of wildland plants. In: Proceedings, Intermountain Nurseryman's Association Conference. Las Vegas, NV. 93 p.

Appendix 2-1

Glossary of Terms

Achene: Small, dry, indehiscent, single-seeded fruit with seed attached to ovary wall at only one point.

Bract: Modified leaf subtending a flower or flower cluster.

Dioecious: Flowering habit in plants in which male (staminate) and female (pistallate) flowers are borne on separate plants as in *Acer*, *Fraxinus*, and *Ilex*.

Equilibrium relative humidity: The humidity established in a sufficiently small sealed test chamber by seeds that indicates the moisture level of those seeds. It is measured by a hygrometer, the humidity sensor of which is sealed in the closed chamber.

Germination: The emergence of the embryo from the seed to the point that it is clear that the embryo has the potential to develop into a normal seedling.

Hard-seeded: The condition of a seed in which the seed is not able to absorb water. Seed coats of hard-seeded species must be broken in order to facilitate water entry.

Imperfect flower: A flower containing only one set of reproductive structures, either male or female.

Live seeds: Seed that germinate or are estimated to be alive by a viability test.

Monoecious: Flowering habit in which male (staminate) and female flowers (pistallate) occur on the same plant.

Mother tree: A tree from which seed is collected.

Orthodox seed: Seed that maintain high viability when dried to low-moisture content. Orthodox seed can generally be stored for long periods of time under the correct conditions.

Pappus: A tuft of delicate fibers or bristles that form a feathery appendance of an achene as in *Baccharis* and *Chrysothamnus*.

Perfect flower: A flower that contains both male and female structures, as in tulip poplar (*Liriodendron tulipifera*).

Polygamous: Bearing both bisexual and unisexual flowers on the same plant, or on different plants of the same species.

Pure live seed (PLS): The number of pure live seeds in a given weight (pound, ounce, gram, or kilogram).

Samara: Dry, indehiscent, winged fruit. Can be 1-seeded as in *Fraxinus* or *Ulmus*, or 2-samaras fused, as in *Acer*.

Scarify: A process to induce germination by disrupting the seed coats, usually with mechanical or chemical means, to increase permeability to water and gases or to lower mechanical resistance to radicle emergence.

Seed Purity: The ratio of pure seeds to the weight of pure seeds plus inert matter, or trash.

Recalcitrant seed: Seed that dies when dried to low moisture content, and generally cannot be stored long-term. Also known as desiccation-intolerant.

Seedlot: A single, uniform collection of seeds.

Seed quality: An assessment of a seedlot that encompasses both the maturity of seed, and the absence of insects or pathogens.

Stratification: A technique to break internal dormancy. During stratification, seed is subjected to cold, moist conditions that release the germinative capacity of the seed.

Seed weight: The weight of 1,000 pure seeds. It is used to determine the number of pure seeds contained in a given weight of seeds.

Viability: The percentage of a seedlot that is estimated to be capable of germination.

Appendix 2-2

Procedures for Seedlot Sampling

1. Number of Samples

If a seedlot is in more than one container, sample every container. A tree seedlot is rarely more than five containers, but if that is the case, contact the National Seed Laboratory for assistance. If only a portion of the seedlot will be sown in a particular season, then only that container or containers should be tested.

2. Sampling Preparation

Seed can be sampled immediately if the seed container has not yet been in cold storage. If the seeds have been kept in a cooler or freezer, however, the first step is to bring the container into ambient conditions and allow the seeds to reach ambient temperature before opening the container. This prevents moisture from condensing on the cold seeds, which will lead to an undesired increase in seed moisture. A 1-quart container or smaller might reach ambient temperatures in about 2 hours, while larger containers would take longer. The safest procedure is to pull the container 16 to 24 hours in advance of opening.

3. Sampling

Using a probe. Open the container and obtain samples, by hand or with a probe. A probe must be able to reach all points in the seedlot and should have uniformly spaced sampling gates. Insert the probe with the gates closed until it reaches the bottom or far side of the container. Open gates and use a slight rotating back and forth to allow seeds to flow into the probe. Gently close the gates so as not to cut or crack any seeds, withdraw the probe, and empty the seeds into a container. If the probe is inserted vertically, it must have divisions forming a separate chamber for each gate opening. If each gate does not have a separate chamber, the probe can only be used correctly in the horizontal position.

Hand-drawn samples. Two methods are recommended for hand-drawn samples. The first method involves collecting handfuls of seeds from the top, middle, and bottom of the container. To reach the middle and bottom of the container, insert an open hand into the seeds and move down to the appropriate level, close the hand around the seeds, and withdraw it. Where the container is too deep, the seeds will be packed too tightly to work the hand down far enough to reach the bottom of the container. If the container is too small, or the seeds are packed too tightly, remove some seeds from the top and pour the remainder into a second container, pausing half-way

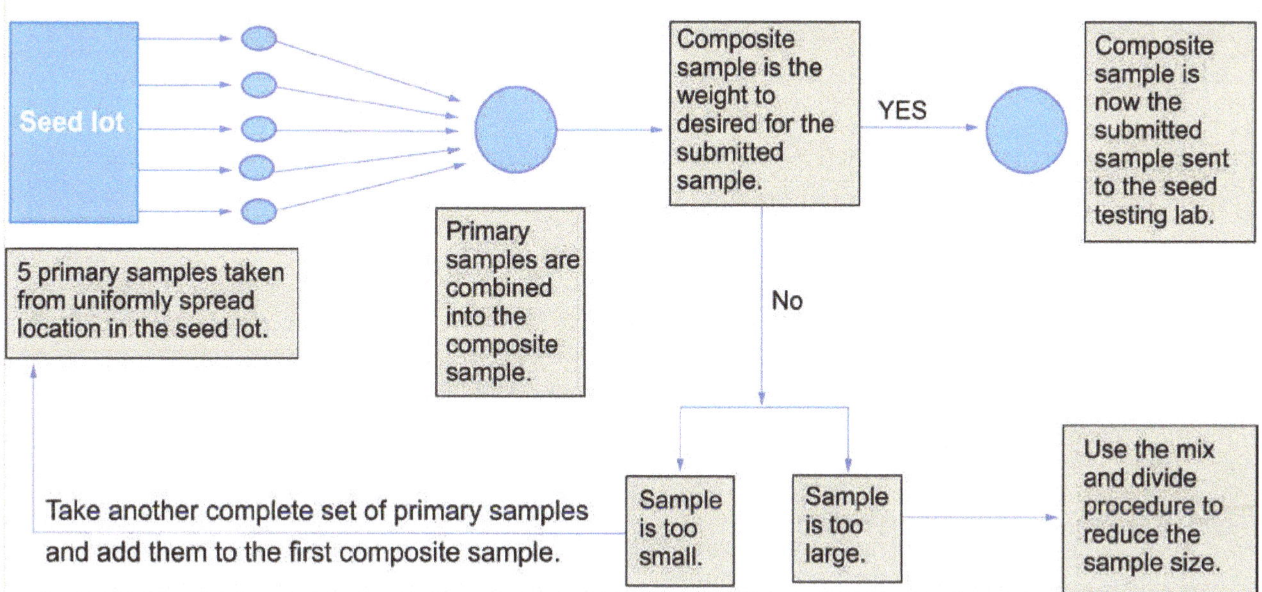

Figure 2.23*—Flow of work in sampling a seedlot for testing its quality.*

through to sample a handful of seeds. Take a third handful of seeds from the top of the second container (which has seeds from the bottom of the original container). To sample more intensely, take five handfuls: a handful of seeds from the top, from one quarter of the way down, half-way down, three-quarters of the way down, and from the bottom. Any number of handfuls over three is appropriate as long as they are evenly spaced down through the container. Alternatively, fill a spoon or small cup at each interval instead of a handful. Figure 2.25 outlines the drawing of samples.

4. Making a Composite Sample

Using table 2.2. Each handful or measure of seeds taken is called a primary sample. These primary samples are combined into a composite sample. For valid seed test results, this composite sample needs to contain at least 5,000 seeds. To determine the count, weigh the composite sample and compare the weight against the weight for the submitted sample in table 2.2. If the sample is too small, draw another complete set of primary samples. Taking only a partial set will bias the sample towards the conditions found in the part of the seedlot from which the partial set was taken and will not represent the values for the entire seedlot. For future sampling, increase the size or number of primary samples to avoid having to take an entire set of primary samples twice.

For species not listed in table 2.2, use the following procedure. First, take small amounts of seeds from at least five evenly spaced points in the composite sample and combine them. Weigh this combined subsample and count the number of seeds. Multiply the weight of the composite sample by the number of seeds in the subsample and then divide by the weight of the subsample to estimate the number of seeds in the composite sample. If the number is less than 5,000, resolve the problem by using the sampling procedures outlined in step 3 above.

5. Preparing the Sample for Testing

The sample to be submitted to the seed testing laboratory should consist of at least 5,000 seeds. However, if the weight of this sample exceeds the 5,000 minimum by more than 10 percent, reduce the sample to avoid an inaccurate test result. Using a soil sample or riffle divider (fig. 2.24), mix and divide the composite, or working, sample. Pour the full sample through the divider twice to mix it thoroughly. After a third division, take one-half of the composite sample from one side of the divider and weigh it to determine if the weight is sufficient to give 5,000 seeds. If not, record the weight and divide the other half into quarters. Weigh one of these quarters and add the weight to the first half. Do not combine the seeds until the weights added together produce a total weight sufficient to give 5,000 seeds. Then, combine the appropriate seeds to form a sample for submission and return the rest to the seed storage container. See figure 2.25 for the flow of this process.

If a riffle divider is not available, use four seamless metal or glass bowls large enough to hold the composite sample. Place the composite sample in one bowl. Then, using a

Table 2.2*—Minimum weights in grams for seed samples submitted for seed tests. The submitted sample is provided by the nursery. The working sample is a subset of the submitted sample used for testing purposes by the lab.*

Common name	Species	Submitted sample	Working sample
Boxelder	*Acer negundo* L	200	100
Japanese maple	*Acer palmatum* Thunb.	100	50
Red maple	*Acer rubrum* L.	100	50
Silver maple	*Acer saccharinum* L	1,000	500
Sugar (hard) maple	*Acer saccharum* Marshall	360	180
Horse-chestnut	*Aesculus hippocastanum* L. *	500	500
Red alder	*Alnus rubra* Bong.	4	2
False indigo bush	*Amorpha fruticosa* L.	300	150
Paper birch	*Betula papyrifera* Marshall	10	3
Silver birch	*Betula pendula* Roth	10	1
Downy birch	*Betula pubescens* Ehrh.	10	1
Hornbeam	*Carpinus betulus* L.	500	250
Catalpa	*Catalpa* spp.	120	60
Cotoneaster	*Cotoneaster* spp.	40	20
Ash	*Fraxinus* spp.	400	200
Honey locust	*Gleditsia triacanthos* L.	800	400
Sweetgum	*Liquidambar styraciflua* L.	30	15
Tulip poplar	*Liriodendron tulipifera* L.	180	90
Apple	*Malus* spp.	50	25
Mulberry	*Morus* spp.	20	5
Sycamore	*Platanus* spp.	25	6
Poplar, cottonwood, aspen	*Populus* spp.	5	2
Mazzard cherry	*Prunus avium* (L.) L.	900	450
European bird cherry	*Prunus padus* L.	360	180
Peach	*Prunus persica* (L.) Batsch *	500	500
Black cherry	*Prunus serotina* Ehrh.	500	250
Cherry, peach, and plum	*Prunus* spp. (TSW ≤ 200 g)	1,000	500
Cherry, peach, and plum	*Prunus* spp. (TSW > 200 g) *	500	500
Pear	*Pyrus* spp.	180	90
Oak	*Quercus* spp. *	500	500
Black locust	*Robinia pseudoacacia* L.	100	50
Rose, briar	*Rosa* spp.	50	25
Willow	*Salix* spp.	5	2
Mountain ash	*Sorbus* spp.	25	10
Littleleaf linden	*Tilia cordata* Mill.	180	90
Bigleaf linden	*Tilia platyphyllos* Scop.	500	250
American elm	*Ulmus americana* L.	30	15
Chinese elm	*Ulmus parvifolia* Jacq.	20	8

TSW = The sample weight.
* Values are number of seeds, not grams of seed.

Figure 2.24—Riffle divider. (Photo by R. Karrfalt, USDA Forest Service.)

small spoon, place a rounded spoonful of seeds alternately into bowl 2 and bowl 3 until the entire composite sample is divided into two equal portions, one in bowl 2 and one in bowl 3. Then, starting with bowl 2, repeat the process by alternately placing one spoonful of seeds from bowl 2 into bowl 1 and then into bowl 4 until bowl 2 is empty. Do the same with bowl 3. Now weigh the seeds in either bowl 1 or bowl 4. Proceed with weighing and dividing the seeds in this manner, as if using the riffle divider, to obtain an acceptable "submitted sample."

6. Forwarding the Sample to the Laboratory

The submitted sample then goes to the laboratory for testing. As moisture control is so important to maintain seed quality, transfer the seed samples to the lab in moisture-proof containers. Use a 4-mil poly bag or a plastic jar with a tight-fitting lid, but avoid glass containers that can break during shipping.

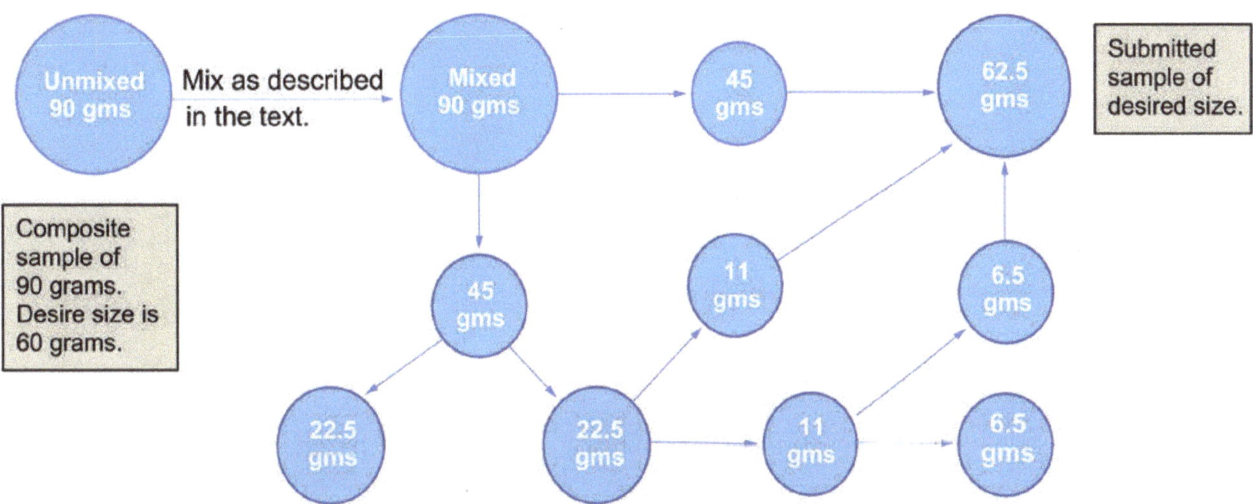

Flow of material using the correct procedure for reducing a composite sample to the desired weight for a submitted sample.

Mix and divide procedure is described in the text.

Figure 2.25—*Flow of work in mixing and dividing a seed testing sample that is too large.*

Fundamental Soil Concepts and Soil Management in Hardwood Nurseries

3

L.A. Morris

Lawrence A. Morris is professor of forest soils in the Daniel B. Warnell School of Forestry and Natural Resources, University of Georgia, Athens, GA

Outline

Facing Page: *A nursery bed prepared for planting. (Photo by Chase Weatherly.)*

The Role of Soil in Nursery Management

Soils provide the foundation of nursery management and are a prime factor in site selection. Hardwood nursery site selection was described in detail by Stoeckeler and Jones (1957), and while many of the factors they describe remain important, some adjustment for the highly mechanized, technological nursery management in today's hardwood nurseries is necessary. These systems rely less on natural growth controls and place more emphasis on the ability to manipulate soils to control growth conditions. For example, while inherent soil fertility is important, inherent fertility must be weighed against the needs to manage nutrient availability and balance, control water availability, limit pathogens, till, plant, and manage root growth. Most nurseries induce hardiness by producing mild water and nutrient stress—a process made easier by coarser-textured surface soils that are more easily manipulated.

A well-sited nursery has soils that are well-drained, flat, and characterized by relatively deep surface horizons (A and E) over subsoil argillic horizons. Slope is a critical consideration and most nurseries are located on slopes of 2 percent or less, which minimizes surface runoff and erosion. The low slopes, however, increase the relative importance of good drainage because lateral subsurface flow is required to move water off site during heavy rainfall periods. Deep surfaces allow grading to be completed while providing enough depth above subsurface horizons for subsurface drainage. In the absence of sufficient surface soil depth, management becomes difficult. For example, in Florida, Phytophthora root rot of hardwood seedlings occurs only in fumigated soils that have shallow surface soils over clay subsoils (Barnard 1996). Loamy sand and sandy loam surface soils are generally preferred, as soils of this texture are relatively easily manipulated without physical degradation. In northern nurseries, they are also less prone to frost heaving (Briggs 2008). Boyer and South (1984) reported 21 of 51 southern nurseries (both pine and hardwood) were on sandy loam soils and only 13 were on clay loam or silt loam-textured soils. Elsewhere in the United States, nurseries on soils more finely textured than sandy loams are more common, but sandy loam textures are still preferred. Finally, a uniform site will tend to produce uniform seedlings. Although precision agricultural techniques enable adjustment for irrigation, fertilization, and pesticide applications within the nursery, uniform soil conditions allow management interventions to optimize seedling growth. Uniform soil conditions allow for more efficient management and lower costs for fertilization and other operations.

In this chapter we review basic soil characteristics and discuss how they affect nursery management.

Soil Physical Characteristics

The Soil Matrix

A handful of soil consists of inorganic minerals, organic debris left by decomposing plants and animals, water, air, and millions of living organisms. Together, these constitute the soil matrix (fig. 3.1). About 50 percent of the matrix consists of solid fragments of inorganic minerals with a small portion, usually 1 to 5 percent, consisting of particulate organic matter or organic coatings on inorganic minerals. The inorganic component of the matrix is stable. The organic fraction is less stable, varying over the course of a year or years depending on the balance between new inputs and loss through decomposition. The remaining 50 percent of the soil matrix is pore space that is filled with water and air. The proportion of the pores filled with water or air is dynamic and changes over the course of individual days.

Soil Particles. ***Texture.*** One important characteristic of the inorganic component of soil is the relative distribution of clay, silt, and sand-sized particles (table 3.1). Grouping by the relative proportions of these particle sizes into soils with similar characteristics is the basis of the textural triangle (fig. 3.2). Note that particles greater than sand-sized (greater than 2 millimeters [mm] diameter) are not included as part of soil texture determination. Loam- and silt loam-textured soils have the best combination of fertility, water retention and release characteristics, and workability for traditional agriculture. Generally, however, soils of these textural groups are difficult to manage in hardwood nurseries. Bed preparation and lifting are both more difficult

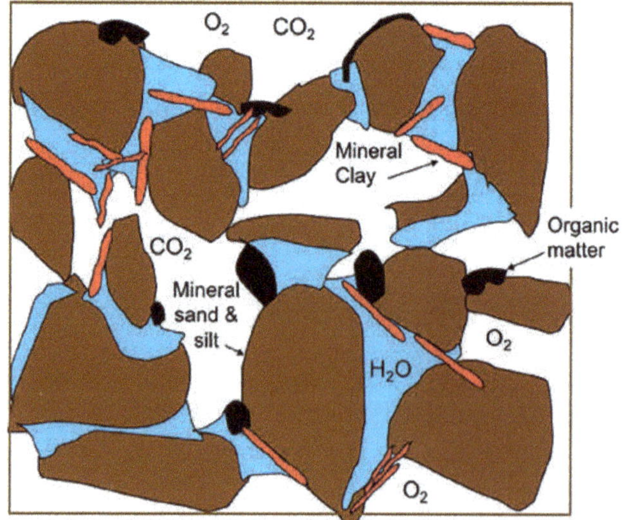

Figure 3.1*—Idealized soil matrix showing inorganic and organic particles and water and air-filled pores.*

Table 3.1—Size range of soil particles.

Particle	Size Ranges		
	Millimeters (mm)	Microns (µm)	Inches (in)
Sand	0.05 to 2.0	50 to 2000	0.002 to 0.08
Silt	0.002 to 0.05	2 to 50	0.00008 to 0.002
Clay	<0.002	< 2	< 0.00008

in these relatively fine-textured soils, and physical conditions are more likely to be adversely affected during tillage and lifting. Lifting can also be a problem when the soils are wet because the soil adheres to the roots (Bosch 1986). Several days of production can be lost after heavy rainfall on these soils in order to avoid compacting or puddling the soil (Hartmann 1970). Consequently, ideal nursery soils generally have sandy loam textures that retain less water and are more easily manipulated than loam-textured soils. Subsoil texture tends to be less of a concern than surface soil texture. Finer-textured subsoils are desirable in nurseries, particularly those with sandy surfaces (Boyer and South 1984).

Mineralogy. Clay has several meanings in soil science. As used above, it refers to the size class of a particle. "Clay" can also refer to the type of mineral. Clay minerals are composed of sheets of silica dioxide and aluminum hydroxide. Clays that have two sheets of silica dioxide for each sheet of aluminum hydroxide are termed 2:1 clays. Clays that have one sheet of silica dioxide for one sheet of aluminum hydroxide are termed 1:1 clays. This second type, 1:1 clays, are less prone to shrinking and swelling and associated problems of frost heaving and are the preferable clay mineralogy in nurseries (Stroup and Williams 1999).

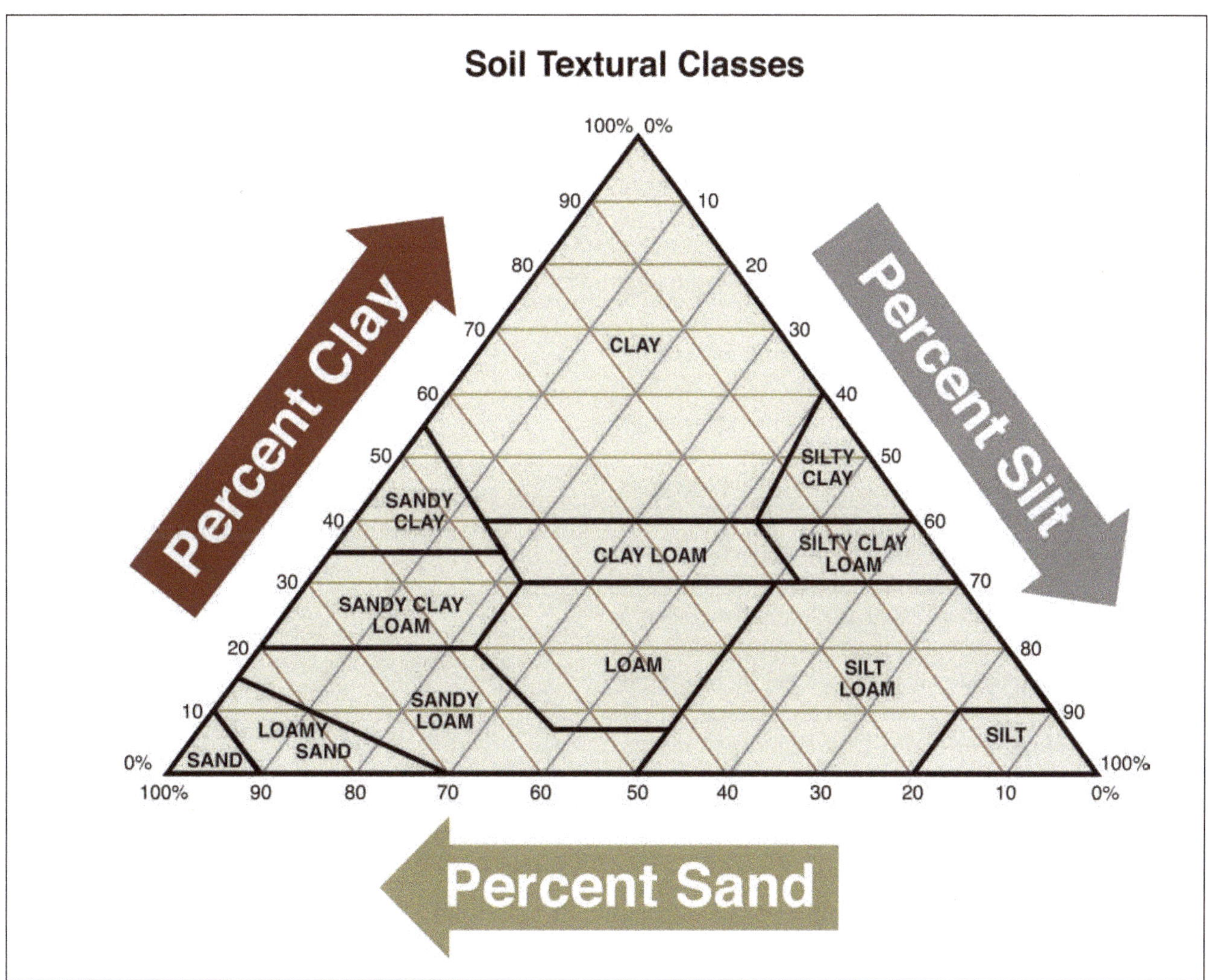

Figure 3.2—The soil texture triangle. Percentages of three soil particle sizes are plotted on the three axes. Texture class is determined from the percentage of any of the two groups.

Organic matter. Organic matter comprises the remaining component of the soil solids. Although it accounts for less than 5 percent, and is usually only 1 to 3 percent of the solid mass, it has a disproportional contribution to soil properties. Organic matter contributes to soil exchange, water-holding capacity, and soil structure. It buffers pesticide activity and is a source of nutrients. Organic matter is removed prior to texture analyses and does not contribute to the determination of soil texture.

Structure. In most soils, individual soil particles do not exist independently, rather, they are bound together by organic matter, metal oxides, and surface charges into groups of particles called aggregates. Soil aggregates are categorized by shape (fig. 3.3), size, and strength. Granular structure is typical of many surface soils, particularly for sandy loam and loamy sand-textured soils characteristic of nurseries. Blocky and sub-angular blocky structures are more common in finer-textured subsoils, but also characterize some surface soils of sandy clay loam and silt loam textures.

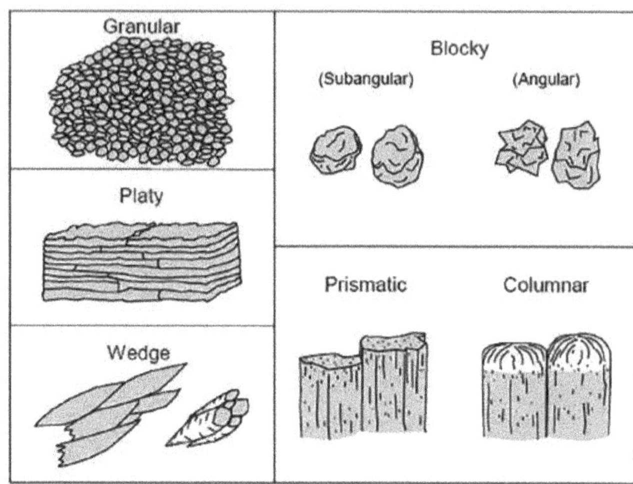

Figure 3.3*—Individual soil particles are organized into structural units. Single-grain and granular structure are common in sandy loam and loamy textured surface soils typical of most seedling nurseries. Block structure is common in subsoils and in some nurseries with finer-textured surface soil (Schoeneberger et al. 1998).*

Structure is particularly important to the development and maintenance of large soil pores that allow rapid infiltration and movement of water within the soil (see following section) and providing open pores that allow gas exchange between the soil and the atmosphere. Additionally, soils with good structure are less susceptible to physical degradation by equipment trafficking or tillage.

Pore space. Pore spaces within the soil are classified by size based on their interaction with water. Surfaces of soil particles contain electrical charge, and water has an affinity for soil surfaces due to its polar nature. The closer the water to the soil surface, the more tightly it is held. In the smallest micropores, the distance between soil surfaces are so short that water does not drain from these pores after the soil is saturated. Water is also held tightly enough that plant roots cannot generate enough tension to remove the water before they wilt. Mesopores are larger than micropores and distances between soil surfaces are greater. Mesopores are small enough that water is held so tightly that they do not drain after wetting but large enough that plants can generate sufficient tension to use this water for transpiration. Macropores are pores too large to hold water against gravitational forces. They drain after wetting and remain open to the atmosphere (fig. 3.1).

Soil Water

Retention and plant availability. The amount of water a soil can hold, expressed as a percent of total soil volume or inches per inch of soil depth, and the portion of this water available to support plant growth, is closely related to texture. This is illustrated in figure 3.4. The total amount of pore space in the soil, or the total porosity, is about 50 percent. When the soil is saturated, all of this pore space is filled with water. If the soil is allowed to drain under gravity, water will drain out of macropores. The amount of water remaining after this drainage is termed field capacity. Field capacity corresponds to water held at tensions (negative soil water potential) of about 0.3 bar (5.0 pounds per square inch [psi]). Plants grown in soil can use a portion of the water held at field capacity for transpiration because they can generate tensions greater than gravity. The lower limit of the water plants can use is termed "wilting point moisture." Below the wilting point, water cannot be withdrawn to supply transpirational needs because the water is held in micropores. This point corresponds to 15 bar (220 psi) tension. The water between field capacity and wilting point is termed "plant available water" and is the water held in mesopores. Sandy soils are dominated by macropores that drain after wetting. Because these soils have few micropores or mesopores that retain water, both the total and available water storage is low. Clay-textured soils retain large amounts of water, but a high percentage of this water is held in micropores and it is not available for transpiration.

While the concept of plant available water is useful, it is important to recognize that all plant available water is not, actually, equally available to plants. As water is removed from soils, the remaining water is held more tightly and moves to roots more slowly. For optimal growth, soil water content is maintained in the upper portion of available water and irrigation typically begins when available water is only 50 percent of the amount available at field capacity.

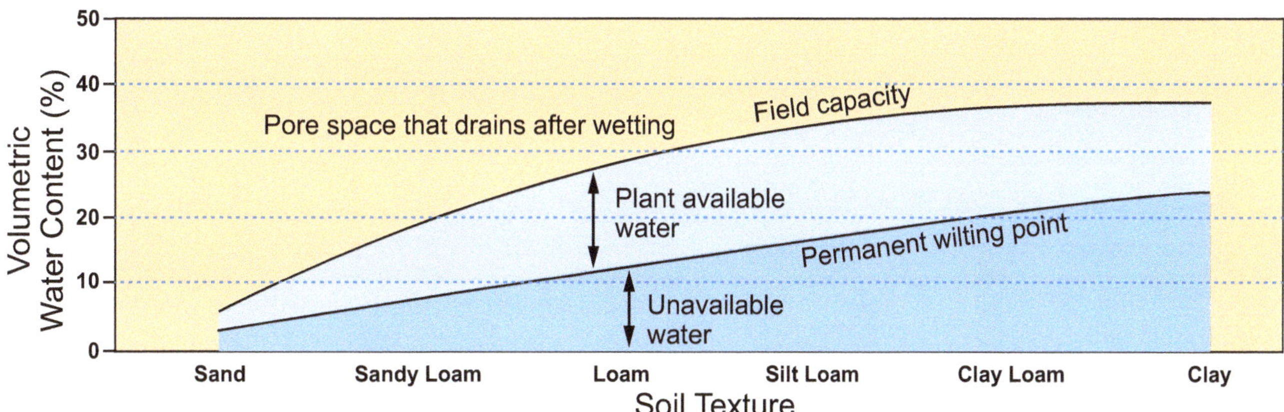

Figure 3.4*—Water retention for noncompacted soils by soil texture class. About 50 percent of the soil is pore space. Macropores drain after rainfall and these air-filled pores are important for gas transfer. Water retained after these macropores drain is termed field capacity. Water held between field capacity and the permanent wilting point is considered plant available water.*

Infiltration rate/hydraulic conductivity. Two other important concepts of soil water are infiltration rate and hydraulic conductivity. Infiltration rate is a measure, usually in inches per hour, that the soil is able to absorb rainfall or irrigation. If rainfall exceeds infiltration rate, runoff will occur. Hydraulic conductivity is a measure of the ease that water can pass through soil. Typically, dry soils have a high infiltration rate but low hydraulic conductivity. As the soil wets, the infiltration rate is reduced and the hydraulic conductivity is increased until the saturated hydraulic conductivity of soil beneath the surface is controlling the infiltration rate (fig. 3.5). In nurseries with fine-textured argillic horizons and shallow surfaces, the saturated hydraulic conductivity may be too low to drain adequately, even with addition of drain tiles (Hartman 1970).

Drainage. Infiltration and hydraulic conductivity depend on intrinsic properties of the soil matrix and the arrangement of soil horizons of different texture and structure. In contrast, drainage is a property related to the natural condition of soils within the landscape. It is an indication of the degree, frequency, and duration of wetness and is inferred from observations of landscape position and soil morphology. A sandy-textured soil with high infiltration capacity and high saturated hydraulic conductivity can be poorly drained if it is located in low landscape position with a high water table. Conversely, a clay-textured soil with poor infiltration and low hydraulic conductivity can be well-drained if it occurs on a ridge.

Eight drainage classes are recognized in the U.S. system of soil taxonomy:

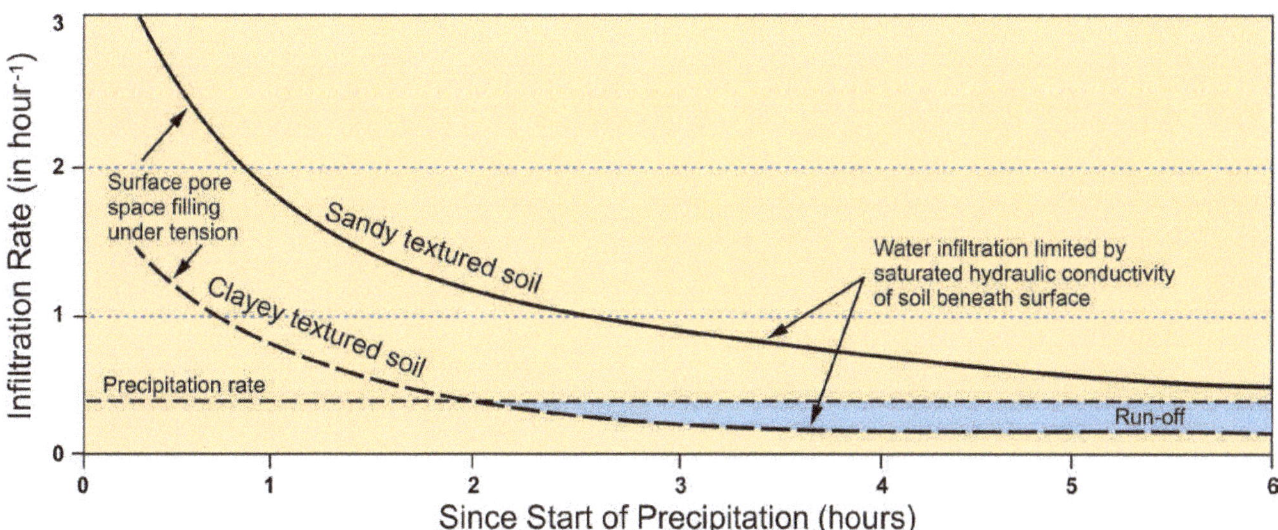

Figure 3.5*—Response of a dry soil to precipitation. Initially, infiltration rate is high and water rapidly enters a soil under tension and fills the air-filled pore space. As the soil continues to wet and air-filled pores fill with water, the ability of the saturated soils to transmit water deeper into the profile begins to control infiltration rate.*

1. Excessively drained
2. Somewhat excessively drained
3. Well-drained
4. Moderately well-drained
5. Somewhat poorly drained
6. Poorly drained
7. Very poorly drained
8. Subaqueous

May (1995) suggests that nursery sites have a minimum depth to the seasonal high water table of 5 feet (ft) (1.5 meters [m]). Excessively drained, somewhat excessively drained, and well-drained soils all meet this criterion. Water moves through excessively drained soils and somewhat excessively drained soils rapidly; they have very low to low available water-holding capacity and a water table seldom occurs within the soil profile. Water movement is slower through well-drained soils and they have higher available waterholding capacity than excessively and somewhat excessively drained soils, but like these soils, they seldom have a water table within the soil profile. Most nurseries are located on well- and somewhat-excessively well-drained soils because they pose little limitation to operations during wet seasons. Moderately well-drained soils typically have a layer of low saturated hydraulic conductivity within 3 ft (0.9 m) of the soil surfaces and are characterized by a water table within the profile during parts of the year. Nurseries located on soils of this drainage class must modify operations to accommodate the periodic wet conditions that occur (Peevy 1976).

Soil Mechanical Properties

Bulk density. Soil bulk density (g/cm3) is defined as the mass (weight) of soil per unit volume. In the United States, SI units of g cm^3 (grams per cubic centimeter) are most often used to express soil bulk density, but English units of lb ft^3 (pounds per cubic foot) are also used. The conversion from grams per cubic centimeter to pounds per cubic inch is: 1 g per cm^3 equals 0.036 lb per in^3. Total porosity can be estimated from soil bulk density using equation 1 (where 2.65 g cm^3 is the assumed particle density).

Porosity % = (1-(Bulk Density/2.65))*100 [Equation 1]

Soil bulk density is easy to measure and is often correlated to other soil physical conditions. Bulk density increases when soils are physically damaged by trafficking, loss of organic matter, and, in many instances, degradation of structure. Because of this, bulk density is often used as an index of soil physical conditions. However, bulk density has little value for assessing soil physical condition unless soil texture is also considered, as the bulk density associated with adverse soil physical conditions varies depending on soil texture. The relationship between soil texture and the bulk densities considered to be restrictive to root growth are provided in table 3.2. For sandy-textured soils, bulk densities of up to 1.69 g cm^3 can occur without root growth restrictions developing. For clay-textured soils with clay contents greater than 45 percent, root growth restriction begins at bulk densities as low as 1.39 g cm^3.

Soil strength. Roots grow through soils by either exploiting pores large enough to accommodate them or by growing into and enlarging small pores. There is a general relationship between the ability of roots to expand pores and grow into soil and soil strength. Root growth is at a maximum when soil strength is low and decreases with increasing soil strength. Root growth essentially stops when soil strength exceeds 20 bars (290 psi). For any given soil, soil strength is lowest when the soil is wet and increases as the soil dries because increased tension of the remaining water tends to hold particles together. Low bulk density is associated with the lowest soil strength and the smallest increase in strength as soils dry (da Silva et al. 1994). The same soil at a higher bulk density has greater strength, and the increase in soil strength under dry conditions tends to be relatively greater than the same soil at a lower bulk density.

Compaction and puddling. Compaction is the reduction of soil volume under pressure. By definition, soil bulk den-

Table 3.2—*Bulk density range associated with initial root growth restriction and full root growth limitation (Adapted from USDA NRCS 2011.)*

Particle	Bulk density of initial root growth restriction	Bulk density above which root growth is limited
	g cm^3	
Sand and loamy sand	1.69	1.85
Sandy loam, loam	1.63	1.80
Sandy clay loam, clay loam	1.60	1.78
Silt loam, silty clay loam, silt	1.54	1.65
Sandy clay, silty clay and clay with clay < 45%	1.49	1.58
Sandy clay, silty clay and clay with clay > 45%	1.39	1.47

cm = centimeter. g = grams.

sity increases when a soil is compacted. Problems created by excessive soil compaction are: (1) increased soil strength and mechanical restriction to root growth, (2) reduced infiltration rate and saturated hydraulic conductivity resulting in reduced drainage, and (3) reduced macropore volume and decreased gas diffusion. Compaction in nursery soils may result from wheel traffic (particularly when soils are moist and strength is low) as well as tillage operations such as disking, undercutting, and lifting (Allmaras et al. 1993). The formation of a compacted zone between 20 and 30 cm (8 to12 in) depth is a predictable consequence of repeated tillage without ameliorative treatment.

Soil puddling is the destruction of soil structure. It occurs when shear force (e.g., spinning wheels, disk harrowing) is applied to wet soils. Although puddling can occur without compaction, typically they occur together. The loss of structure by puddling contributes to the reduced infiltration, water flow, and air exchange essential to root growth observed in compacted soils.

Soil Temperature

Soil temperature is a function of air temperature, incoming radiation, surface albedo (the amount of radiation reflected versus adsorbed), the thermal capacity of the soil, and the thermal conductivity of the soil. Dark-colored surfaces adsorb more radiation than light-colored surfaces (lower albedo). Wet soils transmit heat energy to deeper layers more rapidly and also require more radiation to increase temperature than do dry soils. Thus, dark wet soils will warm to depth more quickly than light-colored wet soils. The surface of dark dry soils will become hotter than the surface of light-colored soils when the soil is dry because the heat energy absorbed at the soil surface is not transferred to deeper in the soil and collects at the surface.

Soil temperature affects root growth both directly and indirectly. Each tree species has an optimum range for root growth. Below this temperature optimum, root growth slows until a minimum temperature is reached (usually 3 to 7 °C; 37 to 45 °F) and growth stops. Above the optimum, respiration increases faster than carbohydrates are made available and net growth is reduced. Lethal temperatures are reached from 40 to 50 °C (105 to 122 °F), again, depending on the species. Lethal temperatures can be reached at the ground line and may kill newly germinated seedlings when high temperatures are combined with low soil moisture and seedbeds covered with dark-colored mulch (Barnard 1990).

Temperature has a profound effect on decomposition and availability of nutrients and on the use of nutrients by trees. Biological zero for decomposition and mineralization processes is about 4 °C (39 °F). Above this temperature, mineralization increases, approximately doubling for each 10 °C (18 °F) increase in temperature to a maximum temperature of about 40 °C (105 °F). Low temperatures reduce mineralization and nutrient availability and, as Dong et al. (2001) showed, may also limit uptake of nitrogen applied as fertilizer. Soil temperature also affects activity of damping-off pathogens. Soils with high clay contents tend to retain more water and warm more slowly in the spring. This increases the period over which seed germination occurs and increases the potential for damping-off (Barnard 1996).

Soil Chemical Characteristics

Nature of Soil Surfaces and Interactions With Soil Solution

Cation and anion exchange. The surfaces of soil particles are electrically charged. Both positively and negatively charged sites occur (fig. 3.6). The total amount of negative charge for a given mass of soil is termed cation exchange capacity (CEC). CEC is expressed in terms of the number of charges in a given mass of soil. In the United States, it is customary to express CEC as milliequivalents (0.001of a mole) per 100 g soil (meq 100 g^{-1}). The amount of positive charge for a given mass of soil is termed the anion exchange capacity (AEC) in a manner analogous to the cation exchange capacity. Positively charged sites that contribute to AEC occur when H+ is added to neutral hydroxyl groups of

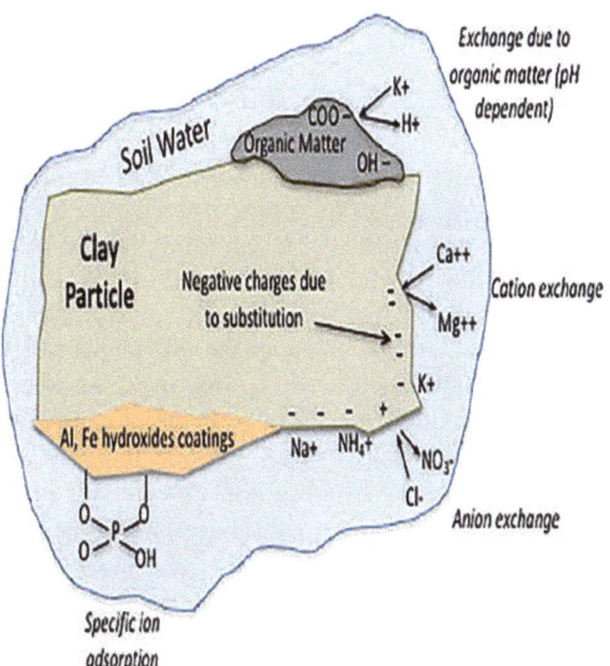

***Figure 3.6**—Adsorption and release of cations and anions on mineral and organic soil surfaces is the primary mechanism controlling availability of most essential elements.*

humus or metal oxides. The anion exchange capacity is typically much smaller than the cation exchange capacity. Although small, AEC contributes to the retention of anions (e.g., Cl^-, NO^{3-}) in soils.

The adsorption of ions to soil surfaces by negative and positive charges of the CEC and AEC is weak and easily reversed. Ions of different types can be replaced by other ions, and the concentrations of exchangeable nutrients in solution are governed by exchange reactions that describe the equilibrium between surface adsorbed cations and cations in solution. Soils with coarser textures, such as loamy sands and sandy loams have lower CECs than finer-textured soils. When fertilizers are added that have an abundance of one cation, it may be preferentially adsorbed to surfaces and displace other cations. This can cause an imbalance and lead to nutritional problems or problems with soil structure.

Potassium (K^+), calcium (Ca^{++}), magnesium (Mg^{++}), and sodium (Na^+) are termed base cations because they are cations of strong bases such as sodium hydroxide (NaOH) and do not contribute protons (H^+) to the soil. H^+ is obviously an acid cation. Additionally, Al^{3+} is considered an acid cation because it combines with water to form $AlOH_3$ and similar compounds that release H^+ and lower soil pH. The balance between basic and acid cations is measured by base saturation (eq. 2), which is the percentage of the CEC occupied by the sum of K, Ca, Mg and Na.

$$BS\% = 100 \Sigma (K,Ca,Mg,Na)/CEC \quad \text{[Equation 2]}$$

Soils with a high base saturation tend to be more fertile while soils with a low base saturation are acidic and of lower fertility.

Specific ion adsorption. In addition to the weak adsorption of ions to soil surfaces by the electrostatic charge of the exchange complex, ions can also be adsorbed to surfaces of soil particles through the process of specific ion adsorption. In this type of adsorption, ions form chemical bonds at one or more locations on the surface of metal oxides or with organic matter (fig. 3.6). As its name implies, sites for this type of adsorption are unique to the compound and the adsorption is much stronger. This type of adsorption tends to be very important for elements that form anionic compounds with oxygen (e.g., $H_2PO_4^-$).

Solubility. The most abundant form of many soil micronutrients, and under some conditions soil P (Phosphorus), is as a component of a compound with low solubility. The concentration of these elements in the soil solution, and hence their availability, is a function of a solubility reaction. The lower the solubility, the less likely an ion will move into the soil solution. The factors affecting solubility, therefore, become increasingly important to manage nutrient availability. For example, a common source of plant-available phosphorus is calcium phosphate, $Ca_3(PO_4)_2$. If the soil pH is high (above 7) then a large amount of Ca^{++} will be available in the soil solution. This makes it difficult for the calcium in calcium phosphate to move into the soil solution. Therefore, the phosphorus remains tied up in a form unavailable to plants.

Soil reaction (pH) and acidity. When pure water disassociates into H^+ and OH^- ions, neither ion occurs in greater concentration and the water is neither acid nor basic. If greater concentrations of H+ ions occur, the water is acidic. If greater concentrations of OH- occur, the water is basic or alkaline. The relative acidity or alkalinity of a solution is its pH. It is determined by measuring the concentration of H^+ in soil solution and expressing it as the negative log of the H^+ ion concentration (eq. 3).

$$pH = - \log10 [H^+] \quad \text{[Equation 3]}$$

Many soil processes are pH-dependent. The disassociation of H^+ from soil organic matter results in a negative charge that contributes to CEC (known as pH-dependent charge). The activity of microorganisms responsible for organic matter decomposition and nutrient mineralization and the formation and stability of compounds that contain and control the availability of some essential nutrients are all affected by soil solution pH.

Soil pH must be kept within an appropriate range to maintain nutrient availability and to control disease. The best balance in nutrient availability occurs when pH is between 5.5 and 6.5. Under more acid conditions, nutrients that occur in solution as anions form low-solubility compounds and are removed from solution. This includes the micronutrient anions boron (B), chlorine (Cl^-) and molybdenum (Mo) as well as the macronutrient phosphorus (P). Under more alkaline conditions, insoluble compounds with copper (Cu), iron (Fe), magnesium (Mg), manganese (Mn), and zinc (Zn) form. For example, Altland (2006) showed that foliar chlorosis of red maple (*Acer rubrum* L.) seedlings in a commercial nursery was due to Mn deficiency in areas of high soil pH. Soil pH also affects disease. The effect of soil pH on damping off (*Fusarium, Rhizoctonia,* and *Phytopthora*) is well known in conifer and hardwood nurseries, and it is standard practice to maintain pH below 6.0 to control this fungal problem (Sutherland and Anderson 1980).

Buffering capacity. Control of pH depends on changing the proportion of the cation exchange complex comprised of H and Al cations. To raise soil pH, elements that can replace (exchange for) H and Al are added to the soil. Typically, Ca and Mg sources are added. To lower soil pH, materials that supply H and Al are added. These are typically elemental S or Al compounds. The amounts added depend not only on the desired pH change, but also the exchange capacity of the soil—its buffering capacity. Soils with a high cation exchange capacity will require more material to be added to effect the same change in pH than soils with a low cation exchange capacity. Thus, sandy soils with low CEC are poorly buffered and relatively small additions of base or acid-forming compounds will change the pH. Soils with greater clay content such as a clay-loam are well buffered and greater additions are required to alter soil pH to the same extent (fig. 3.7). Generally, a soil pH that is too high would only occur in hardwood nurseries when alkaline organic materials (such as some composts) have been inadvertently added in an effort to increase soil organic matter content.

Salinity and Sodicity. Any compound that is made up of positively and negatively charged components is a salt. Examples of salts with high solubility include sodium chloride (NaCl), sodium sulfate (Na_2SO_4), and calcium sulfate ($CaSO_4$). In water, these salts disassociate to their component ions, some of which are essential elements absorbed and used by plants. The sum of the concentration of all of these dissolved ions is termed "soil salinity" and is expressed as total dissolved solids (TDS) expressed as mass per unit volume such as milligrams per liter (mg L^{-1}). Saline soils occur when salt concentrations are so great that plants cannot draw water into the roots. Saline soils develop when salt in low-moderate salt concentration irrigation water builds up in the surface soil because of evaporation and transpiration without adequate leaching. Typically, excess salinity is only a problem for nurseries located in drier climatic regions or with poor-quality irrigation water.

Because charged ions of salts conduct electricity, and it is easy to measure the charge carrying capacity of a soil-water mix, salt concentrations are typically assessed by measuring electrical conductivity. Water is added to soil until the point that the soil is completely saturated and begins to flow and measurements are taken using a conductivity probe. These "saturated paste extracts" can be correlated with TDS. Conductivities greater than 2.0 dS m^{-1} (decisiemens per meter) are considered saline and nursery soils must be maintained below this conductivity. Ideally, the conductivity of nursery soils should be much lower, less than 0.5 dS m^{-1}.

Sodicity refers to the amount of the specific cation, Na, relative to other cations on the cation exchange complex. It is expressed as the exchangeable sodium percentage (ESP). Generally, when more than 15 percent of the cation exchange complex is Na, degradation of soil structure can occur. This is seldom a problem in tree nurseries.

Essential Elements

Thirteen mineral nutrients are recognized as being required for tree growth: the macronutrients nitrogen (N), phosphorus (P), potassium (K), calcium (Ca), magnesium (Mg), sulfur (S), and the micronutrients iron (Fe), zinc (Zn), copper (Cu), manganese (Mn), boron (B), chlorine (Cl), and molybdenum (Mo). Several other elements have been shown to be beneficial for growth, but not essential. These include sodium (Na), cobalt (Co), nickel (Ni), selenium (Se), and silicon (Si). The macronutrients are constituents of proteins, components of cell

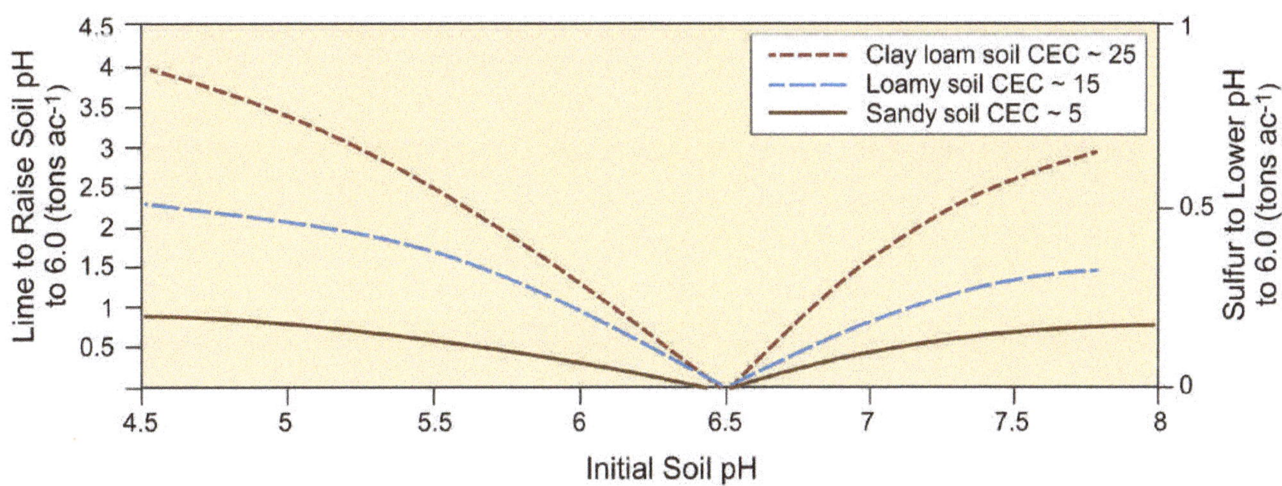

Figure 3.7—Approximate amounts of lime required to raise pH and sulfur required to lower pH to a target pH of 6.5 for soils of different texture. Note the differences in the axes. (Adapted from Havlin et al. 2005, Himelrick 2008.)

walls and are involved in metabolic pathways and occur in plant tissue in high concentrations, normally from several hundredths to more than a percent of plant tissue by mass. The micronutrients occur in low concentrations from a few parts per million to several hundred parts per million.

Essential elements occur in the soil in a variety of chemical forms. The greatest quantity of essential elements is found bound within organic matter, adsorbed to soil surfaces, or in low-solubility compounds. Elements in these solid phases are not available for uptake and utilization by plants until they enter soil solution. Thus, nutrient availability depends on the mechanisms that release elements from solid forms into solution. Although each essential element is unique, it is possible to group elements with similar behaviors.

Nitrogen. Soil organic matter is important in the storage and release of all nutrients, but is always the dominant source of N in soils. When considered relative to annual requirements, little N occurs in plant-available forms at any one time and conversion of organic nitrogen to inorganic forms (mineralization) of NH_4^- (ammonification) and NO_3^- (nitrification), largely controls the quantity of N in soil solution. Factors that affect rates of decomposition such as soil moisture, temperature, and fertility affect mineralization of N.

An understanding of carbon to nitrogen ratio (C:N ratio) is important to understanding the effects of organic matter addition on N availability as it provides a rough estimate of the relative need for N by decomposing organisms involved in decomposition. When the amount of carbon is high and nitrogen low in organic materials (high C:N ratio), there is abundant energy and all available N is used by the decomposer community. Little N is released to soil solution, where it is available for plant uptake. When the C:N ratio is low, energy availability limits decomposer activity and excess N is leaked to the soil solution and can be absorbed by plants (fig. 3.8). Generally, N starts becoming available to the plant when about 35 percent of the original organic matter remains or when the C:N ratio is about 35:1.

Phosphorus. Phosphorus chemistry is complex and not easily grouped with other essential elements. It forms low-solubility compounds with Al and Fe at low soil pH (see below) and with Ca and Mg at high pH. It can be adsorbed on metal oxides and soil humus and its concentration in plant tissue and organic debris is high. In weathered soils of the South, particularly those with finer texture, P storage and availability is dominated by inorganic solubility reactions. However, organic matter decomposition and P mineralization may dominate storage and availability in sandy-textured nursery soils.

Sulfur. Like N, organic matter is usually the dominant source of S in surface soils. This is particularly true in the sandy-textured surface soils characteristic of most tree seedling nurseries. Consequently, S availability in surface soils is affected by factors impacting decomposition rate. Sulfur can be specifically adsorbed on surfaces of Fe and Al oxides coating clay particles, and specific ion adsorption is the dominant storage and availability-controlling mechanism in subsoils.

Base nutrients. The macronutrients K, Ca, and Mg are stored in large amounts in soil on the cation exchange

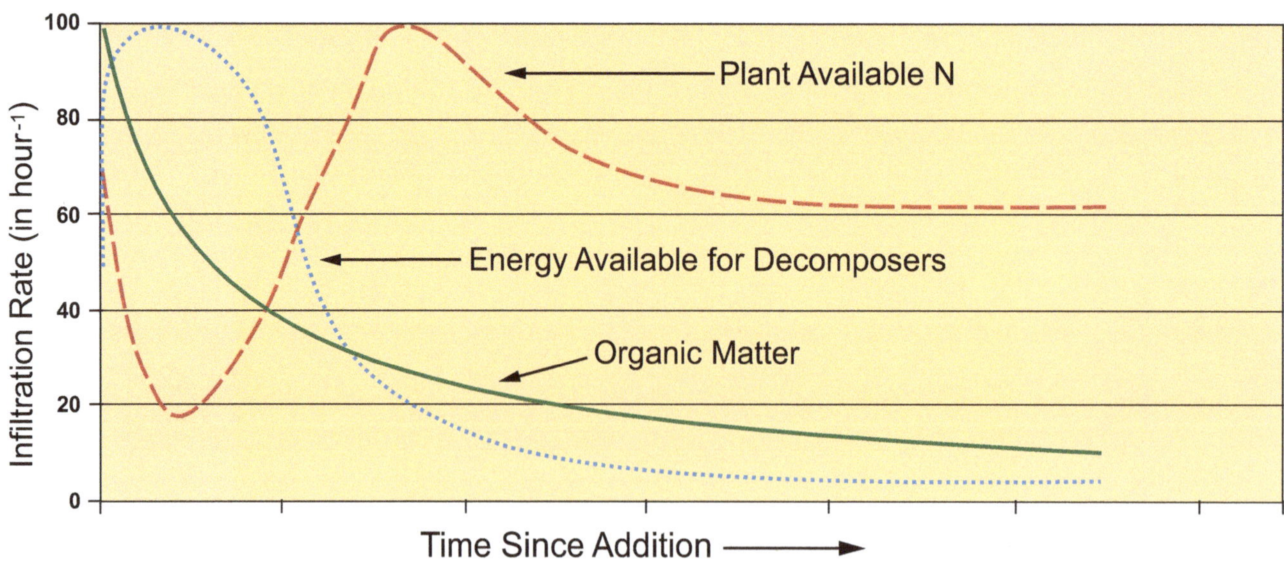

***Figure 3.8**—Relationship among organic matter remaining, energy available for the decomposing community, and plant-available N after the addition of high C:N ratio organics to soil.*

complex; and the CEC is the primary available source of these nutrients. Weathering of primary minerals and mineralization of organic matter also releases these nutrients to solution, but these released nutrients quickly establish equilibrium with the CEC through exchange reactions. Hardwoods have a higher base nutrient demand than conifers and the fertilization of hardwood nurseries will result in the greater incorporation of base nutrients. For example, at high rates of N fertilization, P and K can become growth-limiting in hardwood nurseries (Birge et al. 2006).

Micronutrient cations. Micronutrient cations (Cu^{2+}, Fe^{3+}, Fe^{2+}, Mn^{2+}, Mn^{4+}, Zn^{2+}) can be adsorbed to the exchange complex in a manner similar to K, Ca, and Mg, but this is not the dominant source in soil. Instead, specific ion adsorption to soil organic matter is the major solid-phase storage of these nutrients at typical nursery soil pH. At high soil pH, micronutrient cations form low solubility compounds by combining with hydroxide (OH^-), which greatly reduces concentrations in soil solution. Thus, at high pH, solubility reactions will control plant availability of micronutrient cations. Deficiencies in micronutrient cations can become problematic at soil pH > 7.0.

Micronutrient anions. (B, Cl^-, Mo). The availability of the micronutrient anions is the reverse of the micronutrient cations. Boron and molybdenum both occur as oxyanions in solution. These oxyanions adsorb to metal oxides and form low-solubility compounds under acid conditions. These reactions control soil solution concentrations and plant availability in fine-textured, weathered soils. However, the primary storage and source of B in sandy soils is organic matter and B deficiencies have been reported in Florida, where organic matter concentration of a nursery on sandy soil with few primary minerals was allowed to fall to 1 percent (Stone et al. 1982).

Organic Matter

Contributions of Organic Matter to Healthy Soil

Organic matter concentration of undisturbed upland forest soils typical of the sites where tree nurseries are located could contain anywhere from 2- to 10-percent organic matter on a weight basis, depending on the location. These concentrations reflect the balance between inputs from fallen leaves, branches and bark, root exudates, and root production and mortality. However, organic matter content in forest nurseries is generally at the low end of this range. Undisturbed forest soils in the Southern United States may contain 5-percent organic matter, while tree nurseries will routinely use 1.5 to 3.0 percent as target organic matter content. In the cooler climates of the Pacific Northwest, forest soils can contain over 10-percent organic matter and nurseries may target 5 to 8 percent as a reasonable content (Davey 1996). Target ranges for organic matter depend on soil texture. Nurseries in the Southern United States with sandy-textured surfaces should contain 1.5- to 2.0-percent organic matter, and soils with loam-textured surfaces should contain 2.0- to 3.0-percent organic matter (May 1964).

The organic matter included in these percentages range from recently dead organic debris of obvious origin to amorphous black material that is a mix of fine particulate and colloids with origins that are not possible to determine. Fresh organic matter (corresponding to the Oi horizon of soil taxonomy) contains abundant energy and C and is the food that drives the decomposer community. It is nutrient-poor in relation to its energy content and, in the short-term, can be a sink rather than a source of nutrients. Humus, which is thoroughly decomposed amorphous organic matter, is at the opposite end of the spectrum. It is composed of complex molecules with numerous cross bonds that provide little energy for decomposers and is relatively stable. It contributes to a number of soil properties, but is relatively unimportant as an energy and C source to the decomposer community. Between these two end points exist a range of partially decomposed organic matter that have adequate energy and C to support a thriving decomposer community but that also release mineral nutrients to support plant growth.

Organic matter affects many soil characteristics and processes, and several of these have been previously discussed. Soil organic matter:

- is a primary storage site of N and is an important site for storing other essential elements,
- provides energy and carbon to heterotrophic organisms, including those microorganisms, responsible for nutrient mineralization and transformation and meso- and macrofauna whose activities create soil pores,
- helps bind individual soil articles into aggregates responsible for soil structure,
- influences the chemical activity of important essential elements,
- contributes to soil cation exchange,
- increases soil water-holding capacity,

- partially controls thermal characteristics of soils,
- affects activity and recommended rates of soil-applied pesticides.

Organic Matter Maintenance

The essential role of organic matter in soil processes makes its maintenance a critical goal of nursery soil management. Several factors contribute to the low-organic-matter content typical of nurseries. First, organic matter decomposition is at a maximum when soils are near-field-capacity moisture content and fertility is high. Nurseries are irrigated and fertilized precisely to maintain these conditions. Second, rapid decomposition of organic matter is supported by warmer temperatures. Exposure to the sun and raised beds contribute to more rapid warming of nursery beds in the spring. Third, the frequent tillage that occurs in nursery production breaks up the soil and exposes organic matter protected within structural aggregates to microbial populations. Under these conditions, frequent additions are necessary to maintain soil organic matter with optimal ranges.

Two approaches to organic matter addition are available. The first is to grow a green manure crop that can be tilled into the soil. The second is to add organic soil amendments.

Green manure crops. Crops are grown between seedling rotations for four basic purposes: (1) to protect against erosion, (2) to control weeds, (3) to serve as a "living mulch" to protect sown seeds from injury by wind, rain, or frost, and (4) to act as a green manure that can be tilled into the soil and increase organic matter content. Many combinations of crops and crop rotations are used—almost as many as the number of tree nurseries—and, in most cases, two or more of these four purposes are combined in crop selection.

Grains, such as rye (*Secale cereale* L.), *sorghum-sudangrass* (*Sorghum x drummondi* (Nees ex. Steud.) Millsp. & Chase), and wheat (*Triticum aestivum* L.), are commonly used in hardwood nurseries (Stauder 1993, Ensminger 2002) as both a living mulch and as a green manure. When used as a green manure, however, these crops are tilled into the soil rather than left on the surface. Corn (*Zea mays* L.) is also used as a summer cover crop. Legumes and buckwheat (*Fagopyrum esculentum* Moench.) are less frequently used because they have been associated with increased root disease (Davey 1996). When a 2-year cover crop rotation is used, woodier crops, such as pigeon pea (*Cajanus cajan* (L.) Millsp.), may be used in the first year (Davey 1996). Nurseries in the Pacific Northwest typically use rye and oats (*Avena sativa* L.) as green manures. Use of sorghum sudan grass, which is common in the Midwest and South, is associated with seedling mortality in the Pacific Northwest (Iyer 1979).

The impact that cover crops have on soil organic matter content is limited because the fresh organic matter added by these crops decomposes rapidly. A good cover crop produces 5 to 8 tons/acre (11.2 to 17.9 metric tons per hectare [ha]) of organic matter. If incorporated into the top 6 in (15.2 cm) of soil, this would increase organic matter by a maximum of 0.5 to 0.6 percent, but most of it decomposes rapidly. This is demonstrated by the results of Sumner and Bouton (1981) in their study of organic matter content change in a Georgia nursery following a two-year crop rotation. Summer crops of corn, sorghum (*Sorgum bicolor* L. Moench) and millet (*Pennisetum* spp.) increased organic matter content with the greatest increase—from 1.12 to 1.64 percent—observed for sorghum after the first crop. There was no additional increase after the second summer crop and winter cover crops had little effect on soil organic matter. These authors concluded that the increased organic matter content would be unlikely to persist, a conclusion reiterated by Davey (1996).

Organic amendments. In most nurseries, the use of green manure crops is not enough to maintain sufficient soil organic matter. Consequently, most nurseries also add organic amendments to the soil. Wood wastes such as sawdust and bark, peat moss, agricultural residues and manures are all potential sources of organic amendments (Rose et al. 1995, Davis et al. 2006, Koll et al. 2010).

It is important to distinguish between the two main uses of organic amendments: amendments spread on the soil and left on the surface as a mulch, and amendments tilled into the soil to improve organic matter content. While organic mulches will eventually decompose and be incorporated into soil organic matter, the immediate effects of mulches in nurseries are to protect the surface from erosion, conserve water, moderate surface soil temperature extremes, and reduce weed growth. Mulches have relatively little immediate impact on soil chemistry. In contrast, organic matter tilled into the soil decomposes rapidly and has both immediate and long-term effects on soil chemistry and nutrient availability.

Fresh woody materials such as sawdust or bark have high C:N ratios, typically greater than 100:1 and as high as 300:1. When these materials are incorporated into soil, microbial populations increase because of the abundance of C and energy to support growth and metabolism. However, because of the low amount of N, available N is quickly incorporated into the community of decomposing organisms. Little is available to support plant growth and N deficiency develops due to low plant availability (fig. 3.8). To a lesser extent this microbial demand also reduces availability of other nutrients. Under nursery conditions, the immobilization period that results from the addition of high C:N ratio woody materials ranges from 20 to 80 days, depending on the source of material (Davey 1996). Planting immediately after amendment with sawdust will reduce seedling growth (Koll et al. 2010). Thus, the use of sawdust or bark usually results in the need to either fertilize with N or to leave amended areas out of production until the material is partially decomposed and normal nutrient availability returns. As an alternative to inorganic fertilization, some nurseries mix high C:N ratio organic amendments with manures that have a low C:N ratio and can supply N.

The addition of composted materials will avoid some of the difficulties associated with the use of bark and sawdust amendments. Typically, composts are produced using a mix of organic materials with different C:N ratios, such as sawdust with municipal wastewater treatment plant biosolids or animal manures. Decomposition is promoted by maintaining proper moisture and providing adequate aeration, so oxygen does not limit aerobic decomposition. After a relatively short period of several weeks to several months, a compost is produced that can be incorporated into the soil and immediately planted. Gouin et al. (1978) reported both yellow poplar (*Liriodendron tulipifera* L.) and red maple stem length increased following addition of a compost of wood chips and municipal sludge (fig. 3.9).

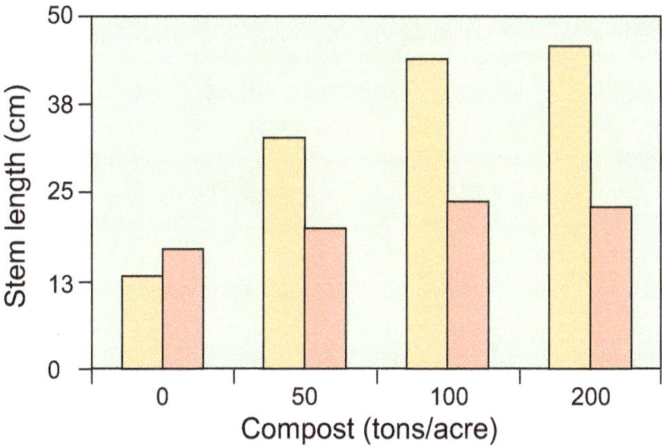

***Figure 3.9**—Effect of compost made from a 3:1 mixture of wood chips and municipal sludge on the growth of yellow poplar (yellow bars) and red maple (red bars) in a nursery (Gouin et al. 1978).*

Composts are characterized by "stability" and "maturity." Stable composts have completed the rapid phase of decomposition and no longer have high nutrient demands and are, instead, slowly releasing N available for plant uptake. "Mature" composts have undergone sufficient decomposition that few volatile compounds or potentially toxic fatty acids or phenols remain. Soil incorporation of unstable or immature composts can result in N deficiency and introduction of weeds to the nursery. Similarly, insufficiently composted materials (immature composts) may introduce allelopathic chemicals. Composts made with cedar (*Juniperus virginiana* L.), eucalyptus (*Eucalyptus* spp.), pecan (*Carya illinoensis* Wangenh. K. Koch), and walnut (*Juglans nigra* L.) are all potentially allelopathic and must be composted before use.

Composts used in nurseries should have a pH between 5.5 and 6.5. Many composts made using biosolids from wastewater treatment facilities or animal manures have a high pH because of the use of lime for pathogen or odor control. Use of such composts as a soil amendment can result in long-term problems due to elevated pH, such as occurred at the Saratoga Tree Nursery in New York (Bicklehaupt 1989).

There is consensus among nursery managers that soil organic matter maintenance is important in tree nurseries and increases in soil organic matter can increase tree growth. If measured immediately after addition, soil organic matter content increases about 0.1 percent for each dry ton of organic amendment added. However, the effects of a one-time addition of organic matter are short-lived. For example, Mexal and Fisher (1987) studied the effects of a single application of sewage sludge, peat moss, pine bark and sawdust on the organic matter content of a nursery soil in New Mexico. Regardless of the amendment or rate applied, nursery soil organic matter contents returned to preapplication levels within 2 years of application. Similarly, Munson (1982) reported that the addition of 245 tons per acre (550 metric tons per ha) of sawdust raised soil organic matter to almost 5 percent in a sandy textured Florida nursery, but in less than 3 years, soil organic matter contents had fallen to pretreatment levels of 1.3 percent. In contrast to these studies, May and Gilmore (1985) showed that increases in organic matter content could be sustained with repeated additions. Thus, it appears that a combination of green manure crops and repeated applications of organic amendments are necessary to maintain nursery soil organic matter content at desired levels.

References

Allmaras, R.R.; Juzwik, J.; Overton, R.P.; Copeland, S.M. 1993. Soil compaction: causes, effects and management in bareroot nurseries. In: Landis, T.D., tech coord. National Nursery Proceedings, Proceedings Northeastern and Intermountain Forest and Conservation Nursery Association. Gen. Tech. Rep. RM-243. Fort Collins, CO: U.S. Department of Agriculture, Forest Service, Rocky Mountain Forest and Range Experiment Station: 19–32

Altland, J. 2006. Foliar chlorosis in field-grown red maples. Hortscience: 41(5): 1347–1350.

Barnard, E.L. 1990. Ground line heat lesions on tree seedlings. Florida Department of Agriculture & Consumer Services, Division of Plant Industry. Plant Pathology Circular 338. 2 p.

Barnard, E.L. 1996. Diseases of seedlings in forest tree nurseries in Florida: history and status. In: Third meeting of IUFRO Working Party S7.03-04 (Diseases and Insects in Forest Nurseries). Orlando-Gainesville, FL.

Bickelhaupt, D. 1989. The long-term effect of a single application of horse manure on soil pH. Tree Planters' Notes. 40(1): 31–33.

Birge, Z.K.; Salifu, D.K.F.; Jacobs, D.F. 2006. Modified exponential nitrogen loading to promote morphological quality and nutrient storage of bareroot-cultured *Quercus rubra* and *Quercus alba* seedlings. Scandinavian Journal of Forest Research. 21: 306–316.

Bosch, L. 1986. Site preparation and soil management in a high silt nursery. National Nursery Proceedings, Southern Forest Nursery Association. Pensacola, FL: 16–17.

Boyer, J.N; South, D.B. 1984. Forest nursery practices in the South. Southern Journal of Applied Forestry. 8(2): 67-75.

Briggs, R.D. 2008. Soil and nutrition: a forest nursery perspective. In: Dumroese, R.K.; Riley, L.E., tech. coords. National Proceedings Forest and Conservation Nursery Associations; 2007. RMRS-P-57. Fort Collins, CO: U.S. Department of Agriculture, Forest Service, Rocky Mountain Research Station. 55–64.

Da Silva, A.P.; Kay, B.D.; Perfect, E. 1994. Characterization of the least limiting water range of soils. Soil Science Society of America Journal. 58: 1775–1781.

Davey, C.B. 1996. Nursery soil management-organic amendments. In: Landis T.D.; South, D.B., tech. coords. National Proceedings, Forest and Conservation Nursery Associations. Southern Forest Nursery Association. PNW-GTR-389. Portland, OR: U.S. Department of Agriculture, Forest Service, Pacific Northwest Research Station: 6–18.

Davis, A.S.; Jacobs, D.F.; Wightman, K.E.; Birge, Z.K.D. 2006. Organic matter added to bareroot nursery beds influences soil properties and morphology of *Fraxinus pennsylvanica* and *Quercus rubra* seedlings. New Forests. 31: 293–303.

Dong, S.; Scagel, C.F.; Cheng, L. [et al.]. 2001. Interactions between soil temperature and plant growth stage on nitrogen uptake and amino acid content of apple nursery stock during early spring growth. Tree Physiology. 21: 541–547.

Ensminger, P. 2002. Nursery practices in Tennessee. In: Dumroese, R.K.; Riley, L.E.; Landis, T.D., tech. coords. National Proceedings Forest and Conservation Nursery Associations; 1999, 2000 and 2001, Western Forest and Conservation Nursery Association Conference. RMRS-P-24. Fort Collins, CO: U.S. Department of Agriculture, Forest Service, Rocky Mountain Forest and Range Experiment Station: 281–283.

Gouin, F.R.; Link, C.B.N.; Kundt, J.F. 1978. Forest tree seedlings thrive on composted sludge. Compost Science. 19(4): 28–30.

Hartmann, H.R. 1970. Results of nursery management on a heavy-textured soil. National Nursery Proceedings, Southeastern Nurseryman's Conference: 69–72.

Havlin. J.L.; Beaton, J.D.; Tisdale, J.D.; Nelson, W.L. 2005. Soil fertility and fertilizers: an introduction to nutrient management. 7th ed. Upper Saddle River, NJ: Pearson-Prentice Hall. p. 63.

Himelrick, D.G. 2008. Home blueberry production in Louisiana. Louisiana State University AgCenter Research and Extension. 7p. (http://www.lsuagcenter.com/NR/rdonlyres/D30270C0-F2DC-4B33-8AB7-036865AB6AAE/43116/pub1978HomeBlueberry-ProductionHIGHRES.pdf). (March 20, 2018).

Iyer, J.G. 1979. Sorghum-sudan grass manure: its effect on nursery stock. University of Wisconsin Short Communication 4082, Madison, WI. 4 p.

Koll, P.; Jurgensen, M.F.; Dumroese, R.K. 2010. Effects of pine sawdust, hardwood sawdust and peat on bareroot soil properties. In: Riley, L.E.; Pinto, J.R.; Dumroese, R.K., tech. coords. National Proceedings Forest and Conservation Nursery Associations. RMRS-P-62. Fort Collins, CO: U.S. Department of Agriculture, Forest Service, Rocky Mountain Research Station: 71–75.

May, J.T. 1995. Chapter 2: Site selection. In: Landis, T.; Tinus, R.; McDonald S.; Barnett, J. eds. The Container Tree Nursery Manual—Volume 1: Nursery Planning, Development and Management. Agric. Handb. 674. Washington, DC: U.S. Department of Agriculture, Forest Service: 27–46.

May, J.T. 1964. The forest nursery and its soils. National Nursery Proceedings, Proceedings Region 8 Forest Nurseryman's Conference: 3–9.

May, J.T.; Gilmore A.R. 1985. Continuous cropping at the Stauffer nursery in Alabama. In: South, D.B. ed. Proceedings of Symposium on Nursery Management Practices for Southern Pines: 213–221.

Mexal, J.G.; Fisher, J.T. 1987. Organic matter amendments to a calcareous forest nursery soil. New Forests. 4: 311–323.

Munson, K.R. 1982. Decomposition and effect on pH of various organic soil amendments. In: Proceedings of Southern Nursery Conference. R8-TP4. U.S. Department of Agriculture, Forest Service: 121–130.

Peevy, C.E. 1976. Hardwood nursery management: problems that can and do occur in the nursery and how these problems can be avoided and solved. National Nursery Proceedings, Southeastern Area Nurserymen's Conference: 4–7.

Rose, R.; Haase, D.L.; Boyer, D. 1995. Organic matter management in forest nurseries: theory and practice. Corvallis, OR: Oregon State University, Nursery Technical Cooperative. 655 p.

Schoeneberger, P.J.; Wysocki, D.A.; Benham, E.C.; Broderson, W.D. 1998. Field book for describing and sampling soils. Lincoln, NE: U.S. Department of Agriculture, Natural Resources Conservation Service. 182 p.

Stauder, A.F. 1993. The use of green over winter mulch in the Illinois State Nursery program. In: Landis, T.D., tech coord. National Nursery Proceedings, Proceedings Northeastern and Intermountain Forest and Conservation Nursery Association. Gen. Tech. Rep. RM-243. Fort Collins, CO: U.S. Department of Agricultures Forest Service, Rocky Mountain Forest and Range Experiment Station: 51–53.

Stoeckeler, J.H.; Jones, G.W. 1957. Forestry nursery practice in the Lake States. Agric. Handb. 110. Washington, DC: U.S. Department of Agriculture, Forest Service. 124 p.

Stone, E.L.; Hollis, C.A.; Barnard, E.L. 1982. Boron deficiency in a southern pine nursery. Southern Journal of Applied Forestry. 6(2): 108–112.

Stroup, M.C.; Williams, H.M. 1999. Frost heaving of container hardwood seedlings planted in an abandoned agricultural field in Sharkey County, Mississippi. In: Haywood, J.D., ed. Proceedings Tenth Biennial Southern Silviculture Research Conference. Gen. Tech. Rep. SRS 30. Asheville, NC: U.S. Department of Agriculture, Forest Service: 148–150.

Sumner, M.E.; Bouton, J.H. 1981. Organic matter maintenance in forestry nurseries. Georgia Forest Research Paper 24. Macon, GA: Georgia Forestry Commission. 6 p.

Sutherland, J.R.; Anderson, R.L. 1980. Seedling disease and insect problems related to nursery soil conditions in North America. Proceedings, North American Forest Tree Nursery Soils Workshop: 182-190.

U.S. Department of Agriculture (USDA), National Resources Conservation Service (NRCS). 2011. Technical Soil Services Handbook. http://soils.usda.gov/technical/tssh/. (August 3).

INTERNATIONAL

Seedbed Preparation and Sowing: A Northern Hardwood Nursery Perspective

4a

R. A. Hawkins

Robert A. Hawkins is nursery section supervisor, Indiana Department of Natural Resources, Vallonia Nursery, Vallonia, IN

Outline

Facing Page: *Operation of a large acorn seeder. (Photo by Jeanie Redicker, Indiana Department of Natural Resources, 2013.)*

Figure 4a.1*—Flail mower used to cut cover crop prior to soil preparation. Mowing is followed by incorporation (disking), fumigation, and bed preparation. (Photo by Jeanie Redicker, Indiana Department of Natural Resources, 2013.)*

Seedbed Preparation

The majority of seed planting in a typical northern hardwood nursery takes place in the fall (September to December) before soil freezes up. Due to the various species of hardwood seed handled in the North, their requirements of cold stratification and the lack of adequate seed storage facilities, most seed need to be fall sown for optimal germination. Seedbed preparation is mainly done just before planting. Species that can be spring sown will have their seedbeds formed before sowing but the actual field tillage and soil preparation for these areas will be done in the fall, with soil management extremely important for subsequent seed germination and seedling survival.

Most northern nurseries start with some type of soil-injected gas for fumigation in late summer or early fall before seeding. For the fumigation equipment and the chemical to work properly, mowing, chopping, and disking of any cover crops are required. Various cover crops are raised in many areas to increase soil organic matter, maintain high soil fertility, and assist with minimizing weed seed buildup. However, cover crops must be well incorporated into the soil. Flail mowers and rotary cutters chop these cover crops in very small pieces that can then be easily incorporated into the soil (fig. 4a.1). This is the first step in preparing the seedbeds for tillage and bedding. Disking and plowing the soil to help bury the cover crop remnants and facilitate decomposition are also necessary. The process may also include deep rippers to break up soil hardpans and chisel plows to assist with clod breakup and cover crop burial. The tools and equipment used to ready the fields for fumigation vary and depend on the individual nursery and the type and amount of cover crop residue.

The type of cover crop will determine the extent of field preparations needed, and plenty of preparation time should be allowed to properly prepare fields for fumigation. Up to 4 to 6 weeks of soil preparation, including weekly disking of cover crop residues, may be necessary to ready the ground for fumigation and eventually bedding (bedforming). A good indication that fields are ready to fumigate is the ability to run a spring-tooth harrow over the fields without dragging up piles of the cover crop residue.

After soil tillage operations and fumigation, seedbed building can begin, within 1 or 2 days of fumigation tarp removal. The benefit to early seedbed preparation is to set the beds and install paths for proper water drainage in the fields. The drier weather typical of the fall results in lower soil moisture and is favorable to seedbed preparation conditions. Various types of seedbed formers or shapers (bedformers) are used to make a raised seedbed to allow equipment access to these seedbeds for various cultural practices. These bedformers also make paths for water to travel away from the sown seed to reduce the potential for germination problems from extremely wet

Figure 4a.2—Bedformers have soil rototilling functions in addition to the formation of a specific bed width. (Photo by Jeanie Redicker, Indiana Department of Natural Resources, 2013.)

soil conditions. Bedformers have changed over the years to better produce a bed for seed sowing (fig. 4a.2). They are now equipped with roto-tiller capabilities as well as rollers to firm up the seedbed. This tilling of the seedbed will assist with the incorporation of all organic matter remnants into the soil, just prior to sowing. A firm, level bed free of clods and large woody materials will allow seed to be planted uniformly at the correct depth over the entire bed and help ensure optimal seed germination. Bedformers are available in varying widths to fit individual nursery requirements. Each seedbed width should match the wheel spacing of tractors and other equipment used in the various cultural practices that are applied to the seedbeds of the individual nursery.

Sowing

Mechanical Hardwood Seeders

Mechanical seeders for hardwood tree seeds are very specialized. Unfortunately, there aren't enough nurseries across the United States to warrant their commercialized mass production, and as a result they tend to be very expensive. Also, while commercially available seeders do an exceptional job, they only handle limited seed sizes: hardwood seed sizes range from smaller than a BB to baseball size and require different sowing depths and densities. (Individual seed depth and density guidelines can be found in *The Woody Seed Plant Manual*, Bonner and Karrfalt 2008). Typically, local nursery operators fabricate hardwood seeders to fit the needs of their nursery. Often each nursery has several homemade seeders that incorporate certain mechanisms from a variety of planters to meet all planting objectives.

Drill sown seeders. This type of seeder usually handles all small-seeded hardwood species, shrubs, and conifer seeds (fig. 4a.3). Seed drills are "ground-driven" so the rate of travel across the seedbeds will have no ill effect on sowing rates. The rate of speed across the field depends greatly on soil conditions. The planter can handle seeds that vary in size from a grain of salt, such as ninebark (*Physocarpus opulifolius* L. Maxim.), to winged seeds like river birch (*Betula nigra* L.), to small stone fruits, like blackgum (*Nyssa sylvatica* Marsh.). Seed drills commonly have double disk openers to create the furrow into which the seed is placed. Individual row covers cover the seed with the correct amount of soil once it has been placed in the furrow. The openers adjust to varying depths (1/8 to 1/4 inch [in]) (3 to 6 millimeter [mm]), based on the sowing requirements of each species.

Seeds are usually sown in five to eight rows across the prepared seedbed. Distribution of seed through this drill ensures equal amounts are sown in all rows. The planter is

***Figure 4a.3**—Operation of the Love seed drill, used for small-seeded hardwood sowing. (Photo by Jeanie Redicker, Indiana Department of Natural Resources, 2013.)*

calibrated by catching all seed in one revolution of the drive wheel, which is a known distance of travel, and weighing it. Individual seed data, specifically "pure live seed" (PLS) per pound, can be used in determining number of seeds sown per linear foot. The drill can be adjusted to dispense the appropriate weight of seed to meet the desired sowing rate. This type of hardwood seeder can easily achieve the desired sowing depth and density for each species. This drill takes two people to operate. The first drives the tractor and focuses on alignment within the seedbed, while the second rides and operates the seeder.

Seeders for large acorns. This type of seeder handles acorns ranging in size from white oak (*Quercus alba* L.) to chestnut oak (*Quercus prinus* L.) or ¾ to 1½ in (19 to 38 mm) diameter. The majority of acorns collected in the North will fall within this range. Nurseries fabricate this type of seeder in-house to meet their specific needs, so the equipment varies based on each nursery manager's ideas and expertise. Most of these seeders are operated from tractor power take-off (PTO) units and are not ground driven. Each tractor must travel a steady speed across the seedbeds (usually 1 mile per hour [mph]) in order to distribute seed at the desired rate (fig. 4a.4). Some type of furrow opener is used to create trenches, usually five or six across the width of the bed, for seed to be placed in as the seeder is pulled over the seedbed. Furrows are made much deeper (1 to 2 in) (25 to 50 mm) when sowing this size of seed, compared to drill-sown hardwood seeders. Double disk openers do not perform well on this type of seeder because of the large seed size and the depth required. Normally, a chain mechanism with attached cups moving through the seed hopper transports seed to the drop tubes and into the furrows. The chain drive operates by hydraulics from the tractor PTO unit. The hydraulic system can be adjusted to increase or decrease the pace of the chains in order to drop the desired amount of seed based on the desired sowing rate for each species. A slight change to the chain speed enables more or less seed to drop while keeping the tractor at a constant speed over the seedbeds.

The furrow opener can also be connected to the hydraulic system, allowing the seed trenches to be deepened or made shallower, depending upon the needs of the seed. The furrow opener can be raised or lowered while the tractor is in motion and seeding is taking place to ensure proper sowing depth when the seedbed level varies. A small-grain drop-type seeder is often incorporated into the hardwood seed planter in order to sow a living mulch cover crop while sowing the hardwood seed. The acorn seeder will also pull some type of drag system to lightly cover the sown seed with soil.

The seeder can be calibrated by collecting seed from the seeder for a set amount of time, such as 1 minute. At 1 mph the tractor will travel a known distance across the seedbed

Figure 4a.4—Operation of a large acorn seeder. This seeder was built at the Vallonia State Nursery in Indiana. A living mulch seed sower attached to the back of the acorn sower sows wheat, rye, or oats simultaneous to acorns. (Photo by Jeanie Redicker, Indiana Department of Natural Resources, 2013.)

(88 feet [ft]) (27 meters [m]). The weight of this collected seed can then be checked against the PLS per pound data estimates. Calculating the number of PLS collected in 1 minute divided by the distance covered provides the sowing rate per unit of linear distance. The speed of the chain drive system can be adjusted to produce the desired sowing rate. This seeder takes two people to operate—one to drive the tractor and monitor speed and straightness and a second to ride and operate the seeder.

Seeder for small acorns and larger stone fruits. Seed sizes for this seeder fall between pin oak (*Quercus palustris* Munchh.) and American plum (*Prunus americana* L.), or between 3/8 in to 5/8 in (9.5 to 16 mm) diameter. This seeder combines the functions of the seed drill with those of the large acorn seeder. The small acorn seeder itself operates by hydraulics from the tractor PTO unit. It is not ground driven but operates through a hydraulic chain drive system with adjustable speed controls. The tractor pulling this seeder is driven at a constant speed (1 mph) over each seedbed. Double disk openers (five to six rows) create the furrows into which the seed is placed. Double disk openers will work with these seeds due to their smaller size. Furrow openers are set fairly deep (½ in to 1 in) (13 to 25 mm) to accommodate the depth requirements of the seed. Finger pickup units designed for soybeans have been slightly modified to allow for the seed size. This enables each individual seed to be picked up and dropped into the furrow, achieving a very uniform seed placement. Individual seed hoppers are used for each row or finger pickup unit. Press wheels follow behind each trench, pressing the seed into the soil and ensuring good soil contact.

A type of wheat/rye dispenser can be incorporated into the seeder to sow a living mulch cover crop while sowing the hardwood seed, or it can be done separately using a different machine. A drag system lightly pulls soil into the trenches and covers the sown seed. This system is separate from the seeder shown but helps incorporate living mulch seed into the trench while lightly covering all seed. Calibration for this type of seeder is identical to that of the large acorn seeders. Personnel requirements and operation are also the same.

As with all mechanical equipment, a good maintenance schedule is needed to assure proper operation. Each piece of equipment should be inspected for proper function every summer, prior to fall use. This includes checking fluid levels and hydraulic systems. Disk openers should move freely and not bind up. Inspect seed metering systems for accurate seed flow. Lubricate chain drive systems regularly to assure that individual seeds will be picked up in the correct manner. All sowing must be completed in a timely manner within a relatively short period, especially when adverse weather and soil conditions are taken into account. When seeding time arrives, mechanical breakdowns can cause havoc, so it is best to ensure proper operation of all equipment before the critical time arrives.

Timing of Sowing

Timing of sowing is crucial for proper germination and is closely tied to the availability of seed in the fall. The fruit of most northern tree species begin to ripen in September or October. Some small seeded hardwoods ripen even earlier. For example, black cherry (*Prunus serotina* Ehrh.) ripens and should be harvested in July and August, while other northern hardwood species, such as cherrybark oak (*Quercus pagoda* Raf.), ripen and fall much later in October and November. The time for seed collection tends to be relatively short, so collection needs to begin when seed ripen and begin to fall. As seed is harvested, a testing procedure must be in place to determine the amount of good seed collected for sowing purposes. Without this knowledge, the accuracy of seeder calibration is very limited.

Seed collected or purchased must be properly cared for until sowing takes place. It must be kept in cold storage to ensure that it does not begin to heat. Some seeds can be cleaned of their fleshy pulp to allow better flow through the seeder (black cherry, for example) and then placed in cold storage until sowing begins. Other large seed—i.e., black walnut (*Juglans nigra* L.)—can have their husk removed to allow seed to be sown by a mechanical seeder. This seed would otherwise have to be sown by another means that may lead to difficulty controlling sowing density.

Fumigation is completed in most northern nurseries in late September, then seeding can commence after the necessary waiting period. Hardwood seed must not be sown too early because of possible early germination if temperatures remain high in late fall. Seeding should begin after a typical fall cool-down has begun. Seedbeds are formed and various species are sown based upon seed availability. Seed can be sown as quickly as it can be harvested and seeders calibrated. This timing of seeding will assure cold stratification periods will be met by the various hardwood seed species. Larger seed, such as acorns, require a large space to store the sheer volume needed to be sown to meet production goals. Sowing this seed as it is harvested eliminates the need to store this large volume of seed any longer than necessary.

The majority of species raised in northern hardwood nurseries are fall sown, but species such as American sycamore (*Platanus occidentalis* L.), which grow quickly to shippable size and do not require a large seed storage space, can be stratified in cold storage for spring sowing. Very small seeded species, such as ninebark, can be held and stratified in cold storage to ensure seed is not lost during winter field conditions. Frost heaving, bird predation, and soil and wind erosion can all affect the availability of this seed to remain sown at the correct depth to germinate in the spring. Spring sowing of this stratified seed gives some assurance that this small seed will be in the seedbeds and found at the correct depth to germinate a few weeks later.

Seed Handling

Field handling of seed to be sown is also important for seed viability. Keep seed out of direct sunlight so it will not dry to the point that it would inhibit germination. Once the seed has been sown, irrigation can be used to moisten the seed if rainfall is not sufficient. This will also help secure the soil around the seed so loose soil will not be lost in a heavy downpour shortly after seeding. Various types of mulches can also be used to protect seed from drying out and inhibit seedbed erosion.

Mulching

Mulches are commonly used in northern hardwood nurseries as they provide several benefits to both seed and seedbed. Sawdust, wood chips, hyrdo-mulch, and wheat straw are common mulches used in northern hardwood nurseries. The primary benefit for using mulch is to hold the seed in place on the seedbed during the winter months. The mulch also provides secondary benefits such as covering seed at the proper depth, reducing seed predation, and protecting it from extreme cold temperatures. Typically, hardwood seed germinates up through this mulch layer in the spring.

Living mulches are also commonly used in northern hardwood nurseries. Common living mulches are rye, winter wheat, and oats. Each mulch species has its benefits and nursery personnel have to determine what works best in their environment. Living mulch seed is sown along with the tree seed during fall seeding. Rye and wheat seed will fall into the furrows made with the seeder and are covered along with the tree seed (fig. 4a.4). Seeders with this ability can plant crop and living mulch seeds with one pass over the seedbeds. Irrigation after sowing will assist with quick germination of the living mulch seed. This enables the mulch to grow in size to hold the seedbed in place as well as provide winter protection to the seed. In late February or early March, living mulches are sprayed with a grass herbicide to kill the vegetation. Several types of chemical are available to kill this living vegetation; selection and use depends on the condition of hardwood seed germination. If hardwood seedlings have not emerged at the time of herbicide application, an over-the-top application of a glyphosate-based product may be used. On the other hand, if hardwood seedlings have emerged, then the herbicide choice is limited to products that are not soil active and affect only grasses (see chapter 8).

Soil protection continues as the mulch begins to die. Shading the seedbed lowers soil temperatures and helps to avoid early hardwood seed germination, which may result in seedling damage caused by a late spring frost. Germinating hardwood seed has the ability to shoot up through this dying vegetation and continue normal development. Oats are usually killed by cold temperatures, which is a benefit over the use of wheat or rye. This could save time and money by not having to spray this vegetation in early spring. However, oat seed typically does not have sufficient time in the fall to germinate and grow due to the short degree days remaining after seeding. This is a definite disadvantage when using oats as a living mulch because hardwood seed will not be protected from wind and water erosion to the degree necessary throughout the winter months. Also, soils may warm early and possibly result in early seed germination.

The use of a living mulch and wheat straw combination provides excellent protection from extreme cold temperatures, seed predation, and soil erosion (fig. 4a.5). This unique combination may be used over seedbeds sown to large hardwood seeds such as oaks (*Quercus* spp.), hickory (*Carya* spp.), and walnut (*Juglans* spp.). Wheat or rye seed is sown at the time of seeding and covered along with the large hardwood seed. At completion of the seeding, a layer of clean wheat straw is applied, 2 to 3 in thick, over these seedbeds (fig. 4a.6). Wheat or rye seed will germinate and grow up through the wheat straw, creating a very thick mat over the seedbed. This not only provides excellent protection from extreme cold temperatures, but also creates a layer that animals have a difficult time pawing through. This virtually eliminates seed predation in these seedbeds. As with the other living mulches, this must be sprayed with herbicide in late winter. Chemical choice will depend on the degree of crop seed development. After the living mulch is killed and before hardwood seed emergence, a prescribed burn can be used as a relatively easy way to remove the majority of the wheat straw layer and allow for the large hardwood seed to germinate in a normal manner. A prescribed burn also reduces annual weeds and their seed.

Figure 4a.6—*Hardwood seedbeds covered with wheat straw after sowing of both hardwood and living mulch seed. The combination of a living much and wheat straw provides excellent protection for hardwood seed against cold temperatures, erosion, and animal predation. At the appropriate time both mulches are removed by a combination of herbicide application and fire. (Photo by Bob Hawkins, Indiana Department of Natural Resources, 2014.)*

Figure 4a.5—*A living mulch of rye growing over seedbeds. (Photo by Bob Hawkins, Indiana Department of Natural Resources, 2014.)*

Reference

Bonner, F.T.; Karrfalt, R.P. 2008. The woody plant seed manual. Agric. Handb. 727. Washington DC: U.S. Department of Agriculture, Forest Service. 1,223 p.

Seedbed Preparation and Sowing in Southern Hardwood Nurseries

4b

R. Rentz
Randy Rentz, retired Nursery Manager, Louisiana Department of Agriculture and Forestry, Columbia, LA

Outline

Facing Page: *Seedbed preparation. (Photo by Randy Rentz.)*

Soil Tillage

Objectives and Sequence

The primary objective of soil tillage is to provide a stable seedbed with good external and internal drainage. Several factors affect the ways in which the soil is prepared for bedding. Soil type, whether a silt, sandy loam, or a deep sand, will determine the amount, type, and at what time of year many soil tillage operations are performed.

Cover crops are typically disked under in August and allowed to breakdown in preparation for fumigation in the fall or early spring. Most nurseries in the South prefer fall fumigation. Any cover crop needs to be incorporated into the soil well before fumigation. Fields may then be sub-soiled, harrowed, and lay fallow until time to fumigate. Many nursery managers prefer to work the soil into shallow beds ("hipping") during the fallow period between cover crop and fumigation, while other managers fallow the field flat. Factors that may figure into this decision are soil type and external drainage. On fields with finer-textured soils, hipping allows equipment back in the field faster.

Subsoiling is performed with a two- or three-shank subsoiler designed to shatter any hardpan but not pull soil from lower zones up into the tillage zone. Subsoiling is performed before fumigation and when fields are dry so as to enhance the shattering of the lower zones and increase internal drainage. Fields are harrowed to the desired fumigation depth with a spring-tooth harrow fitted with a clod buster in the back. Harrowing depth after fumigation should not be greater than fumigated soil depth. This prevents unfumigated soil from being introduced into the bedding zone. Fields should not be disked before bedding in order to help retain soil structure.

The following is the general sequence of tillage operations.

1. Cover crop incorporated in mid-summer by disking, which could take multiple passes.
2. Subsoil or chisel plow and harrow
3. Lay-by awaiting fumigation (hipped or flat)
4. Fumigation (fall or spring)
5. Fertilize according to recommendations (fall or spring)
6. Prepare seedbeds
7. Sowing

Preplant fertilization can take many forms. Some managers apply phosphorous and potassium to fields in the cover crop area preceding the seedling crop and apply nitrogen after fumigation when bedding. Others apply the complete regimen following fumigation and prior to bedding, while some prefer to fertilize at bedding prior to sowing. Many factors play into each scenario, such as soil type, organic matter, and pH. Perhaps the most common is the personal experience of the nursery manager and what seems to work best under the conditions at each site.

Equipment

Seedbed preparation is one aspect of nursery management that has changed considerably through the years. This is due in part to the sandier sites where most nurseries are now located and, more importantly, the advances in equipment availability. There are currently many different models of bed shapers on the market. These range from the Whitfield pull type, which hips and shapes beds, the rotary tiller types, and the combined rotary cultivator-fertilize distributor-bed shaper. These are all used in bed preparation and provide satisfactory results. The Whitfield pull type (fig. 4b.1) must have a well-broken soil and requires disking and harrowing before shaping beds. Equipment that combines a rotary cultivator, fertilizer distributor, and bed shaper, such as the Fobro Kulti-Rotor (figs. 4b.2a and 4b.2b) can prepare beds with limited precultivation practices. This results in less soil compaction and substantial fuel savings by eliminating at least one pass over the field with a harrow or disc and one pass over the field when fertilizing. It also saves on fertilizer cost, as only the beds are fertilized, thus

Figure 4b.1—*The Whitfield bed-shaper lifts and shapes to create a raised bed. (Photo by Doug Gillett, Louisiana Department of Agriculture and Forestry, 2001.)*

Figure 4b.2a—*The Fobro Kulti-Rotor, front view. (Photo by Denise Barnette, Louisiana Department of Agriculture and Forestry, 2011.)*

Figure 4b.2b—*The Fobro Kulti-Rotor, side view. (Photo by Denise Barnette, Louisiana Department of Agriculture and Forestry, 2011.)*

reducing the amount used over the entire field. All of these bed shapers are suited to a wide range of soils.

Seedbed Preparation

Seedbeds are typically laid out in compartments consisting of nine beds per compartment. Beds are 48 to 54 inches (in) (1.22 to 1.37 meters [m]) across the top and middles are at 6 ft centers. Most nursery equipment is manufactured to accommodate 6 ft centers. The seedbed should be raised to a height of 4 to 6 in (10 to 15 cm) and flat across the top to allow for uniform sowing depth across the entire bed width. Lighter, very sandy soils do not need to be raised as long as they have good internal drainage. Generally, a raised bed is needed to facilitate good drainage and bed aeration, especially in finer-textured soils or soils with a clay subsoil (fig. 4b.3).

Figure 4b.3—*The finished product—prepared and sown beds. (Photo by Denise Barnette, Louisiana Department of Agriculture and Forestry, 2005.)*

***Figure 4b.4**—A Love seeder showing drop tubes and rear packing wheels. The seeder accommodates up to eight drills and can be precision adjusted. (Photo courtesy of Louisiana Department of Agriculture and Forestry, 2005.)*

Sowing

Equipment

With the various seeders and planters on the market, one can be found to meet the needs of just about any hardwood nursery operation. Planters such as the Love Oyjord (fig. 4b.4) have been modified to accommodate a wide variety of small- and light-seeded hardwood species. Planters such as the Whitfield (fig. 4b.5) are capable of sowing seed ranging from sweetgum (*Liquidambar styraciflua* L.) to black walnut (*Juglans nigra* L.). Planters or sowers consist of a feeder hopper (a device to regulate the rate of seed drop), drop tubes (a form of drill to open the ground and regulate depth), and some form of covering apparatus. Many are fitted with front and rear drum rollers. The front rollers help prepare the bed just ahead of the drills and the rear rollers assist in packing and closing the drills after sowing. Metering devices used to regulate seed drop are either ground-driven and gear-calibrated, or hydraulic driven. Seed plates or adjustable openings accommodate different seed sizes. Adjustments regulate the seed density.

All of these planters require a relatively low level of maintenance. All bearings, gears, and chains need to be lubricated daily when in use. At the end of the day, all dust should be blown out and drop tubes inspected. Regularly check drop tubes for blockage and proper seed flow. The planter's drum roller needs to be kept clean and free of buildup to assure a smooth, flat bed. Inspect coulters regularly to remove any soil buildup and ensure proper rotation. If coulters are not rotating properly, this will affect seed drop and proper sowing depth.

At completion of sowing, thoroughly clean the entire unit and properly lubricate all moving parts. Cover the drum

***Figure 4b.5**—A Whitfield planter designed specifically for sowing hardwood seed. (Photo by Doug Gillett, Louisiana Department of Agriculture and Foresry, 2001.)*

roller and coulter with a light coating of grease or oil. Inspect seed plates and drop tubes for warpage, cracking, and general wear. Check all belts, chains, bearings, and gears for excessive wear and replace as needed before placing the unit in storage awaiting another sowing season.

Timing

Sowing of hardwood seed in the Southeastern United States ranges from September to November for fall sowing and February to June 1 for spring sowing. This is species-dependent as some species can be readily sown in fall and spring, while others must be spring planted after the chance of heavy frost has past. In either case, the South is blessed with a relatively long growing season and a wide window of opportunity for sowing. Species whose seed mature in the spring, such as red maple (*Acer rubrum* L. *var. drummondii* Hook. & Arn. ex Nutt.) and American elm (*Ulmus americana* L.), generally do better if sown as soon as possible after seed is collected. Other species, like yaupon (*Ilex vomitoria* Ait.) and fringe tree (*Chionanthus virginicus* L.), which show dual dormancy as a result of two or more factors such as seedcoat and embryo dormancy, require special handling to break dormancy. Still others that show a light dormancy of some type will be handled in different ways.

The oaks (*Quercus* spp.) may be planted in either fall or spring, depending upon species. White oak species fare better if fall planted immediately after collection as they do not store well and much seed viability is lost if stored until spring sowing. The red oak species, which show signs of light dormancy, may be fall or spring planted. These store well and under proper conditions may be kept at a temperature of 36 °F (2.2 °C) for up to a year before any appreciable loss of viability. When spring sowing oaks, the order of sowing is determined by how readily each species germinates. Some species such as Shumard oak (*Quercus shumardi* Buckl.) and cherrybark oak (*Quercus pagoda* Raf.) readily germinate while others take longer. Most nursery managers plant the slower germinating species first, followed by the faster germinators. Spring sowing in the South can start as early as the middle of February and last until the end of May. It is usually too hot by June 1 for adequate germination and growth of many hardwood species.

Consideration must also be given to the growth patterns of individual species. Red mulberry (*Morus rubra* L.), sycamore (*Platanus occidentalis* L.), and green ash (*Fraxinus pennsylvanica* Marsh.) are usually sown later in the season, due in part to the accelerated growth they show in the nursery bed. Species that exhibit slower patterns of growth perform better when planted earlier in the growing season. Other factors that affect timing of sowing are length of stratification, soil type, weather patterns, and weed pressure. Recommended guidelines for sowing order may be found in table 4b.1, recognizing the order may be subject to change at different sites and based on the experience of each nursery manager.

Field Handling of Seed

Proper care in seed stratification is essential to ensure a quality stand of hardwood seedlings. Stratification times usually range from 30 to 120 days. Proper care and types of stratification of each species may be found in *The Woody Plant Seed Manual* (Bonner and Karrfalt 2008).

Table 4b.1*—General guideline for the sowing order of spring-sown hardwoods.*

1. Native sweet pecan, *Carya illinoensis* (wangenh,) K. Koch
2. Bitter pecan, *Carya aquatica* (Mich f.) Nutt.
3. Black walnut, *Juglans nigra* L.
4. Water oak, *Quercus nigra* L.
5. Any white oak species left over from fall Sowing
6. Willow oak, *Quercus phellos* L.
7. Laurel oak, *Quercus laurifolia* Michx.
8. Post oak, *Quercus stellata* Wangenh.
9. Overcup oak, *Quercus lyrata* Walt.
10. Nuttall oak, *Quercus nuttallii* Palmer
11. Shumard oak, *Quercus shumardii* Buckl.
12. Cherrybark oak, *Quercus pagoda* Raf.
13. Southern Red oak, *Quercus falcata* Michx.
14. Red Maple, *Acer rubrum var. drummondii* Hook. & Arn. ex Nutt.
15. Sweetgum, *Liquidambar styraciflua* L.
16. Hawthorn, *Cratagus* Spp.
17. Elm, *Ulmus* Spp.
18. Persimmon, *Diospyros virginiana* L.
19. Plums, *Prunus* spp.
20. Tupelo gum, *Nyssa aquatic* L.
21. Blackgum, *Nyssa sylvatica* Marsh
22. Yellow poplar, *Liriodendron tulipifera* L.
23. Red mulberry, *Morus rubra* L.
24. Sycamore, *Platanus occidentalis* L.
25. Baldcypress, *Taxodium distichum* (L.) Rich.
26. Green ash, *Fraxinus pennsylvanica* Marsh.

Seed need to be readied for sowing once it has been properly stratified. Hard mast seed such as pecan (*Carya illinoensis* Wangen. K. Koch) and oak need little to no preparation before sowing, while most of the soft mast species such as green ash and sweetgum need some form of preparation. Soft mast and smaller seeded hardwood are often treated with some type of bird repellent or other treatment. Afterwards, the seed is carefully surface-dried on screens or in a blower. During the drying process, it is very important not to overdry seed and reverse the stratification process. Seed may then be treated with talcum powder or some other material that allows the seed to more uniformly flow through the planter.

Proper Depth and Distribution of Seed

Depth. All mechanical sowers are fitted with some type of sowing depth adjustment. Some, like the Oyjord, have coulters that can be adjusted up or down and can sow as shallow as 1/8 in (3 mm) to as deep as 2 in (51 mm). Others, such as the Whitfield, are fitted with rollers or shanks just ahead of drop tubes that open the drills to varying depths and cover and roll seed with devices located on the seeder. The texture of the bed must allow for proper sowing depth and covering of seed.

The desired sowing depth will be affected by the type of mulch used, soil texture, and time of year. Sowing depth will be shallower if heavy mulch is used to cover the beds. The seed may be planted a little deeper where a soil-binding agent is used. Seed will need to be planted shallower in heavier soils than in light, sandy soils, where seedlings can emerge easier. When fall sowing, it is usually desirable to plant a little deeper to compensate for overwinter washing of seedbeds. The old rule of sowing depth being 1 to 1 ½ times the diameter of the seed is still a good one to follow.

Seed is sown in drills in most bareroot nurseries with four or five drills per bed with drills 6 to 10 in (15 to 25 cm) apart (depending upon the number of drills sown). Some lighter seeded species may not require as much bed area to reach desired seedling specifications. In these cases, as many as eight drills may be sown per bed. The number of seedlings grown per square foot of bed space is determined by growth characteristics of each species and the desired product. Most species are sown to produce 8 to 10 seedlings per ft^2 (86 to 108 seedlings per m^2), although several species can be grown 15 to 20 seedlings per ft^2 of bed space (161 to 215 per m^2). The desired caliper, height, and root mass of seedling to be produced will initially determine bed density.

Sowing rates. The following formula (Stoeckeler and Jones 1957, Williams and Hanks 1994) can be used to calculate the total amount of seed needed for each species or seedlot.

$$P = \frac{A \times D}{G \times S \times Y}$$ [Equation 1]

Where P is the total pounds of seed needed for sowing. The term A x D equals the total number of seedlings desired, where A is the area of bed space in square feet and D is the target density expressed as the desired number of seedlings per square foot. G is percent seed germination expressed as a decimal. S is the number of seeds per pound as they come from the container. Y is a "survival factor" that varies by species and is an experience-based estimate of the percentage of viable seed that will produce plantable seedlings at the end of the growing season, expressed as a decimal.

As an example, Williams and Hanks (1994) assume a nursery production target of 100,000 yellow poplar seedlings and a nursery target density of 10 plantable trees per square foot. Meeting these targets will require 10,000 square feet of seedbed. The percent germination of the seed is 8 percent and there are 14,000 seeds per pound. Based on the nursery manager's experience with this species and seedlot, the "survival factor" is estimated at 50 percent.

$$P = \frac{10{,}000 \times 10}{.08 \times 14{,}000 \times .50}$$ [Equation 2]

$$P = \frac{10{,}000}{560} = 178.57 \text{ pounds.}$$

Seed counts must be made periodically to ensure the number of seeds dropped from the sower is on target. The number of seeds to sow per linear foot of drill can be computed using the formula of Williams and Hanks (1994):

$$N = \frac{D}{GY}$$ [Equation 3]

N is the number of seeds to sow per linear foot. D is the desired number of seedlings per linear foot. G is the seed germination percent expressed as a decimal. Y is a "survival factor" that varies by species and is an experience-based estimate of the percentage of viable seed that will produce plantable seedlings at the end of the growing season, expressed as a decimal.

Mulching

Many nurseries in the South use some form of bedding mulch in the form of living mulches or other organic materials. Other nurseries have opted to use a soil-binding adhesive sprayed directly over the bed. Each approach has advantages and disadvantages.

Living Mulches

Living mulches work well on fall-sown seedbeds, as they do not wash during the winter. After the beds are sown, they are seeded with rye, wheat, or some other form of winter cover. This provides cover for seed overwintering in the beds, as well as protection from freezing and animal depredation such as deer, crow, and feral hogs. The winter cover can be killed with glyphosate in late winter or early spring if seedlings have not begun germination. If seedlings have emerged, a postemergent grass herbicide such as fluazafop-p-butyl, or clethodim may be used to kill back the living mulch. It is important to kill mulch back before it gets too large and overpowers seedlings. One disadvantage of living mulches is that windblown seed and contaminated cover seed is introduced to beds. Therefore, after the mulch has been burned back, any preemergent and postemergent herbicides need to be applied as soon as possible to control weed pressure.

Adhesives

A second option is not a mulch at all, but to spray on an adhesive that acts as a soil-binding agent. Spray adhesives are applied by converted hydromulchers or tanks and tips designed to apply 250 to 500 gallons of mixed material per acre (2338 to 4677 liters [L] per hectares [ha]). Adhesives come in 50-gallon (189 L) drums and are usually applied with one drum mixed with enough water to properly cover and bind 1 acre (0.404 ha) of ground. How much mixed material is applied over a given area depends on soil types and the nursery manager's own experience.

Adhesives provide an easy, reliable, weed-free binding agent to maintain seedbed integrity. In addition, preemergent herbicides and fungicides may be mixed with adhesive agents and applied at the same time. Another advantage is that adhesives can be used with all seed types, large or small. This allows easier seed depth control while sowing and results in better overall germination. The drawback to adhesives is that they provide little, if any, moisture-holding capacity. More frequent watering and monitoring of soil moisture is needed to assure proper germination. The ease of adhesive application and ability to provide weed-free soil binding, along with its use on all types of seed, outweighs this drawback for many nursery managers (fig. 4b.6).

Standard Mulches

Most of the many types of standard mulches are byproducts of agriculture or forest product operations. Examples include wheat straw, oat straw, pine straw, sawdust, wood chips, pine bark, and grit. Each of these can effectively protect seed and seedbeds from the elements. These types of mulches have a certain amount of moisture retention capability and work well as a cover for seedbeds. These may also introduce unwanted weed seed to the beds. The straws may be fumigated before spreading, but many of the other forms are very difficult to fumigate adequately. Since these will be hauled and spread mechanically, time and expense are considerations. Added care must be taken with the spreading of mulch. If too thin, it may tend to float away and not provide adequate protection from washing. If too thick, it may hinder germination of some species. The nursery manager needs to determine which is the most economical and effective cover for their situation.

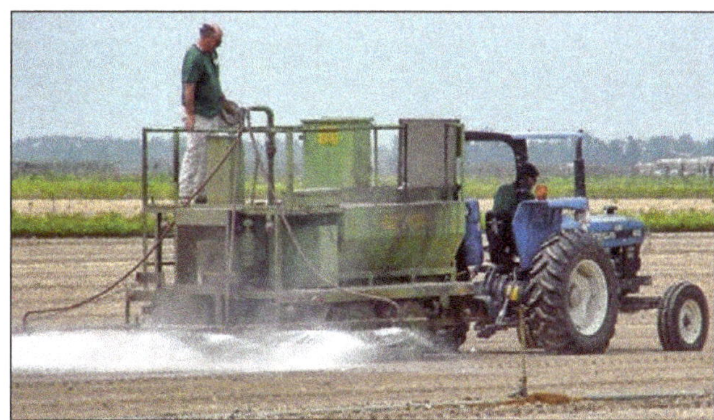

***Figure 4b.6**—A converted hydro-mulcher applying a soil-binding agent. (Photo by Ginger Bonner, Louisiana Department of Agriculture and Forestry, 2001.)*

References

Bonner, F.T.; Karrfalt, R.P. 2008. The woody plants seed manual. Agric. Handb. 727. Washington, DC: U.S. Department of Agriculture, Forest Service. 1,223 p.

Stoeckeler, J.H; Jones, G.W. 1957. Forest nursery practice in the Lake States. Agric. Handb. 110. Washington, DC: U.S. Department of Agriculture, Forest Service. 123 p.

Williams, R.D.; Hanks, S.H. 1976. Hardwood Nursery Guide (formerly Hardwood nurseryman's guide; slightly revised July 1994). Agric. Handb. 473. Washington, DC: U.S. Department of Agriculture, Forest Service. 78 p.

Irrigation Management

J. Robbins
Jackie Robbins is founder of Irrigation-Mart, Ruston, LA

5

Outline

Facing Page: *Sprinklers on hardwood beds. (Photo by Jackie Robbins.)*

Irrigation Basics

Irrigation is used in bareroot hardwood nurseries to enhance both germination percentages and uniformity, and to grow seedlings with well-developed root systems that have good survival and growth when outplanted. Irrigation can be used to prepare beds for root pruning and for harvesting. Sometimes irrigation is used for micro-climate control, to limit heat and freeze injury. When limited or withheld, irrigation can condition ("harden-off") seedlings for harvesting and to withstand cold weather. Although not common in bareroot nurseries, irrigation can be used to apply fertilizers (fertigate) or pesticides and other additives, including soil sterilants (chemigate). Sometimes sprinkler irrigation systems are used to move surface-applied materials into the soil and to wash materials from seedling foliage. Except for freeze protection, which requires 50 to 100 gallons per minute per acre (gpm/ac) (468 to 935 liters per minute per hectare [Lpm/ha]), each of these uses of irrigation can be fully met with a pumping flow rate of less than 10 gpm (38 Lpm per minute) per acre of the entire area (Ae) irrigated by a system.

Several terms are critical to the understanding and discussion of irrigation systems. Many of these terms are defined in appendix 5-1. Three terms essential to understanding the design, operation, and performance of irrigation systems are precipitation rate (PR), irrigation efficiency (IE), and application uniformity (AU).

Precipitation rate is how fast an irrigation system applies water to an irrigation zone, usually reported as inches per hour. Table 5.1 shows the recommended maximum sprinkler precipitation rate for various soil textures. In those few cases when sprinkler systems apply water at rates exceeding the soil infiltration rates, surface runoff from the nursery beds can be controlled by providing sufficient surface storage to allow adequate time for the water to infiltrate. Tillage practices that create small reservoirs in the beds to capture and hold the water can increase infiltration time. Placing permeable mulches such as straw on the beds increases surface storage and helps maintain a high infiltration rate. Equation 1 provided in appendix 5-2 is used to calculate precipitation rate.

Irrigation efficiency is the amount of irrigation water stored in the crop's root-zone that is available for beneficial use by plants divided by the total amount of all the irrigation water pumped (assuming the crop's root zone covers all the area being irrigated). IE accounts for all losses of the irrigation water in getting it to where it is available for plant uptake: (1) for water not being applied uniformly to the irrigation area; (2) for evaporation that occurs as water travels from the sprinklers to the irrigation area and from wetted plant and soil surfaces; (3) for water falling outside of the irrigation area; and (4) for water moving out of the crop's root-zone via surface runoff and deep percolation. The water ending up where it is not crop-available may carry materials such as fertilizers, which are subsequently lost. If IE were 75 percent, an additional one-third (100/75 = 1.33) of irrigation water would have to be pumped to meet the needs of plants located in the irrigated area that receives the least water.

Application uniformity is a measure of how evenly irrigation water is applied over the irrigation area. AU is often the largest component of IE but only deals with the part of the irrigation water that is applied rather than pumped. If AU were 80 percent, an additional 25 percent (100/80 = 1.25) of irrigation water would have to be applied to meet plant needs.

Bareroot Nursery Layouts

Irrigation systems for bareroot hardwood nurseries are the same as those used to produce bareroot conifer tree seedlings. Often both hardwood and conifer seedlings are produced in the same nursery, using the same or very similar irrigation scheduling criteria. Layout, equipment, and cultural practices have become somewhat standardized over the past 70 or so years to use solid-set, impact sprinkler irrigation systems and components similar to those pictured in figures 5.1, 5.2, 5.3, 5.4, and 5.5. The essential components of such systems are: (1) a pressurized water source, (2) a piping network of main lines, control valves, laterals, and sprinkler risers, (3) impact sprinklers, and (4) monitoring equipment including pressure gauges, flow meters, and soil moisture status indicators, such as tensiometers. Some systems include submains, which feed more than one lateral through a single control valve from the main line rather than each lateral being fed directly from the main. The following are some control items added on the sprinkler risers to improve the system performance.

- **Quick coupling/connect valves** (www.webstermatic.com, www.travispattern.com). These are placed between the laterals and the risers to allow the risers to be removed for repair even while the system is operating. They can also help prevent damage when the laterals are moved (fig. 5.4).
- **Spring loaded check valves.** These are placed under each sprinkler to prevent flow through the sprinklers at the beginning and end of each irrigation event, until the pressure is large enough (maybe 5 pounds per square inch [psi]) to make the sprinklers turn. They also maintain pressure in the laterals between irrigation events to keep the lateral coupler gaskets set and prevent unwanted drain-down/emptying of the system. They minimize bed erosion, puddling, and poor irrigation efficiency (fig. 5.4).

- **Part-circle shields.** These may be placed on the risers at the boundaries of the nursery to prevent throw of water beyond the beds from full-circle sprinklers; e.g., to prevent wetting roadways (fig. 5.5).
- **Pressure regulators.** These may be placed in each riser to limit discharge variations caused by different pressures at the sprinkler nozzles; they are particularly useful in fields with varying elevations and on systems that operate at lower pressures.

In a typical bareroot nursery, impact sprinklers are spaced 40 feet (ft) apart along sprinkler laterals. The laterals are assembled using lengths of aluminum tubing with integral, quick couplers. Sprinkler laterals are located with nine, 4-ft wide (1.2 meters [m]) beds between them. The beds are spaced 6 ft (1.6 m) on center (OC) except where sprinkler laterals are placed, whereby the OC spacing is increased by 4 ft (1.2 m), making the spacing between laterals 58 ft (17.7 m) (fig. 5.1). Note that in such a nine-bed layout, the beds cover only 36 ft (11 m) of the 58 ft (17.7 m) width, or 62 percent of the irrigation area. Because lateral layouts are not exact, the laterals are usually assumed to be spaced at 60 ft (18.3 m), and not 58 ft (17.7 m), when estimating the precipitation rate and how efficiently and uniform these systems operate.

Some nurseries space sprinkler laterals closer to assure adequate watering of beds midway between laterals and to increase application uniformity. For example, under a common set of no-wind operating conditions, a typical nine-bed layout with sprinklers spaced 40 ft by 58 ft (12.2 by 17.7 m) has an application uniformity of 77 percent. Under the same conditions, but with sprinkler nozzles changed to main-

***Figure 5.1**—Typical layout of a bareroot hardwood nursery. Beds are 4 ft (1.2 m) wide and spaced 6 ft (1.8 m) on center. Where sprinkler laterals are placed between two beds, the spacing between beds is increased by adding 4 ft (1.2 m). With one lateral per nine beds, the spacing between the laterals is 58 feet (17.7 m). Usually the spacing of sprinklers along the laterals is 40 ft (12.2 m). (Photos by Chase Weatherly, ArborGen, Inc. 2011.)*

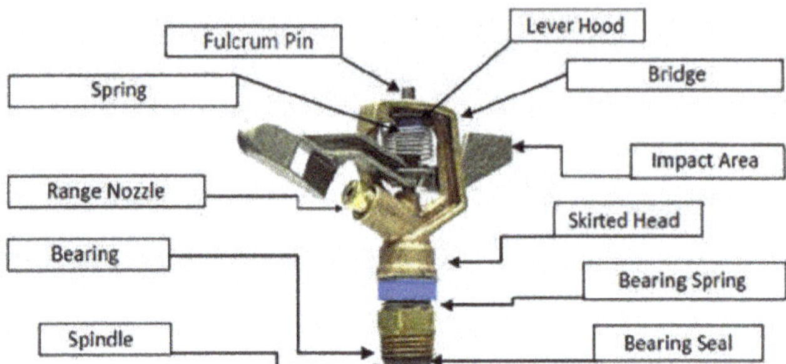

Figure 5.2—*Standard impact sprinkler: Some have a second outlet (for a spreader nozzle) that is usually plugged when used in bare-root hardwood nurseries. Some are part-circle to prevent applying water beyond the nursery (e.g., to roadways). Some are made of engineering grade plastic and others are brass. All should include stream straightener vanes (fig. 5.3) placed just before the nozzle to increase the throw distance. (Photo courtesy of WeatherTec, 2011.)*

Figure 5.3—*Sprinkler nozzle with stream straightener vanes installed. A sprinkler's throw distance will be increased by 3 to 4 feet (.9 to 1.2 m) and the application uniformity will be greater if the streamlines exiting the sprinkler nozzles are straight. (Photo courtesy of Irrigation-Mart. 2011.)*

tain the same precipitation rate, the application uniformity of a six-bed layout with sprinklers spaced 40 ft by 40 ft (1.2 by 1.2 m) is 86 percent. If the nozzles were not changed, the application uniformity would be 89 percent, but the precipitation rate would be 1.45 times greater. Note that the beds in the six-bed layout cover 60 percent of the irrigation area, or 24 ft of the 40 ft width (7.3 of 12.2 m), which is about the same as the 62 percent for the nine-bed layout. Under increasingly windy conditions, the application uniformity for a six-bed layout decreases less than that for a nine-bed layout, and this difference increases as the wind speed increases.

Sprinkler System Basics

Sprinkler System Limitations

The generic limitations of all sprinkler systems relate to several factors.

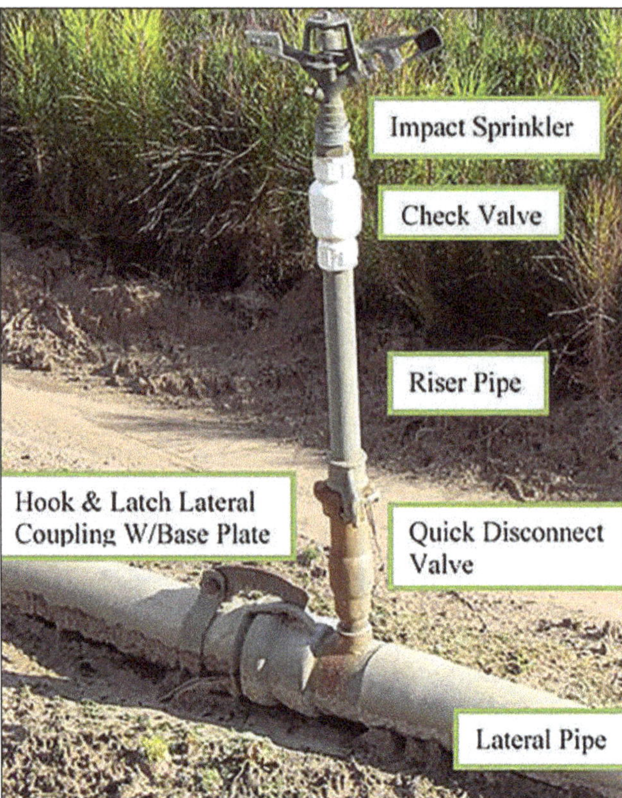

Figure 5.4—*Typical sprinkler riser with a quick disconnect valve and a check valve on an aluminum lateral with a hook and latch type quick coupler. Sprinkler risers should be vertical, even at the expense of adding stakes to support them; otherwise the distribution pattern will be skewed, and the application uniformity will be decreased. (Photo by Chase Weatherly, ArborGen, Inc., 2011.)*

Figure 5.5—*Sprinkler shields can be used on full-circle sprinklers to prevent full-circle application. Some shields use solid splash plates and drop all the deflected water near the sprinkler, others use splash plates made of expanded metal to control overwatering near the sprinkler. (Photo courtesy of Irrigation-Mart and Chase Weatherly, ArborGen, Inc., 2011.)*

1. The entire plant and soil surfaces is wetted leading to significant evaporation losses, disease susceptibility, and removal of pesticides and other agricultural chemicals, and leaving of deposits on the seedlings that can reduce photosynthesis, growth, and marketability.
2. There are high power and energy requirements. These may be minimized by using low pressure and high irrigation efficiency systems. Decreasing the total dynamic head (pressure) of the irrigation system by one-half (e.g., from 70 psi to 35 psi, or 482 to 241 kilopascal [kPa]) lowers the power and energy requirement by 50 percent. Improving the irrigation efficiency from 65 percent to 75 percent not only saves 13 percent of the water needed to be pumped, but also lowers the amount of pumping plant energy required by more than 13 percent, depending on the efficiency of the pumping plant (pump and motor combined). (See also equations 3 and 4 in appendix 5-2.)
3. There are difficulties in obtaining uniform distribution, particularly in wind.
4. There is a high labor requirement. This may be reduced by mechanization and automation.
5. There is limited layout flexibility, which makes management changes difficult to implement.
6. Cultural practices may be hindered by wetted soils and by exposed system components that are subject to damage and must be worked around.

A major disadvantage of sprinkler irrigation in nursery operations is that water is applied to the entire irrigation area (A_e), and not just the bed area. This alone results in about 40 percent of the irrigation water being wasted (not available to the crop). Likewise, the same portion of any materials, such as fertilizers, carried by the water is wasted. Also, cultural practices must be delayed until the water applied between the beds has drained sufficiently to allow trafficking.

Nursery sprinkler irrigation efficiency (IE_N) is usually less than 50 percent. Even with the best design and no-wind conditions, irrigation efficiencies of more than about 90 percent are difficult to obtain for impact sprinkler systems. When system cost restraints are added, the solid-set sprinkler irrigation systems used in bareroot nurseries are generally established with irrigation efficiencies of less than 80 percent under no-wind conditions. With reasonable maintenance and scheduling, common in-field irrigation efficiencies are less than 70 percent under winds up to 8 mph. (Wind speeds greater than this are very common throughout the Eastern United States.) When using a realistic in-field irrigation efficiency of 67 percent and including the loss of all of the water applied between the nursery beds, only about 40 percent of the water pumped ends-up where it can be beneficially used by the crop.

Effect of Wind on Sprinkler Application Uniformity

Wind skews sprinkler distribution and is one of the most important factors governing the arrangement and spacing of sprinklers (and laterals). High wind conditions and winds from all directions should be assumed in the design of bareroot nurseries in the Eastern United States. Failure to do so has been one of the main causes of inadequate watering of beds midway between laterals and along the boundaries, and for low distribution uniformities and irrigation efficiencies in general.

Higher wind conditions require closer spacing of sprinklers to maintain a given level of application uniformity. The following is an example of recommended maximum spacing between fixed-location impact sprinklers as a percent of the sprinkler's diameter of throw for varying wind speeds:

no-wind	65 percent
0 to 4 mph (6.4 kph)	60 percent
4 to 8 mph (12.9 kph)	50 percent
over 8 mph (12.9 kph)	30 percent.

kph = kilometers per hour
mph = miles per hour

Whenever possible, laterals should be installed perpendicular to the wind direction; then just spacing sprinklers closer along the laterals, without spacing the laterals closer, maintains good application uniformity. Wind effects may be reduced by using pressure and nozzle combinations that produce larger droplets and/or using a single nozzle only, which concentrates all the sprinkler flow in just one nozzle stream. Sprinklers with lower discharge angles also limit the distortion of distribution patterns caused by wind.

Characteristics of Impact Sprinklers

Generally, bareroot nursery sprinkler systems use impact sprinklers because they provide larger diameters of throw than other overhead irrigation devices (e.g., jets, rotators, spinners, and off-center rotators) for a given set of operating conditions (pressure, discharge rate, discharge angle, etc.). Most impact sprinklers used in bareroot nurseries are a ¾-inch (in) (19 millimeters [mm]) base series with just one nozzle. They are installed on ¾- or 1-in (19 or 25 mm) diameter metal risers at regular intervals along the laterals (fig. 5.4). They are operated with pressure near 50 psi (345 kPa) at the nozzle, and they are nozzled to discharge 6 to 10 gpm (22.7 to 37.9 Lpm). Under a no-wind condition and with stream straightener vanes installed (fig. 5.3), the sprinklers have an effective throw radius of around 45 to 50 ft (13.7 to 15.2 m).

Impact sprinklers apply water in a stream as the head rotates either in a full- or part-circle. All other factors being the same (nozzle size, operating pressure, etc.), full- and part-circle sprinklers do not give the same precipitation rate because their areas of coverage are different. Therefore, to get good application uniformity, only full-circle sprinklers are recommended. Part-circle shields can be used on full-circle sprinklers at the ends of beds and along the boundaries of the nursery to prevent throw of water beyond beds if desired, such as to prevent wetting roadways (fig. 5.5).

Impact sprinklers with larger nozzles produce higher precipitation rates and require higher pressures to obtain a good distribution pattern. The application depth from a typical impact sprinkler decreases with distance from the nozzle. The flow rate and the distribution pattern of an impact sprinkler are governed by the size of the nozzle orifice and the operating pressure, with the shape of the nozzle (e.g., straight bore or taper bore) also having some influence. If the pressure at the sprinkler is adequate, the discharge pattern is approximated as triangular for one nozzle (a range nozzle) and elliptical for two nozzles (a range nozzle and a spreader nozzle). When the pressure is too low, the distribution pattern becomes donut shaped, which is unacceptable. When the pressure is too high, the portion of small droplets increases, increasing the depth of water applied closer to the sprinkler, evaporation, and the potential for skewing the application pattern by wind.

Impact sprinklers are available with trajectory angles ranging from 0 to 32 degrees, although some single-nozzle sprinklers have adjustable trajectory angles. The most common trajectory angles for range nozzles are from 21 to 27 degrees, and 5 to 7 degrees for spreader nozzles. For trajectory angles common to range nozzles, the diameter of throw will increase about one percent for each degree increase in trajectory angle upward from horizontal. Smaller trajectory angles result in higher precipitation rates. Sprinklers with larger trajectory angles reduce the impact of droplets on the soil and maximize coverage, but their distribution pattern can be greatly distorted by wind, especially by winds greater than 10 mph (16 kph). The distribution patterns of sprinklers with low trajectory angles are less distorted by wind, but their droplet impact on soil is more severe and their coverage is reduced.

Bareroot Nursery Irrigation Systems

Solid-set sprinkler irrigation systems used in bareroot hardwood nurseries are either permanent or nonpermanent, depending on whether the laterals are removable. Usually the main lines of both types and the laterals of permanent systems are polyvinylchloride (PVC) pipe and are installed underground. Outlets from the mains to the laterals include control valves. Permanent systems limit changes in nursery layout and they often require more time and expense to repair when damaged. Therefore, they are not very common in bareroot nurseries.

Nonpermanent sprinkler irrigation systems use portable, aboveground laterals that are placed in the field near the time of planting and not removed until the time seedlings are lifted. Although some moveable laterals are PVC or polyethylene (PE), most are made by coupling together 20-, 30-, or 40-ft (6.1, 9.1, or 12.2 m) lengths of aluminum tubing. The length of tubing is chosen to correspond to some multiple of sprinkler spacing along the laterals.

The thickness or gauge of the aluminum lateral tubing is chosen to withstand operating pressures. A 0.050-in (1.27-mm) wall thickness is common. Sprinkler spacing is typically held constant and all lateral tubing in a system is one diameter and one length. For example, a system might use 3-in (7.6 centimeters [cm]) diameter, 20-ft (6.1-m) long tubing with sprinklers spaced 40 ft (12.2 m) apart along the lateral. To save on material, laterals are often spaced further apart than the sprinklers along the laterals; e.g., laterals might be spaced 60 ft (18.2 m) apart, while sprinklers along the laterals might be spaced 40 ft (12.2 m) apart.

The diameter of the piping used in bareroot hardwood nursery irrigation systems is selected according to some predetermined design criteria which should be chosen to limit flow velocities to below 5 feet per second (fps) (1.52 meters per second [mps]) and pressure variations in sprinkler laterals due to friction and slope to less than some value, maybe 10 percent. Usually, the flow velocity restriction (5 fps maximum) (1.52 mps) governs for 4 in (10 cm) and larger pipes, while friction loss governs in smaller pipes. Many texts, tables, charts, calculators, and websites are available to aid in sizing pipe, including lateral pipe (chapter 7 of Stetson and Mecham 2011; USDA NRCS 2003, USDA NRCS 2008.)

Aluminum lateral tubing most often comes from the supplier with couplers attached. The couplers require gaskets, with fast-drain, slow-drain, and nondrain gaskets available for most coupler styles. Generally, nondrain gaskets should be used in nurseries to prevent drain-down of the laterals between irrigation events. Usually the couplers for aluminum lateral tubing are a hook and latch, quick-connect type, and include a threaded outlet for installing a riser pipe to serve a sprinkler; any outlet not needed is plugged. The couplers include a base or plate to help keep the riser and sprinkler upright. Risers may require additional support, however, to remain vertical and control skewing the sprinkler distribution (fig. 5.4).

System Capacity

System capacity addresses the ability of an irrigation system to deliver both the required rate (gpm, gpm/ac, inches/hour [in/h]) and volume (gal, acre-feet [ac-ft]) of water necessary to produce a crop, including the losses and inefficiencies encountered during the irrigation process. In other words, it is the gross amount of water the system must deliver and the rate at which it must be delivered.

Crop Water Requirement

The volume of irrigation water needed to produce a bareroot hardwood seedling crop in the Eastern United States is poorly known, extremely variable, and depends on numerous factors including weather. Equation 2 in appendix 5-2 may be helpful in estimating the volume of irrigation water that should be available, if needed, to assure a successful hardwood seedling crop. Equation 2 is only as good as the estimate of the volume of water needed to be supplied by irrigation during the entire growing cycle, and might best be based on meeting all of the crop's gross water needs during a crop cycle assuming no rainfall, maximum evapotranspiration, and no contribution from stored soil moisture.

Pumping Rate Required

While the moisture stored in the soil and the rainfall during the growing season are important to determine the amount of irrigation water needed to produce a crop of seedlings, they are not factors involved in determining the required system pumping rate. Instead, evapotranspiration and irrigation efficiency are the key factors. A nursery irrigation system should have a large enough pumping rate to replenish the peak soil moisture use that occurs during the production cycle. Based on peak evapotranspiration, the minimum rate at which water is to be supplied by a nursery irrigation system is:

$$Q_{min} = [k_3(A_e)(ET_{cp})/(T_i)(IE)] \quad \text{(Equation 3)}$$

where:

Q_{min} = minimum pumping capacity or flow rate [gpm],

A_e = entire nursery area irrigated by the system [ac],

ET_{cp} = average peak evapotranspiration for the crop [in/day],

T_i = a decimal representing the portion of time that the system operates,

IE = a decimal representing the irrigation efficiency, and

k_3 = a constant: (27154 gal/ac-in) / [(24 h/day) (60 min/h)] = 18.86 gal-day/ac-in-min.

Equation 3 assumes that water losses during conveyance from the source to the emitting devices are negligible (i.e., no leaks).

The term A_e does not include any areas that receive irrigation water (sprinkled) beyond the defined irrigation boundaries. Irrigation water applied outside the nursery area is addressed through the IE term. In nursery sprinkler irrigation systems, A_e is the entire crop production area, including the area between the beds.

The term ET_{cp} is the average of the peak daily evapotranspirations that are expected to occur during the crop cycle. In hotter, dryer regions of the Eastern United States, evapotranspiration from irrigated hardwood seedling nurseries occasionally reaches 0.5 in/day (12.7 mm/day), and often reaches 0.3 in/day (7.6 mm/day) for a period of several days. In cooler and more humid regions, ET_{cp} may be as low as 0.2 in/day (5.1 mm). Absent better information and depending on region, 0.2 to 0.3 in/day (5.1 to 7.6 mm/day) is recommended as the minimum ET_{cp} value to use for design/planning purposes.

The operation of a nursery irrigation system is never continuous (i.e., T_i is less than 1.0) because of the need for downtime for system maintenance, to allow for cultural operations, or other reasons such as operator convenience. Still, for design purposes, one might use a T_i value of 1.0, assuming that irrigation will be continuous during the peak demand period.

If deficient irrigation is acceptable or if rainfall can be depended on to supply part of the water needed by the crop during the peak demand period, an irrigation system with a flow rate of less than Q_{min} would be adequate. However, before accepting such a system, a good appreciation is required of the rainfall frequency and amounts, the dependable amount and ease of soil moisture removal from the crop's root zone, and the importance of meeting the peak water use of the seedlings. Also, a firm commitment to precise irrigation scheduling, plus overall good management (e.g., weed control), is needed to limit production losses under such irrigation schemes.

Equation 3 can be used to size pumps for nurseries. Assuming that a 10-ac (4 ha) irrigation zone uses an impact sprinkler system with an IE of 67 percent (a common value for a well-maintained and operated system with sprinklers spaced 40 ft by 58 ft [12.1 by 17.7 m]), and wind speeds under 8 mph (12.9 kph), a design ET_{cp} of 0.3 in/day (7.6 mm), and a $T_i = 1$ (i.e., irrigation will be continuous during the peak demand periods), then the minimum pumping rate needed, regardless of the number and size of zones involved, would be:

Q_{min} = (18.86 gal-day/ac-in-min) (10 ac) (0.3 in/day) / (1) (0.67) = 85 gpm

Even though ET_{cp} quite often exceeds 0.3 in/day (7.6 mm/day) during hot, dry periods throughout much of the Eastern United States for short periods, the damage caused by the deficit irrigation during these times may not justify the cost of a system with a larger pumping rate. Also note that if IE were increased to 75 percent (e.g., by spacing the sprinklers 40 ft by 40 ft, or 12.1 by 12.1 m), the Qmin would be decreased to 75 gpm (284 Lpm).

Example calculations of the power needed for pumping (equation 3) and the subsequent energy consumption (equation 4) are provided in appendix 5-2.

Irrigation Scheduling

Effective and efficient irrigation systems limit plant stress, seedling problems, pollution, and the wasteful use of energy, water, fertilizers and other resources. Such systems are capable of making applications so that watering can be correct with respect to: (1) when it is applied, (2) how much is applied during each event, (3) precipitation rate (the number of inches applied per hour), and (4) irrigation efficiency. For practical purposes, once a system is designed and installed, precipitation rate and irrigation efficiency are fixed. But when and how much to apply are operational and/or scheduling factors determined by the irrigator.

Irrigation scheduling plans (when and how much to irrigate) are an integral part of an irrigation system. Irrigation scheduling is governed by the crop water requirement (evapotranspiration, ET) and the ability of the soil to hold and release water. ET includes both the soil water that the crop and weeds transpire and soil water that is drawn from below the soil surface and evaporated. Numerous factors govern ET, including solar radiation, day length, air temperature, wind speed, humidity, crop species, crop growth stage, canopy size and shape, and leaf size and shape. The ability of a soil to hold and release water is related to texture, as indicated in table 5.1. Irrigation scheduling can be based on nonprecise methods such as observing the plants and/or feeling the soil. But even with years of well-developed experience, efficient and effective irrigation cannot be achieved without using some type of soil moisture measuring tool and monitoring technique.

The objective of irrigation based on soil moisture criteria is to keep soil moisture content between field capacity (FC) and some portion of plant available water (PAW). Soil moisture above field capacity will drain away due to gravity and may be harmful to the plant. The portion of PAW (e.g., 75 percent of PAW) is set by the nursery manager. Then, irrigation is managed and scheduled to maintain plant available water between these two levels. (Often the portion of PAW is imprecisely referred to as a portion of FC [e.g., 70 percent of PAW as 70 percent of FC], ignoring the amount of water that the soil contains at permanent wilting point [PWP].)

Frequent irrigation events are important to consistently maintain soil moisture near field capacity (FC) so that plant stress is kept at a minimum. This is particularly true for seedlings grown in soils with little water-holding capacity, such as the sandy soils so common to bareroot nurseries. Frequent applications are also needed to keep the seed moist during germination and the young seedlings turgid and cool during the early growth periods.

How much water to apply during an irrigation event is governed by the length of the event, because the precipitation rate is fixed. Over- and under-irrigating can definitely lower yield and quality and increase waste and the cost of production. Applying too little water per irrigation event increases the likelihood of stressing the crop and usually results in reduced efficiencies and the need for extra irrigation events. Applying too much water per event decreases irrigation efficiency because the excess water ends up wasted outside the crop's rootzone. Precisely timed applications are needed to assure that a high portion of the irrigation water ends up where it is readily available for beneficial use by the plants; e.g., with 50 percent ending up in the top 3 in (7.6 cm) of the bed and 30 percent in the 3 to 7 in (7.6 to 17.8 cm) zone, and with little deep percolation. See appendix 5-3 for an example of how to develop an irrigation schedule based on soil moisture.

Automated irrigation systems have been shown to be highly desirable in bareroot nursery production because of the need for frequent and precise irrigation events, the need to frequently vary the length of irrigation events in response to ET changes, the use of multiple irrigation zones, and the need to operate the systems for a high percentage of time during high water use periods. Continuous operation is

Table 5.1—The impact of soil texture on the maximum depth of water to pump per irrigation event and maximum sprinkler precipitation rate (partially from Hoffman et al. 2007).

Soil texture	Total plant available soil water at field capacity (Inches per foot of soil depth)	*Maximum amount of water to pump per irrigation event, based on 25% allowable depletion (Inches per foot of root-zone depth)	**Maximum precipitation rate using sprinklers (Inches per hour)
Coarse sand	0.60	0.15/IE	1.97
Fine sand	0.80	0.20/IE	1.57
Loamy fine sand	1.00	0.25/IE	1.38
Sandy loam	1.40	0.35/IE	0.98
Fine sandy loam	1.70	0.42/IE	0.79
Very fine sandy loam	1.80	0.45/IE	0.59
Loam	1.90	0.48/IE	0.51
Silt loam	2.00	0.50/IE	0.51
Sandy clay loam	1.80	0.45/IE	0.39
Clay loam	1.90	0.48/IE	0.31
Silty clayloam	1.90	0.48/IE	0.31
Clay	1.80	0.45/IE	0.20

IE = irrigation efficiency.

*The numbers in column 3 are 25 percent of those in column 2. Removal of this amount of plant available water (PAW) might be chosen by the irrigator as the driest acceptable soil moisture content for growing a crop. Dividing the numbers in column 3 by the irrigation efficiency, IE, gives the amount of water that must be pumped to bring PAW back to field capacity. Any additional water would be wasted. The same procedure may be used for other levels of allowable depletion.

**The rates in column 4 assume little or no soil slope. These rates should be reduced by at least one-half for bare or crusted soils or where plants are small.

common during peak irrigation demand periods. Experience has shown that manually operated systems are not operated as frequently and precisely as planned, especially on weekends and around holidays. Furthermore, more effort can be devoted to improving system monitoring, scheduling, inspection, and maintenance when an irrigation system is automated.

Monitoring

Irrigation monitoring is necessary to optimize bareroot nursery operations. Irrigation monitoring includes not only monitoring the performance of the physical irrigation system to determine how well the system is operating, but also monitoring soil moisture levels to determine when to irrigate and how much water to apply.

Monitoring System Performance

To help diagnose operational problems such as leaks, plugging, irrigation efficiency, and application uniformity, emphasis should be given to measuring both flow rate (gpm) and total flow (gal), as well as pressures at key locations throughout the system. When the flow rate, Q, is known, the length of irrigation gives the amount of water applied. Total flow records (volume pumped) are useful for further planning, water budgeting, and calculating irrigation efficiencies. Monitoring pressures throughout the irrigation system is helpful in determining where problems such as leaks, plugging, and nonuniform application exist.

Monitoring for Irrigation Scheduling

Irrigation scheduling addresses the issue of when to irrigate and how much water to apply. Quality seedling production can be obtained by basing irrigation scheduling on soil moisture monitoring alone. But adding weather data such as temperature, solar radiation, wind speed and direction, and in- and above-canopy humidity can improve irrigation scheduling. Weather data helps predict how fast the crop is using water and may give early indications of whether irrigation events are needed or should be delayed or even omitted. Augmenting soil moisture data with salinity and/or electrical conductivity readings may reveal additional information on where the irrigation water (and fertilizers, etc.) collect in the soil profile and whether it is available to the seedlings.

Soil moisture monitoring is necessary for scheduling irrigation and should include data from both within and below the crop's root zone. The root zone data is important when determining the need for more or less irrigation by revealing how much water is plant-available and the ease with which the plant can obtain it. Data from below the root zone reveals if the amount of water applied per event has been so much as to have caused excessive losses to deep percolation.

If the soil moisture status at just one location in the nursery is representative of the entire nursery and if the irrigation scheduling scheme is the same for all zones, monitoring just one site would be adequate. Otherwise multiple sampling sites should be established so that data is collected where soil moisture status and/or irrigation schemes differ. See May (1985) and chapter 3 of Stetson and Mecham (2011) for more discussion on the location of monitoring sites.

Soil moisture status is expressed as soil moisture content or soil moisture tension, depending largely on how it is measured. The dryer the soil, the lower the soil moisture content and the higher the soil moisture tension. Soil moisture content is the percent of water in the soil, which may be expressed on a weight basis (weight of water per weight of soil) or on a volume basis (the volume of water in a given volume of soil). Soil moisture tension expresses the energy level of water in the soil system, or the ease with which water can be removed by plants. It is the amount of suction needed to extract water from a soil. It is a pressure term and commonly measured and reported in centibars (cb). Soil water potential is another term expressing the same thing as soil water tension, but it has an opposite sign (e.g., a soil water tension of 9 cb is a soil water potential of -9 cb). A soil water retention curve (also called a soil moisture characteristic curve) gives the relationship between soil water content and soil water potential. This curve is unique for each type of soil. A good summary and discussion on the principles of soil moisture monitoring is provided by Shock and Wang (2011).

The standard method of measuring soil water status involves collecting a physical sample of the soil, weighing it before any water is lost, and drying it in an oven before weighing it again. This is relatively inexpensive and easy to conduct, and requires very simple field and laboratory equipment. However, it is also labor and time-consuming and leads to errors if the soil sample size is too small. Additionally, the sampling method is destructive, preventing repetitive measurements at the same location. Therefore, only indirect methods using instruments are routinely used for measuring soil moisture status in nursery operations, mainly because instruments require less labor and give frequent, reliable, and accurate data. Most give continuous readings and can be automated. Three reliable instruments recommended for use in bareroot nurseries are (1) tensiometers (e.g., Irrometer™), (2) electrical resistance-based sensors (e.g., Watermark™), and (3) capacitance-based sensors (e.g., TriSCAN™). See chapter 3 of Stetson and Mecham (2011) for more on these and other field monitoring methods to monitor soil water status.

Both tensiometers and electrical resistance-based sensors continuously measure soil moisture. They quantify the level of difficulty of removing water from soil. This is much like what a root senses. The data they provide can be collected manually or it can be collected automatically and transmitted electronically (fig. 5.6). Detailed information on how to use these instruments and the information they provide is readily available from many sources.

Capacitance-based sensors are commercially available in soil probes, which include multiple sensors set at different depths to measure the volumetric water content in the soil profile. Some probes include salinity sensors, which give data that is useful in tracking the movement of water and fertilizers in the soil profile. These sensors are often combined with weather and other sensors to make field stations (fig. 5.7). In addition to soil moisture and salinity sensors, field stations usually include in-canopy and above-canopy weather sensors (wind, solar radiation, humidity, and temperature) and irrigation line pressure sensors (indicating pressure and duration of irrigation). Sensors, probes, and field stations can be purchased or leased by the end user. The data from these can be collected automatically, transmitted electronically, and analyzed onsite or off-site. This allows the user to frequently and easily monitor soil moisture, site-specific weather events, and irrigation events from any location that has internet access. The number of individuals and companies that analyze the data and provide recommendations for irrigation scheduling via phone, email, and/or the internet is increasing (www.irrigation-mart.com, www.servitech.com).

Figure 5.6—Field station automatically measuring and transmitting tensiometric soil moisture and other soil indices at various depths. (Photo courtesy of Irrigation-Mart, 2011.)

Planning for an Irrigation System

The planning for a bareroot hardwood nursery irrigation system includes considerations of soil-plant-water relationships in addition to land slopes, hydraulics, weather and climate factors, economics, and system layout schemes, along with details on how the system is to be operated. Some items to address are: (1) amount of irrigation water that may be needed to produce the crop; (2) pumping rate and system pressure; (3) water quality; (4) amount of water to apply during each event, when to apply it, how fast to apply it, and the application uniformity and irrigation efficiency; (5) auxiliary uses of the system (e.g., fertigation, chemigation, and micro-climate control); and (6) how to monitor soil moisture (e.g., tensiometers) and system performance (water meters and pressure gauges). Comprehensive irrigation texts such as Hoffman et al. (2007) and Stetson and Mecham (2011) provide guidance for planning a system.

Also, a nursery irrigation system plan should consider possible expansion and changes. Failure to recognize and plan for how an irrigation system will be used in the future or how that usage may change over time, can lead

Figure 5.7—Field station continuously measuring and transmitting volumetric soil moisture and salinity at various depths, in and out of canopy weather, and irrigation system pressure when irrigation is occurring. (Photo courtesy of Irrigation-Mart, 2011.)

to excessive operational and modification costs, wasteful use of energy and other resources, inefficient labor utilization, and poor seedling production and quality.

The following outline lists factors that may have a bearing on the evaluation of irrigation system alternatives and the selection of a particular system. The outline can serve as a checklist to prevent overlooking important factors, and will be particularly helpful when dealing with regulatory agencies and irrigation providers such as consultants, designers, and dealers.

Physical considerations:

- **Seedling species and cultural practices**
- **Soils**
  - Texture, depth, and uniformity
  - Water intake or infiltration rate
  - Erosion potential
  - Internal drainage
  - Salinity
  - Bearing strength
- **Topography**
  - Slope percentages
  - Irregularities, such as ditches and wetlands
- **Water supply**
  - Source and delivery schedule
  - Quantity available and reliability
  - Quality
  - Chemical constituents
  - Suspended solids
- **Climate and microclimate**
- **Land value and availability**
- **Boundary constraints and obstructions**
- **Flood hazard**
- **Water table**
- **Pests**
- **Energy availability and reliability**

Economic considerations:

- **Capital investment required**
- **Credit availability and interest rate**
- **Equipment life and annualized cost**
- **Costs and inflation**
  - Energy, operation, and maintenance
  - Labor (various skill levels)
  - Supervision and management
- **Cash flow**
- **Efficiency factors**

Social considerations:

- **Legal and political issues**
- **Local cooperation and support**
- **Availability and reliability of labor**
- **Skill and knowledge level of labor**
- **Local and governmental expectations**
- **Level of automatic control desired**
- **Potential for damage by vandalism**
- **Health issues**

References

Hoffman, G.J.; Evans, R.G.; Jensen, M.E. [et al.]. eds. 2007. Design and operation of farm irrigation systems. 2nd ed. St. Joseph, MI: American Society of Agricultural Engineers (now American Society of Agricultural and Biolgical Engineers).

May, J.T. 1985. Soil moisture. In: Lantz, C.W., ed. Southern pine nursery handbook. Atlanta, GA: U.S. Department of Agriculture, Forest Service, Southeastern Area State and Private Forestry.

McDonald, S.E. 1991. Irrigation in forest-tree nurseries: Monitoring and effects on seedling growth. In: Duryea, M.L.; Landis, T.D., eds. Forest nursery manual. The Hague/Boston/Lancaster: Martinus Nijhoff / Dr. W. Junk Publishers.

Shock, C.C.; Wang, F. 2011. Soil water tension, a powerful measurement for productivity and stewardship. HortScience. 46(2): 178–185. http://hortsci.ashspublications.org/content/46/2/178.full.pdf

Stetson, L.E.; Mecham, B.Q., eds. 2011. Irrigation. 6th ed. Falls Church, VA: Irrigation Association.

U.S. Department of Agriculture (USDA), Natural Resources Conservation Service (NRCS). 2003. Conservation Practice Standard 442. Irrigation system, sprinkler. Washington, DC.

U.S. Department of Agriculture (USDA), Natural Resources Conservation Service (NRCS). 2008. Sprinkle irrigation. In: National Engineering Handbook. Washington, DC. Section 15, Chapter 11.

Appendix 5-1

Commonly Used Irrigation Terms

Acre feet (ac-ft). A unit of volume, commonly used to designate the amount of water applied to an area. One ac-ft of water is 325,848 gallons, and the volume of water 1 foot deep covering 1 acre. (Metric conversion: 1 ac ft = 0.1233 ha m)

Acre inch (ac-in). A unit of volume, commonly used to designate the amount of water applied to an area. One ac-in of water is 27,154 gallons, and the volume of water 1 inch deep covering 1 acre. (Metric conversion: 1 ac in = 0.0103 ha m)

Allowable depletion. The amount of soil moisture depletion allowable between irrigation events that is set by the irrigation manager. It is the amount of soil water between field capacity (FC) and some portion of plant available water (PAW); it is usually reported just as a percent of PAW. Often the portion of PAW is imprecisely referred to as a portion of FC (e.g., 40 percent of PAW as 40 percent of FC), disregarding the amount of water the soil holds at PWP. When irrigation scheduling is based on soil moisture criteria (content or tension), the objective is to keep the soil moisture between the selected percent of PAW and FC. Then irrigation is to begin before the soil moisture is depleted beyond the selected percent of PAW, and to stop before the soil moisture exceeds FC. Note: the smaller the selected percent of PAW, the less energy the plant must use to get water and the less the plant is stressed.

Application uniformity (AU). A measure of how evenly irrigation water is applied over the irrigation area. Except in some nongermane cases of deficit irrigation, AU is a part/component of irrigation efficiency, often the largest. AU only deals with the part of the irrigation water that is applied rather than the gross amount, or amount pumped. If AU were 80 percent, an additional 25 percent (100/80 = 1.25) of irrigation water would have to be applied; e.g., if the plant available water needed were 0.7 in (17.8 mm), a total of 0.875 in (22.2 mm) would have to be applied; 0.175 in (4.4 mm) would be not available for beneficial use by the crop.

Centibar (cb). A unit of pressure, commonly used to quantify the energy level of water in the soil system or the ease with which water can be removed by plants. It is a unit of measurement for soil moisture tension and soil water potential. One cb is the same as one kPa, and is about 1/100 atmosphere.

Crop root zone. As used in irrigation matters, the volume of soil where plant-available soil moisture is stored; it usually increases in depth throughout the crop cycle as the crop grows.

Drain down. The partial or complete emptying of all or part of the irrigation system after an irrigation event.

Field capacity (FC). The maximum amount of water that a soil will hold under the force of gravity, or the water held in the soil after being saturated and allowed to freely drain for 2 or 3 days. At FC the soil contains 100 percent of plant available water (PAW), plus that held at permanent wilting point (PWP) which is not available for plant use. Soil moisture content near FC is ideal for plant growth.

Feet per second (fps). A unit of speed and velocity, commonly used to designate the speed of water flowing in a pipe. Metric conversion: 1 fps = 0.3048 mps (meters per second).

Gallons per minute (gpm). A unit of flow rate, commonly used to designate the flow rate of water in a pipe. Metric conversion: 1 gpm = 3.785 Lpm (liters per minute).

Impact sprinkler: A hydraulically operated mechanical device that rotates as it discharges pressurized water through a nozzle or nozzles. To cause rotation, momentum is transferred to the sprinkler body which is intermittently hit/impacted by a swinging, spring-loaded arm that gets its energy from contact with the water stream exiting a nozzle (fig. 5.2).

Irrigation area (A_e). The entire area desired/planned to be watered by an irrigation system.

Irrigation efficiency (IE). The amount of irrigation water stored in the crop's root zone that is available for beneficial use by plants, divided by the total amount of irrigation water pumped, assuming the crop's root zone covers all the area being irrigation. Thus, if the IE is 75 percent, an additional one-third (100/75 = 1.33) of irrigation water would have to be pumped. For example, if the plant available water needed were 0.7 in (17.8 mm), a total of 0.93 in (23.6 mm) would have to be pumped and 0.23 in (5.8 mm) would not be available for beneficial use by the crop, and would be wasted. Except for the portion of water applied between the beds in bareroot nurseries that would otherwise be crop-available if planted, IE accounts for all losses of the pumped water in getting it to where it is available for plant uptake. This includes: (1) water not applied uniformly to the irrigation area, (2) evaporation that occurs as water travels from the sprinklers to the irrigation area and from wetted plant and soil surfaces, (3) water falling outside of the irrigation area, and (4) water moving out of the beds via surface runoff and deep percolation.

Jet. A device that does not rotate as it distributes water through the air as a spray or streams after the water passes through a nozzle and strikes a pad.

Nozzle: A device with a hole/passageway through which pressurized water passes as the pressure is converted to stream velocity.

Nursery irrigation efficiency (IE_N). The same as irrigation efficiency (IE) when the crop root zone covers the entire irrigation area. When this is not the case, the irrigation efficiency is decreased by the portion of the irrigation area that has no crop, multiplied by IE. For bareroot hardwood nurseries that have no nursery plants between the beds, IE_N is less than IE by IE times the portion of the irrigation area that is between the beds; that is, $IE_N = IE\ [(1 - A_{bb}/A_e)]$, where A_{bb} is the area between the beds and Ae is the entire area. For example, if a bareroot nursery irrigation system has an IE of 0.75 and 40 percent of the irrigation area is between the beds, IE_N is [(0.75)(1 - 0.40)] = 0.45; that is, only 45 percent of the pumped water ends up available to the crop, and 2.22 times (100/45) as much irrigation water would have to be pumped to meet the needs of plants that receive the least water.

Off-center rotator. A sprinkler that distributes water through the air as rotating streams after the water passes through a nozzle and strikes a pad which rotates off-center (wobbles).

Permanent wilting point (PWP). The soil moisture content at which plants wilt to the extent that they will die. Even though the soil contains water at PWP, plants cannot remove it easily or fast enough to survive.

Plant available water (PAW). The amount of water held in the soil between field capacity (FC) and permanent wilting point (PWP), commonly reported as inches of water per foot of soil depth. Often a portion of PAW is imprecisely referred to as a portion of FC (e.g., 40 percent of PAW as 40 percent of FC), ignoring the amount of water the soil holds at PWP.

Precipitation Rate (PR): The rate at which an irrigation system delivers water to an irrigation area, usually reported as in/hr.

Range nozzle. The nozzle or the larger of multiple nozzles on a sprinkler. The range nozzle is used to throw water as far as possible (under the operating conditions), while any smaller, spreader nozzle(s) is used to apply water near the sprinkler, resulting in a more uniform application over the throw range of the sprinkler.

Riser. A length of pipe placed on an irrigation lateral to supply pressurized water to and to support a sprinkler.

Root zone. The same as the crop root zone.

Soil moisture tension. Expresses the energy level of water in the soil system, or the ease with which water can be removed by plants. It expresses how much suction is needed to extract water from a soil. It is a pressure term and commonly measured and reported in centibars (cb). Even though soil moisture tension is a negative pressure (suction), by convention it is usually reported as a positive value; i.e., a soil water tension of -9 cb is usually reported as 9 cb. Soil water potential is another term expressing the same thing as soil water tension, but it has an opposite sign; i.e., a soil water tension of 9 cb is a soil water potential of -9 cb.

Soil water retention curve. Also called a soil moisture characteristic curve, gives the relationship between soil water content and soil water tension. This curve is unique for each type of soil.

Spinner. A hydraulically operated mechanical device that rotates as it discharges water under pressure through a nozzle (or nozzles). Rotation is caused by directing the water stream exiting the nozzle through a curved path.

Spray head. A device that does not rotate as it distributes water through the air as a spray after the water passes through a nozzle and strikes a pad.

Spreader nozzle. One or more of the nozzles of a multiple-nozzle sprinkler. The smaller spreader nozzle(s) is used to apply water near the sprinkler, while the larger range nozzle is used to throw water as far as possible (under the operating conditions). This gives a more uniform application over the throw range of the sprinkler than would be possible with just one nozzle.

Sprinkler. A device that distributes water through the air as a stream(s) after it passes through a nozzle or nozzles, which converts water pressure to stream velocity.

System capacity. The ability of an irrigation system to deliver both the net required rate (gpm) and volume (gallons) of water necessary to meet a crop's needs, including all the losses that occur related to the irrigation process.

Appendix 5-2

Useful Calculations for Irrigation Management

Equation 1

Precipitation Rate of an Irrigation System:

PRavg = $[k_1(Q)/(Az)]$

where:

PRavg = average precipitation rate in an irrigation zone [in/hr],

Q = flow rate at which water is applied to the zone [gpm],

A_z = area of the zone being irrigated [ft^2], and

k_1 = a constant: (60 min/hr)(12 in/ft)/(7.48 gal/ft^3) = 96.25 in-min-ft^2/gal-hr.

Equation 1 assumes that all the water is applied within the boundaries of the irrigation zone. Then, the average precipitation rate of a one-acre (43,560 ft^2) zone irrigated by an 85 gpm pump is:

PRavg = [(96.25 in-min-ft^2/gal-hr) (85 gpm) / (43,560 ft^2)] = 0.188 in/hr.

Equation 2

Amount of Irrigation Water to Grow a Seedling Crop:

$V_{app} = [k_2(d_{ieu})(A_e)/(IE)]$

where:

V_{app} = volume of irrigation water needed to produce a crop of seedlings [gal],

d_{ieu} = amount/depth of irrigation water effectively used/evapotranspired to produce a crop of seedlings [in],

A_e = entire area irrigated by the system [ac], and

IE = a decimal representing the irrigation efficiency, and

k_2 = a constant: 27,154 gal/ac-in.

If an irrigation system with an IE of 0.67 is to supply 8 inches of water to be beneficially used by a crop of seedlings growing in a 10-ac nursery, the volume of irrigation water that must be supplied is:

V_{app} = [(27,154 gal/ac-in) (8 in) (10 ac)] / (0.67) = 3,242,268 269 gal. = 120 ac-in.

Thus, to apply the 8 inches of water for use by the seedling crop, 12 in must be supplied to the entire 10 ac nursery area.

Equation 3

Size of Power Source (Pump Motor)

The power required for irrigation depends on the rate water is pumped (Q), the efficiency of the pumping plant, and the total dynamic head of the system as follows:

$P = [(Q)(TDH)d/(Epp)k_4]$,

where:

P = pumping power (size of motor) required by the irrigation system [hp],

Q = flow rate at which water is supplied by the irrigation system [gpm],

TDH = total dynamic head (pressure) of the irrigation system [ft, 1 ft = 0.433 psi],

d = density of water [taken to be 8.33 lb/gal],

E_{pp} = a decimal representing the efficiency of the pumping plant (pump and motor combined), and

k_4 = a constant: 33,000 ft-lb/min-hp.

Assume that the TDH for a sprinkler system used for the 1-acre nursery zone previously discussed (Equation 1) is 139 feet (60 psi) and that the pumping plant has a 65 percent efficiency. Then the size of electric motor/power unit required to supply the 85 gpm flow rate is:

P = (85 gpm) (139 ft) (8.33 lb/gal) / (0.65 eff) (33,000 ft-lb/min-hp) = 4.6 hp, or 5 hp.

Equation 4

Irrigation Energy Consumption

$E = [k_5(P)(V_{app})/Q]$

where:

E = energy consumed/used by the pump to produce the crop [kilowatt hours (kW-hr)],

P = power used by the pumping plant [hp],

V_{app} = volume of irrigation water needed to produce a crop of seedlings [gal],

Q = flow rate at which water is supplied to/by the irrigation system [gpm],

k_5 = a constant: (0.745 kilowatts per horsepower [kW/hp]) / (60 min/hr) = 0.012417 kilowatts per horsepower kW-hr/hp-min.

So, the amount of irrigation energy needed to produce the 10-ac seedling crop previously discussed (Equations 1, 2, and 4) is:

E = (0.012417 kW-hr/hp-min) (4.6 hp) (3,242,268 gal) / (85 gal/min) = 2,178 kW-hr.

At an energy cost of $0.10/kW-hr, this amounts to $217.30, or $21.73 per acre.

Appendix 5-3

Example Calculations for Irrigation Scheduling Based on Soil Moisture

A sprinkler irrigation system with a pumping rate of **150 gpm** and an irrigation efficiency **(IE) of 0.73** is to irrigate a **10-ac** nursery crop using **five 2-ac zones**. The soil is **sandy loam** and the **crop's root zone is 6 in**. The allowable soil moisture depletion is chosen to be **25 percent of plant available water (PAW)**, meaning that irrigation will be initiated when soil moisture is depleted to 75 percent of PAW and continued until reaching field capacity (FC).

*What is the pumping rate in units of in/hr?

[150 gal/min / (2 ac) (27154 gal/ac-in)] [60 min/hr] = 0.1657 in/hr.

*What is the amount of plant available soil moisture between 75 percent of PAW and FC.

From column 3 of table 1, 25 percent of PAW is 0.35 in per foot of soil. Thus, the amount of plant available soil moisture between 75 percent of PAW and FC in the crop's 6-in root zone is:

(0.35in/ft) (6 in) (1/12 ft/in) = 0.175 inches

and, over the 10 acres this is:

(0.175 in) (10 ac) (27,154 gal/ac-in) = 47,519.5 gal.

*What is the volume of irrigation water to pump to replace the 25 percent depletion?

Since IE is 0.73,

(0.35/0.73 in/ft) (6 in) (1/12 ft/in) = 0.24 inches

and, over the 10 acres this is:

(0.24 in) (10 ac) (27,154 gal/ac-in) = 65,170 gal.

*What is the pumping time required to irrigate each of the 2-ac zones to replace the 25 percent depletion?

Using the pumping rate of 150 gal/min,

[(0.24 in) (2 ac) (27154 gal/ac-in)] / (150 gal/min) = 87 min.

*How often must irrigation occur not to exceed the allowable depletion of soil moisture if the **ET is 0.10 in/day**?

[(0.35 in/ft) (6 in) (1/12 ft/in)] / (0.10 in/day) = 1.75 days.

*But if a **frequency of irrigation** is chosen to be **once per day**, what is the total daily amount of water to pump for the 10 acres, and the length of the daily irrigation event for each 2-ac zone?

The amount to pump each day is:

(0.10 in/day) / (0.73) = 0.137 in/day,

or (0.137 in/day) (10 ac) (27,154 gal/ac-in) = 37,197 gal/day.

The length of the irrigation event per day for each 2-ac zone is:

[(0.137 in/day) (2 ac/zone) (27154 gal/ac-in)] / (150 gal/min) = 50 min/zone-day.

However, if the **ET were 0.33 in/day**, the frequency of irrigation would need to be more than once per day because the daily ET is greater than the allowable depletion of soil moisture, 0.175 in. If two irrigation events per day were chosen and the length of each event were the same, the volume of irrigation water to pump would be:

[(0.33) / (0.73 in/day) (2 ac/zone)] / (2 events/day)]= 0.45 ac-in/event-zone,

or (0.45 ac-in/event-zone) (27,154 gal/ac-in) = 12,275 gal/event-zone,

and for the entire 10-ac nursery:

(12,275 gal/zone) (5 zones) = 61,375 gal/event,

and the daily amount to pump for the 10 acres would be:

(61,375 gal/event) (2 events) = 122,750 gal.

The pumping time required per event per day for each zone would be:

(12,275 gal/zone) / (150 gal/min) = 82 min/zone;

The pumping time required for one event on the entire 5-zone nursery would be 409 min, or 6 hr and 49 min. And the total pumping time for the two events per day would be 13 hr and 38 min.

The Management of Seedling Nutrition

6

C.B. Davey and K. McNabb

C.B. Davey was professor emeritus, Department of Forestry and Environmental Resources, North Carolina State University, Raleigh, NC

Ken McNabb is W. Kelly Mosley Professor Emeritus, School of Forestry and Wildlife Sciences, Auburn University, Auburn, AL

Outline

Facing Page: *Field of pecan seedlings. (Photo by Greg Hoss.)*

General Considerations

Fertility management for the large-scale production of hardwood seedlings is a difficult and complex challenge. Research-based recommendations specific to the fertility management of individual species or even genera are lacking or very limited. As a result, hardwood fertility management tends to take a generalized approach, where many species are lumped together and managed in similar fashion (Stone 1980, Davey 1994, 2005), and a few general principles applicable to hardwood fertility management have developed.

First, it is generally accepted that hardwood crops require substantially more nutrients than do pine crops. Most eastern hardwood species are native to temperate deciduous forests. Natural temperate hardwood forests require substantially more nitrogen, phosphorus, potassium, calcium, and magnesium than do temperate conifer forests for tree growth (Cole and Rapp 1981). These higher nutritional requirements have implications for the amount and nature of fertilizer applications in nurseries. In addition, many hardwoods are deciduous and have evolved to efficiently recycle essential nutrients. A study conducted in a Tennessee hardwood nursery (dos Santos 2006) found that 19.5, 65.0, and 26.5 pounds per acre (lb/ac) (21.9, 73.2, and 29.8 kilograms per hectare [kg/ha]) of nitrogen was deposited through leaf litter in nursery beds during the growing season by Nuttall oak, yellow poplar, and green ash, respectively. This has implications for nutrient availability, the balance between nutrient removal and addition, and soil organic matter maintenance.

When compared to conifer forests, hardwood forests typically occur on soils with a higher pH. Hardwood physiological demand for base cations such as calcium and magnesium and subsequent nutrient recycling results in soils less acidic than conifer forests (Reich et al. 2005, Brady and Weil 2000). There is probably not an "ideal" soil pH for hardwood nurseries and there is still much research needed in this area, however, it seems likely that temperate hardwoods evolved within and contributed to ecosystems where soil pH was less acidic than temperate pine forests. Current nursery practice suggests nursery managers should maintain a soil pH between 5.0 and 6.0 when growing eastern hardwoods. This may or may not be the "ideal" pH for each of the many species grown across the Eastern United States, but this pH range both matches the general pH characteristics of soils in the eastern hardwood forest and provides a soil pH range where all soil nutrients are relatively available.

Finally, hardwood nursery crops require nearly twice as much water (rainfall plus irrigation) compared to pine crops. Faster growth, larger seedlings, increased transpiration potential as a result of different leaf structures, and more efficient water transpiration structures in stem xylem result in a higher water demand for hardwood crops than for pine. The difference is sufficient that nursery managers should physically separate hardwood crops from pine crops so the manager can water each crop differently.

While providing a helpful starting point, such generalized principles are limited in their applicability across the many hardwood species cultivated by nursery managers and the specific edaphic and climatic conditions encountered in individual nurseries. Appropriate fertility management should be based on the particular conditions of the nursery and the application of fertility recommendations as specific to the crop as information and experience allow. The following discussion is meant to assists managers to develop such an approach.

Macronutrients

Nitrogen

Hardwood seedling culture requires nitrogen fertilization. Not only do the seedlings require nitrogen for proper growth and development (table 6.1), nitrogen compounds tend to be easily lost through leaching and volatilization so that soil reserves must be replenished each growing season. Leaching losses (table 6.1) are increased by coarse-textured soils, low organic matter content, low cation exchange capacity, and heavy rainfall. As a general rule of thumb, a total of 225 lb/ac (252 kg/ha) of elemental nitrogen is needed each year to grow a crop of "1-0" hardwood seedlings. This is around 50 percent more nitrogen than required for pine crops.

Nitrogen fertilizers should be applied to hardwoods over the growing season to ensure a steady supply of elemental nitrogen, due to both the increased demand for nitrogen during the growing season and the loss of plant-available nitrogen compounds through leaching. For spring-sown species, application typically begins at 6 weeks after sowing. In the case of fall-sown species, application begins at the same time as seedling development, but depends on time of emergence and seasonal weather. Some fall-sown seed have nitrogen supplies that will support seedling development during the first few weeks after germination.

The total amount of recommended fertilizer nitrogen should be divided among several growing season applications until late August. To match seedling development, application equipment can be set to put out smaller amounts in greater frequency or larger amounts in less frequency. Soil texture also affects the frequency of application, with coarse-textured soils requiring more frequent applications. Nursery managers must learn to observe their trees for any change in color or development that might indicate a nitrogen deficiency, with the frequency and intensity of rainfall strongly

Table 6.1—Characteristics of the nutrients essential for plant growth. (Sources: Tisdale et al. 1993, Brady and Weil 2000, Goldy 2013.)

Element	Symbol	Uptake form	Use by plant	Plant mobility	Potential soil mobility
Nitrogen	N	NO_3^- NH_4^+	Formation of amino acids, proteins, chlorophyll, and multiple other plant components and processes	Yes Yes	High Low*
Phosphorus	P	$H_2PO_4^-$ HPO_4^{2-}	Energy storage and transfer for virtually all plant metabolic pathways	Yes Yes	Low Low
Potassium	K	K^+	Enzyme activation, water relations, transpiration, and multiple other plant activities	Yes	High in sandy soils with low CEC
Calcium	Ca	Ca^{2+}	Structure and permeability of cell membranes, plant growth	No	Medium
Magnesium	Mg	Mg^{2-}	Chlorophyll, several plant metabolic functions	Yes	Medium
Sulfur	S	SO_4^{2-}	Amino acid and protein syntheses and functionality	No	High
Iron	Fe	Fe^{2+} Fe^{3+}	Enzymatic activity and structure	No	Low
Manganese	Mn	Mn^{2+}	Reagent in various plant metabolic pathways	No	High in acidic soils
Zinc	Zn	Zn^{2+}	Enzymatic activity	No	Low
Boron	B	H_3BO_3	Meristematic cell development, other multiple metabolic functions	No	High in sandy soils
Copper	Cu	Cu^{2+}	Enzyme structure and functionality	No	Low
Chlorine	Cl	Cl-	Not clear, may be involved in water retention and movement	Yes	High
Molybdenum	Mo	MoO_4^{2-}	Essential component of the nitrate reductase enzyme, a component of the N fixing process in legume nodules	Yes	High in alkaline soils

CEC = cation exchange capacity.
* Compounds and elements may leach from very sandy soils regardless of their affinity for soil particles and low mobility.

influencing the movement of nitrogen down the soil profile. In the case of liquid fertilizers, the frequency of application may be as high as weekly. This provides an effective way of maintaining a stable nitrogen supply, which is important over the growing season.

Plants take up nitrogen primarily as the positively charged ammonium ion (NH_4^+) and the negatively charged nitrate ion (NO_3^-). The ammonium ion is often referred to as the "reduced" form of nitrogen, while the nitrate ion is an "oxidized" form. Studies have well established that pines thrive best on fertilizers that supply the reduced form of nitrogen, such as urea, diammonium phosphate, and ammonium sulfate. And, some studies have so far indicated that hardwoods also thrive best on fertilizers that provide a reduced form of nitrogen (Deines 1973, Villarrubia 1980). The research support is far from definitive, however, and it cannot be assumed that hardwoods will not do just as well with the oxidized forms of nitro gen. South (1975), for example, observed taller sweetgum seedlings when seedlings were fertilized with ammonium nitrate (vs. urea).

Other formulations of nitrogen fertilizer include ammonium thiosulfate (table 6.2) which is entirely a "reduced" form of nitrogen, and although containing sulfur, has limited, if any, effect on soil pH. Slow-release fertilizers are also available but are expensive and cost more than liquid forms of N. Furthermore, each has distinctive characteristics and fertilizer release curves. Unfortunately, the release curves for slow-release fertilizers have proven very difficult to match to the needs of hardwood seedlings over the typical seedling growing season.

Liquid nitrogen formulations are becoming a more popular source of fertilizer nitrogen in hardwood nurseries. Urea-ammonium nitrate (UAN) is one such fertilizer material that

The Mineralization of Organic Compounds

The soil is a dynamic matrix where chemical transformations constantly occur in both the organic and inorganic components. These transformations can have profound effects on the amount, nature, and availability of nutrients. The chemical transformations affecting soil nitrogen availability are especially important. In natural systems, organic matter is decomposed and nitrogen released through the process known as "mineralization" which transforms the nitrogen in organic compounds to the ammonium ion NH_4^+ then oxidizes it to NO_3^-. This process is mediated by soil microorganisms and as such the process is greatly affected by soil temperature and moisture conditions. The soil microbes associated with mineralization prefer warm temperatures, moist soil conditions, and abundant oxygen. These conditions are typically present in nursery soils during the growing season.

The mineralization process may be further stimulated when nitrogen fertilizer materials are added, resulting in important effects on soil properties. Because hydrogen ions are released during the chemical reactions associated with mineralization, the repetitive application of nitrogen fertilizers, particularly those containing ammonium sources, will lower soil pH over time (Tisdale et al. 1993, Darusman et al. 1991). Also, because NO_3^- is highly soluble and mobile in the soil, the loss of nitrogen through leaching will likely increase when conditions are optimal for microbial mediated mineralization. The potential for nitrogen loss through mineralization simultaneous to increased demand during the growing season requires that nursery managers remain especially vigilant to ensure plant requirements are being met.

Sulfur has a similar mineralization process where soil microbes transform organic sulfur-containing compounds to the plant available and highly leachable form SO_4^{2-}. These microbes thrive best in the same environmental conditions favored by nitrogen mineralization. Other essential plant nutrients such as phosphorus, potassium, and the micronutrients are also incorporated into the process of organic matter decomposition and released back into the soil environment. However, their chemical nature, movement, and plant availability are mostly affected by their complex interaction with the surfaces of soil colloids.

can be applied as a liquid. Ranging from 28- to 32-percent nitrogen content and applied over the top of seedlings during the growing season, UAN can quickly provide needed seedling fertilizer nitrogen requirements. UAN offers certain advantages, such as application uniformity, compatibility with many pesticides, and relative ease of handling and storage (Tisdale et al. 1993), but managers need to be aware of certain possible disadvantages, as well. Both the ammonium and urea components of UAN may volatilize, and the nitrate component is susceptible to leaching and denitrification (when microbes change the nitrate to nitrogen gas). Primarily because of the volatility issue, UAN should not be applied on hot, dry, and windy days. Leaf scorch can also be a problem, because high concentrations of ammonium may be toxic to seedlings. Younger seedlings will be most sensitive, but resistance should improve over the growing season as seedlings produce more mature leaves. The use of at least 1/2 inch (in) (12 millimeters [mm]) of irrigation, either during or immediately after application, can be particularly important for the effective use of UAN fertilizers. Not only can irrigation reduce the risk of leaf scorch, it can also help incorporate the fertilizer into the soil and reduce ammonium volatility. Finally, managers need to be aware that UAN fertilizers can "salt out" at low temperatures. The 32-percent formulation, for example, will begin to form fertilizer salt crystals at temperatures of 32 °F (0 °C). The 28-percent formulation begins to salt out at 1 °F (-18 °C).

Nitrogen-fixing trees, such as black locust, are the exception to the preceding general recommendations. Nursery managers should check seedling roots in early summer (June) to verify that nodulation is occurring. If so, and growth seems to appear on schedule, then further nitrogen fertilization is not usually required. On the other hand, if nodulation is not present or is weak, and the seedlings appear to lag behind the desired growth curve, then the seedlings should be put into the normal nitrogen fertilization regime with the other hardwoods. Some nitrogen-fixers can be sensitive to the presence of nitrogen in the soil, slowing nodulation, even when the nitrogen availability is not enough to maintain the desired growth curve.

Phosphorus

Unlike nitrogen, phosphorus tends to stay where it is placed. As an anion (negatively charged) it readily combines with many soil components such as organic matter, iron, and aluminum, to form stable compounds that resist leaching. Phosphorus compounds generally move only with the physical displacement of soil. Historically, in fact, solubility and plant availability presented a challenge for development of suitable phosphorus fertilizers. Unlike nitrogen, however, and similar to all other fertilizer elements, a soil test is useful for developing a phosphorus fertilizer recommendation.

Soil test results provide an estimate of "available" fertilizer nutrients in the soil. Unlike tissue samples, which are

Table 6.2—Nutrient content of various commercially available fertilizers (shown as percentage). (Source: Magdoff and Van Es 2009, Tisdale et al. 1993.)

Chemical	N	P_2O_5	K_2O	Ca	Mg	S	Cl
Nitrogen Materials							
Ammonium nitrate	34						
Ammonium sulfate	21					24	
Ammonium thiosulfate	12					26	
Calcium ammonium nitrate	27			4-8	4		
Urea	46						
Urea-Ammonium nitrate (UAN)	28-32						
Phosphorous and N+P Materials							
Superphosphate		20		20		12	
Triple superphosphate		46		14		1	
Diammonium phosphate (DAP)	18	46					
Monoammonium phosphate (MAP)	11-13	48-52					
Potassium Materials							
Potassium chloride (muriate of potash			60				47
Potassium-magnesium sulfate ("sul-po-mag")			22		11	23	2
Potassium sulfate			50		1	18	2
Other Materials							
Gypsum				23		18	
Limestone, calcitic				25-40	0.5-3		
Limestone, dolomitic				19-22	6-13		1
Magnesium sulfate				2	11	14	
Potassium nitrate							
Elemental sulfur						30-99	

chemically analyzed for total elemental content, soil test results provide an estimate of the amount of fertilizer element available for plant uptake, and not the total amount in the soil. This measure of availability greatly depends upon the chemical methodology employed to extract the element from the soil matrix. The Mehlich 3 extraction gives a reliable phosphorus and minor-element extraction for sandy acidic soil conditions—typical of most forest tree nurseries. Hardwood nursery crops need a little more phosphorus that do pine crops. Using a Mehlich 3 extraction, phosphorus fertilization is recommended when the level is less than 45 parts per million (ppm).

Phosphorus fertilizer compounds are often applied during the soil tillage phase and before bed shaping. In fact, once phosphorus soil levels are corrected, fertilizer phosphorus may not need to be further applied for 3 years or more. If a growing season addition of phosphorus fertilizer is needed, the most commonly used soluble formulation is diammonium phosphate ($(NH_4)_2HPO_4$), which may be used as a top dressing. Hardwood seedlings have been reported to respond faster to the application of liquid forms of phosphorus than granular DAP (Weatherly 2018). A growing season application of phosphorus might be needed when fumigation has decreased endomycorrhizae levels or, in the case of "new ground syndrome," where ectomycorrhizae have not had a chance to establish on species like oaks. Both endomycorrhizae and ectomycorrhizae may be found on hardwoods, depending upon species, and either may be affected by fumigation. (See accompanying discussion of Soil Fumigation and Hardwood Seedling Production.)

Potassium

Common fertilizer forms of potassium are potassium chloride (KCl) and potassium sulfate (K_2SO_4). Both are

Soil Fumigation and Hardwood Seedling Production

Scott Enebak

Mycorrhizae are beneficial soil-borne fungi associated with the roots of most forest nursery seedlings. These fungi have been shown to increase absorption of numerous macro- and micro-nutrients necessary for plant growth, particularly phosphorus. In fact, seedlings lacking in mycorrhizal fungi become purple due to the lack of available phosphorus. Because of the enhanced plant nutrition, seedlings with mycorrhizal fungi will grow more rapidly and appear healthier than non-mycorrhizal seedlings which often are stunted, with chlorotic foliage that becomes necrotic along the margins with corresponding sparse, limited and minimal root growth.

There are two types of soil mycorrhizae, ectomycorrhizae and endomycorrhizae, with the latter also known as Vesicular-Arbuscular (VAM). Ectomycorrhizae form and are found, on the outside of seedling roots and are commonly associated with conifer seedlings. These fungi produce spores on fruiting bodies that are easily dispersed in the wind and can quickly colonize and infest nursery soils. Two common nursery ectomycorrhizae are Telephora terrestris and Pisolithus tinctorius. These mycorrhizal fungi typically result in the formation of a mycelia around the seedling roots called a Hartig net that often results in root forks or bifurcations of the seedling roots. It is this Hartig net and multiple root forks that assist the tree in nutrient and water absorption, thereby increasing seedling growth. In contrast, endomycorrhizae (VAMs) form inside the root tissue cells, forming vesicles, thus the VAM designation. Endomycorrhizae are commonly associated with hardwood seedling root systems. These mycorrhizae do not produce fruiting bodies like the ectomycorrhizae and therefore do not spread by wind-blown spores, but rather by infected seedling root pieces. Therefore, endomycorrhizae do not spread and colonize nursery soils as effectively as ectomycorrhizae, and endomycorrhizal deficiencies in nursery soils are more pronounced and take longer to build up soil populations.

The production of conifer and hardwood seedlings without the use of soil fumigants is simply not possible in many bareroot nurseries. Weeds, nematodes, and damping-off fungi all take their toll on seed efficiency and seedling quality. The use of soil fumigants has long-been known to significantly reduce the levels and type of mycorrhizae in nursery soils resulting in the stunting and discoloration of both hardwood and conifer seedlings. Seedlings rarely die, but remain alive in a stunted condition, generally becoming culled in the lifting process and negatively affecting seedling densities and thereby seedling uniformity. Fortunately, conifer seedlings tend to be quickly colonized by ectomycorrhizae spores from surrounding, non-fumigated soils. However, the lack of spore production by endomycorrhizal fungi tends to result in hardwood seedlings being more susceptible to stunting due to soil fumigation.

Fortunately, most nursery soils that are fumigated do not result in the elimination of 100% of the soil-borne fungi, and if stunting does occur, it does not appear on the entire field site. This is demonstrated by the patches of healthy seedlings scattered among the stunted seedlings which will serve as an inoculum source. VAM mycorrhizae will be embedded in the root materials that remain in the soil after lifting. In addition, studies have shown mycorrhizae surviving days of methyl bromide exposure at rates commonly used in soil fumigation. There is also some evidence that ectomycorrhizal fungi recolonization speed increases after the second and third soil fumigation, indicating that some populations resistant to fumigation were being selected. Numerous studies monitoring VAM recolonization after soil fumigation have shown that it takes at least 2 months for mycorrhizae to reappear in soil samples after fumigation and up to 13 months in some soils for populations to return to prefumigation levels. Endomycorrhizae are also spread and moved around by earthworms, small mammals, and insects. The roots of weeds also help recolonize the field prior to sowing the hardwood seedling crop. Therefore, cover crops that favor endomycorrhizae (winter wheat, for example) can also increase the levels of VAM's prior to soil fumigation.

Nursery managers have other options to minimize or eliminate the effect of fumigation on soil endomycorrhiza populations. Where possible, fall fumigation allows more time for the soil to become reinfected with mycorrhizae. When managers must fumigate in the spring they may want to consider lowering the rate of methyl bromide if they use totally impermeable film (TIF) during fumigation. When the stunting of pines occurs due to a lack of mycorrhiza, quickly adding P in one or two top-dressings (25 lb of P / acre) will mitigate the P deficiency. With endomycorrhizal hardwoods that often have problems with mycorrhiza such as yellow poplar and sweetgum, adding P in June with the first top-dressing of N is a rapid and inexpensive method to address mycorrhizae issues. Several types of P fertilizer can be used in this case. Diammonium phosphate (DAP) may be used for those preferring granular applications, while soluble monoammonium phosphate (MAP) may be used for those preferring liquids. Either granular or liquid materials are suitable if applied accurately and timely. Applying mycorrhizal spores at the time of sowing is not recommended because of the added expense of the fungal inoculum and the low probability of success.

highly soluble and subject to loss through leaching, particularly in coarse-textured soils with low cation exchange capacity and low organic matter. While nitrogen is critical to the growth of new foliage, potassium is essential to all growth and is therefore needed even after autumn leaf fall, when root and stem growth can be fueled by the photosynthesis of green branches. The demand for potassium may therefore extend beyond the summer growing season. The most common timing of potassium chloride (KCl) applications is preplant, at a maximum of 150 lb/ac (168 kg/ha).

A mid-summer application may be needed in some soils because of potential losses through leaching during the growing season.

Calcium

Hardwood seedling crops tend to take up more calcium (per unit of biomass) than pine species. When analyzed for total nutrient content, hardwood seedlings typically show a relatively high level of calcium in their tissue due to the formation of calcium pectate used in the lignification process, when forming woody branches and stems. Calcium must therefore be available as long as the seedling is growing woody tissue. Once incorporated into the stem structure, the calcium is trapped and is no longer mobile in the plant. Although relatively higher concentrations of calcium are required by hardwoods, it does not necessary follow that they need higher soil pH to supply that calcium. Adequate calcium can be provided by the appropriate application and balance of soil nutrients. Some nurseries may accumulate soil calcium, particularly if the nursery water source is a deep limestone well.

A soil test will provide an estimate of available soil calcium and indicate the need and amount of calcium necessary for application. A level of 300 ppm is appropriate for most hardwood nursery soils. However, the pH and buffering capacity determine the type and amount of soil amendment used to raise soil calcium levels. If the soil acidity is already at pH 5.5, then a form of calcium should be used that will not affect soil acidity when applied. In this case, gypsum, also known as calcium sulfate ($CaSO_4$-$2H_2O$), can be applied at a rate of 400 to 500 lb/ac (448 to 560 kg/ha). On the other hand, if the soil test indicates an acidic soil condition—for example pH 4.4—where decreasing soil acidity may benefit soil properties, then dolomitic lime (calcium magnesium carbonate ($CaMg(CO_3)^2$), should be used. On typical sandy nursery soils a common application rate is 1,000 pounds per acre (1,120 kg per ha). In some areas of the country, dolomitic lime has limited availability and calcitic lime ($CaCO_3$) may be substituted, although calcitic lime lacks the Mg component.

An important consideration in the application of any of the lime additives is that they be incorporated soon after application. Calcium does not readily leach in the soil and will have limited effect if left on the surface. To become available, it must be adequately mixed and incorporated into the root zone (i.e., the top 6 in [15 centimeters (cm)] of nursery soil). In addition, most lime products are fine powders that are easily moved by wind, causing uneven distribution over the area or even movement off the field, reducing application rates. Pelletized formulations greatly reduce wind-associated movement. Lime application is made during the soil tillage phase and before bed formation in the fall and spring. The time required for adequate soil reaction is around 3 weeks prior to sowing for dolomitic lime, while gypsum is faster acting and may be incorporated 2 days or even 1 day before sowing.

Magnesium

Magnesium is absorbed by plants as Mg^{2+} and is necessary for chlorophyll formation and therefore essential to photosynthesis and growth. Seedlings need magnesium as long as they are growing new foliage, but need little, if any, after leaf fall. Available soil magnesium should be 30 ppm. Magnesium is very similar to calcium in terms of reactivity in the soil and plant uptake. Both occur in the soil as positively charged divalent cations and may "compete" for sites on negatively charged soil colloids. Fortunately, hardwood seedlings tolerate calcium/magnesium ratios as high as 10 to 1 and as low as 1 to 1. The total amount of plant-available calcium and magnesium is substantially more important than their ratio (Koppitte and Menzies 2007, Schulte and Kelling 1985).

Besides dolomitic lime, there are two other sources for magnesium soil amendments. The first is magnesium sulfate, or Epsom salts, $MgSO_4$. (CAUTION: Magnesium sulfate is a strong purgative and applicators should conscientiously minimize respiratory inhalation and oral ingestion.) The second compound is a mixture of magnesium sulfate and potassium sulfate, and may be sold as either "sul-po-mag," "Kmag," or "sulfate of potash magnesia." Application rates depend upon the objectives and are typically 200 to 250 lb/ac (224 to 280 kg/ha), depending on the soil test.

Sulfur

Sulfur is a macronutrient used primarily in the formation of essential amino acids required for building proteins and is essential to virtually all plant metabolic activities. Although sulfur can be found in the soil in a large variety of reduced and oxidized states, it is taken up by seedlings in the sulfate form, SO_4. The process of oxidation, which produces the form taken up by plants, is regulated by soil microbes and affected by oxygen availability. Sulfur uptake may be limited in conditions of low soil oxygen.

The required amount of available soil sulfur is 10 ppm. When sulfur amendments are necessary, two commonly used fertilizer materials are elemental sulfur and ammonium sulfate. Elemental sulfur is a finely ground powder that must be evenly and accurately applied, then incorporated into the root zone for maximum effectiveness and speed of reaction. In a well-aerated soil, microbial activity changes the sulfur to SO_4, which reacts with water to form sulfuric acid ($H_2SO_4^{2-}$), which lowers the pH value. This reaction is relatively quick and effective. Both plant-available sulfates and pH-modifying acids are formed quickly. (Avoid applying elemental sulfur immediately before sowing to reduce any chance of an acid burn to the roots or cotyledons of germinating seedlings.) On the other hand, the addition of ammonium sulfate occurs at a slower pace, with the SO_4 being released as the plant takes up the NH_4. Bacteria are not required for this activity. Elemental sulfur application produces a measurable effect after only 3 weeks, while the addition of ammonium sulfate may take an entire season.

Micronutrients

Micronutrients are necessary for plant growth and development but are required in relatively small amounts. These small amounts do not indicate small importance. Micronutrient deficiencies can and will impact plant growth as surely as will macronutrient deficiencies, so managing micronutrient fertility is essential to proper hardwood seedling production.

Iron

Any hardwood species can show iron deficiencies, although hardwoods seem to be more effective at absorbing iron from the soil compared to pines. Iron deficiencies in hardwoods seem to be most common in green ash and the oaks. Deficiencies show up as a foliage chlorosis and because iron does not translocate, deficiencies are seen in the new shoots of growing plants. This is different from nitrogen chlorosis, as nitrogen is highly mobile and may move from older leaves to younger leaves, leaving a chlorotic condition in the older leaves, or in severe cases the entire plant. A soil test of 20 ppm using the Mehlich 3 extraction is considered the threshold for deficiency, although such a low value is rarely encountered. Interpreting soil test results and correcting iron deficiency therefore depends on other factors.

Iron mobility in the soil results from a complex interaction between inorganic soil chemistry and the activity of soil microbes. Iron is one of the most abundant soil minerals but is not readily available for plant uptake. Plants absorb iron as both the Fe^{3+} (ferric) and the Fe^{2+} (ferrous) forms, but iron is often present in the soil as unavailable insoluble precipitates, particularly at high pH. The chemistry of iron solubility, transport, and absorption is complex and not entirely understood, however iron chelation by soil microbes has been shown to be closely associated with increased mobility and availability to plant roots. Plants have developed specific mechanisms to remove the iron from chelates present in the soil solution, actively transport the Fe^{2+} ion across root cell membranes, and then rechelate it for internal plant transport. Summer temperatures can be high enough to kill soil microbes and slow the process of chelation, making iron even less available to plant roots than it normally would be and resulting in chlorosis. On the other hand, cooler periods of the growing season may not have visible signs of iron deficiency. Obviously, a soil test is limited because a test may indicate adequate soil iron content only to have iron moved from available to unavailable forms during the high temperatures of summer.

Iron deficiency may be corrected through foliar application of iron fertilizer. Direct application to the soil solely on the results of a soil test may or may not prevent deficiency symptoms from appearing once microbial activities decrease in the summer. A direct foliar application of 2 lb/ac (2.24 kg/ha) of elemental iron in late June or early July is directly absorbed into the plant and will normally resolve iron deficiency problems. Irrigate the seedlings within 8 to 12 hours after application to wash off any residual salts found in the fertilizer that might "burn" the leaves. Much of the iron in the fertilizer should have been absorbed into the leaves within 8 hours after application.

Boron

Boron is used in cell wall formation, and deficiencies are seen primarily in a chocolate-colored pith of small branches, weak stems, and apical meristem death, although different species may show different symptoms. It is taken up by the plant in the form of borate H_3BO_3. Boron is an anion (negatively charged) while most other micronutrients are cations (positively charged). As such, boron is more easily leached from the soil, particularly coarse soils, where deficiency symptoms may occur. Much of the boron available to seedlings comes from the organic matter fraction of the soil and is made available through microbial activity. A minimum soil test level should be considered 0.4 ppm (0.8 lb/ac, 0.9 kg/ha).

Correction of boron deficiency in hardwood nurseries can be made through a foliar application of 2 lb/ac (2.24 kg/ha) of elemental boron in the form of sodium borate ($Na_2B_3O_7$-$10H_2O$) in late June or early July. In this case, an irrigation rinse should be applied 8 to 12 hours after application to wash off any salts that may have been present in the fertilizer. Boron may also be applied directly to the soil using 2.25 lb/ac (2.52 kg/ha) of elemental boron in the form of sodium borate during the soil preparation phase prior to sowing. Foliar applications tend to resolve deficiency symptoms relatively quickly, producing an effect on seedling appearance within weeks, sometimes even days. Presowing soil applications, on the other hand, are intended to prevent any deficiency from occurring.

Unlike other micronutrients, the range from boron deficiency to toxicity is relatively narrow. Boron toxicity can be produced by improper calibration or excessive application of fertilizer materials. In the case of boron, follow application recommendations as closely as possible. Calcium levels affect boron toxicity. Seedlings growing in soils with high calcium levels seem to tolerate higher levels of boron than would otherwise be toxic.

Manganese

Manganese is used by plants in enzyme functionality and is important in a variety of metabolic processes, but does not seem to be necessary for plant structure formation. Manganese deficiency usually produces a plant with "bronze" colored leaves, sometimes greenish grey, and smaller than normal. Manganese is similar to iron in that it is not mobile in the plant and deficiency symptoms appear in new shoots. Plants take up available soil manganese in the manganous form (Mg^{2+}), with soil availability increased in acidic soils. The soil test threshold level for available (Mehlich 3 extraction) manganese is 5 ppm (10 lb/ac, 11.2 kg/ha). Seedling deficiencies can be treated by a foliar application of manganese sulfate ($MnSO_4[H_2O]$) at 20 lb/ac (22.4 kg/ha) in late June or July (followed by an irrigation rinse 8 to 12 hours after application), or using a presowing incorporated soil application of 40 lb/ac (44.8 kg/ha). Plants tolerate a high level of manganese seemingly without any adverse effect and toxicity symptoms have not been reported for hardwood nurseries.

Zinc

Zinc (Zn^{2+}) is used by plants as a catalytic and structural component of enzymes and is taken up from soil as the Zn^{2+} divalent cation. Zinc deficiencies seem to be more common in large seeded hardwood species such as hickory (including pecan) and the oaks. A minimum threshold level for available soil zinc (Mehlich 3 extraction) is 1 ppm or 2 pounds per acre (2.24 kg per ha). Deficiency symptoms may be treated through a presowing incorporated soil application of 40 pounds per acre (44.8 kg per ha) of zinc sulfate ($ZnSO_4$) or a late June, early July foliar application of 20 pounds per acre (22.4 kg per ha) followed by an irrigation washing at eight to twelve hours after application. Toxicity problems have not been reported for hardwood nurseries.

Copper

Copper is essential to several enzymatic reactions and lignification, and is taken up from the soil as the cupric form (Cu^{2+}). Seedling copper deficiencies show up as "droopy" foliage and weak branch formation. The soil test threshold level (Mehlich 3 extraction) for available soil copper is 0.8 ppm or 1.6 lb/ac (1.8 kg/ha). Deficiencies may be treated using a foliar application of 12 lb/ac (13.4 kg/ha) of copper sulfate ($CuSO_4$)—also known as blue vitriol—in late June or early July (followed by a foliar rinse at 8 to 12 hours after application), or a presowing soil incorporation of 15 lb/ac (16.8 kg/ha) of copper sulfate.

Molybdenum

Molybdenum (Mo) is necessary for enzymatic functionality, particularly for nitrogen fixation and is considered essential for plant growth. A deficiency of molybdenum in forest tree nurseries of the Eastern United States has not yet been reported.

Chlorine

Along with boron and molybdenum, chlorine (Cl^-) is one of the three micronutrients that is an anion. While considered essential to plant growth, its metabolic function is not clearly understood. A deficiency in nursery soils has not yet been reported.

Soil Acidity

Soil acidity, which is measured in units of pH, profoundly affects the availability of all plant nutrients. First, acidity has strong influence on the movement of nutritional elements from the surface of soil particles into the surrounding soil solution. Since nutrients must be in the soil solution to move to the plant root where it might be taken up, the interchange between soil particle surfaces and the soil solution is fundamental to nutrient availability. Secondly, soil acidity greatly influences the oxidation/reduction state of individual elements, not only through the direct chemical reaction caused by available H^+, but also through the activity of microbes that may be positively or negatively impacted by soil acidity. These reactions determine if the nutrient exists in the soil solution in a form the plant can use. The understanding and management of soil acidity is fundamental to proper plant nutrition.

The hardwood species produced in nurseries of the Eastern United States are native to a wide range of soil conditions (Burns and Honkala 1990), but for the most part evolved over time on moderately acidic soils. It is a challenge, however, to specify an ideal pH value for hardwood nursery culture. Not only must hardwood nursery managers work with a large number of species and genera native to a variety of soil types with a wide range of characteristics, but those species also may vary in their sensitivity to pH. Londo et al. (2006), for example, indicated that black cherry (*Prunus serotina* Ehrh.) will grow best on a site with a soil pH between 3.0 to 5.0, while dogwood (*Cornus florida* L.) prefers a rage of 5.0 to 8.0, with sweetgum (*Liquidambar styraciflua* L.) doing well on a pH range of 3.6 to 7.5. Soil pH ranges applicable to silvicultural decisions, however, may or may not be applicable to the more artificial and intensely managed conditions of the hardwood nursery, but until better and more complete research and field trials show the way, managers must do their best with the experiences they have shared. A good target for hardwood nursery management, therefore, would be a pH range of somewhere between 5.0 and 6.0. This range generally matches the moderately acidic conditions favored by most hardwoods in their native habitat and provides optimal nutrient availability, including N and the cations K, Ca, and Mg, which hardwoods require in large amounts compared to pine. While some nutrients may become more available in more acid soils, and other nutrients may become more available under more alkaline conditions, the availability of both macro- and micronutrients is maximized around pH 5.5. Soils with pH values below 5 and above 6 are candidates for corrective soil amendments.

Measures To Raise Soil pH

With pH values below 5, adding lime can raise soil pH values nearer to the target range (i.e., decrease soil acidity). This can be done by adding either dolomitic or calcitic lime. The choice of compound depends on the ratio of available calcium to magnesium. Dolomitic lime contains magnesium, while calcitic lime does not. A desirable calcium to magnesium ratio is around 4 to 1, and if the current soil test indicates this to be the case, then a lime application to adjust soil acidity should use dolomitic lime, as it would tend to maintain this desirable ratio. If, on the other hand, the ratio is considerably lower, say around 1 or 2 parts calcium to 1 part magnesium, then calcite should be used to adjust soil acidity. In many locations, calcitic lime is also the cheaper alternative. However, the ratio of calcium to magnesium should be considered when weighing the two options.

Application rate depends on the buffering capacity of the soil, which is mostly controlled by texture. The typical application rate for lime for sandy soils is 1,000 lb/ac (1,120 kg/ha). The lime is applied in the spring, during soil tillage and before bed formation. It must be incorporated to a depth of 4 to 6 in in order to activate the lime, which is a simple chemical interaction with soil particles and is not mediated by microbial activity. In the case of finer textured (10-percent clay) or high organic matter soils (4 percent), the rate may be raised to 1,500 or 2,000 lb/ac (1,680 or 2,240 kg/ha). Nursery managers should take a conservative approach in their acidity correction measures. It is better to apply a small amount twice than to over-correct in a single application.

Measures To Lower Soil pH

If soil pH values are above 6, then the addition of elemental sulfur can bring pH values down closer to the targeted range (increase soil acidity). Typical application rates for sandy nursery soils range between 400 to 800 lb/ac (448 to 896 kg/ha) of elemental sulfur applied during soil tillage and several weeks, if not months, before bed formation in the spring. Elemental S needs to be incorporated to a depth of 4 to 6 in. Generally, 2,000 lb/ac (2,240 kg/ha) of lime has approximately the same degree of change on soil pH as does 800 lb/ac (896 kg/ha) of elemental sulfur. As in the case of lime application, soil buffering capacity has a strong effect on application rates. Organic matter content is particularly important because the reaction producing the acidifying affect is mediated by soil microbes.

$S \rightarrow$ microbial activity $\rightarrow H_2SO_4 \rightarrow$ microbial activity $\rightarrow \mathbf{2H^+}$ plus SO_4

Environmental conditions that increase microbial activity will hasten this process. On the other hand, environmental conditions that decrease microbial activity (such as dry weather) will slow the process.

Soil Sampling

Proper management depends on obtaining an accurate assessment of soil fertility conditions. Reliable analytic laboratories can generally provide an accurate and replicable soil analysis report. However, the accuracy of their results is only as valid as the samples they analyze. If the soil sampling technique does not accurately reflect soil conditions in the nursery, then any nutrition management prescription based on those samples will most likely be erroneous, a waste of time and resources, and possibly damaging to the crop. A suitable soil sampling procedure is essential to proper nursery fertility management.

There is no hard and fast rule dictating a specific number of soil samples per unit of area. Sampling intensity depends on the variability of the units to be sampled; the objective is to provide enough detail in the soil fertility report to achieve crop production goals across the area of production. Differences in soil texture and cropping history should be reflected in the sampling protocols. Cover crop areas should also be sampled if time and resources allow. Then any needed corrective action (sulfur or lime) can be taken before the field returns to seedling production. Once the sample units have been determined, take 30 to 50 subsamples in a representable pattern across each unit using a standard 1-in soil probe

The Interpretation of Soil Tests

David B. South

Once soil test reports arrive, the next step is interpreting the numbers. By themselves, numbers have no meaning, so an interpreter can help to develop an operational fertilizer regime. This individual should have knowledge of soil testing procedures, an understanding of how hardwoods respond to various soil conditions and which fertilizers are available from the dealer at reasonable prices. Professionals with different backgrounds, training and experience will interpret soil and foliage test results differently, and nursery managers should expect different recommendations when identical reports are sent to various interpreters. Soil agronomists rely on scientific studies to make fertilizer prescriptions for various agronomic crops and this helps explain why yields from genetically improved row-crops are typically high. However, an experienced hardwood nursery manager once said that although soil testing laboratories make good cover-crop recommendations, they do not know the best rates for hardwood seedlings. Unfortunately, useful fertilizer trials for hardwood nurseries are rare in the eastern United States.

Hardwood nursery manuals may provide estimates of desired foliar nutrient values for growing hardwood seedlings, but most do not provide information on when managers should apply fertilizers to nursery soils. In the absence of fertilizer rate trials, experience and intuition are used to set "trigger values" for hardwood seedbeds. If the soil test is below the "trigger value" for a certain nutrient, then a fertilizer is recommended. Typically, the "trigger value" is at the low end of what is considered an adequate nutrient range for growing hardwoods. Some call this minimum value a "target value" while others may set a higher level for the desired fertility level (e.g. trigger = 75 ppm K; target = 100 ppm K). There are many factors to consider when determining if the "trigger value" has been met and how much fertilizer should be applied to achieve the target soil fertility level. Some professionals take soil texture into account when setting a "trigger value" while others use the same values for all soil textures and all hardwood species. The buffering capacity of a particular soil can strongly influence the amount of sulfur or lime necessary to reach the target soil acidity level.

The laboratory test methodology used to determine soil nutrient levels must be taken into account when interpreting soil test results. Different laboratories may use different chemical extractants when conducting their tests. A good soil test interpreter must take into account the methodologies used to produce the values on the soil test result. Likewise, when reviewing a foliar nutrient test, the timing of the test is an important consideration. Was the foliage sampled in July to make a growing season correction because leaves appeared purple or yellow? If so, then the interpretation of the results may be very different than for an analysis made in the fall, just before leaves are about to drop from the seedling. Also, the interpreter should be able to identify obvious typographical errors that occasionally occur in results.

The interpreter should consider the individual history of the nursery fertilization program and previous soil amendments that have been applied. Row-crop fertilization recommendations are made based on research specific to individual soil series. No such specific soil series information exists for hardwood seedling culture. Site familiarity, soil tests and nursery records are often the best information available.

Familiarity with operational hardwood seedling production can be an important component of soil test interpretation and fertilizer program development. For example, when growing certain endomycorrhizal species on fumigated soil, a nursery manager may apply monoammonium phosphate to young seedlings even when the soil contains more than 60 ppm of extractable phosphorus. This "insurance" application allows non-mycorrhizal seedlings access to readily available phosphorus and sometimes produces a more uniform crop (especially after newer, more effective soil fumigation has been accomplished).

In summary, there are many considerations to making appropriate soil and foliage test interpretations, and many times it is more of an "art" than "science." While test results are presented as a series of numbers, the exact meaning of those numbers and the management actions they may initiate, are subject to a great deal of interpretation.

to a depth of 4 to 6 in. The sampling often takes the form of a crisscross or "W"-shaped pattern across the unit (May 1984). Place the subsamples in a plastic (NOT galvanized or metal) bucket and mix thoroughly. If field conditions are suitably dry, place a sample of the thoroughly mixed soil directly into the laboratory-provided sample boxes for shipment. Label each box with enough detail so that same specific area could be located for a second sample if needed. If soil conditions are wet, place the samples in well-labeled open plastic bags and spread them out in the packing shed or other building to air dry. When dry, place them in the boxes for shipping to the laboratory.

Carefully selecting the areas to be sampled can help avoid sampling problems. For example, do not take a subsample from the end of a riser line area where agricultural lime was stored the previous year because this material could strongly bias the sample and result in an erroneous recommendation for the entire management unit. The objective is to obtain soil analysis values that are representative of the entire sample unit.

Finally, the importance of careful recordkeeping cannot be overemphasized. As May (1984) suggests: "Nursery managers should have a map showing the location of samples, crops, and fertilizers since the last analysis and any other relevant information such as deficiencies observed, quality of last crop and unusual summer rainfall."

Diagnosis of Nutrition Problems

Under ideal conditions, a nursery fertility program is based on representative soil sampling, accurate analysis, well-conceived fertility recommendations, and proper application procedures. Invariably, however, the unexpected happens and problems occur. Hardwood seedlings may show signs of inadequate nutrition anytime between 4 weeks after sowing up to leaf fall. Nursery managers should be inspecting their crop at least weekly for signs of anything negatively affecting proper seedling morphological developments, such as inadequate coloration, leaf shape, and stem development. A proper and timely diagnosis of the problem is essential to corrective action. Insect damage is usually easy to spot and diagnose, either by seeing the insect, signs of feeding on leaves or stems, or the presence of frass. Disease is typically found as irregular patches in seedling production areas, as opposed to a general impact caused by a fertility issue. And drought effects, while possibly difficult to see in conifers, causes wilting in hardwoods and the observant nursery manager can quickly alleviate the problem. But, not all growth problems can be quickly diagnosed or resolved.

The possibility of herbicide toxicity must be considered when morphological abnormalities appear in hardwood seedling crops. Herbicide damage can cause discoloration, leaf and stem deformation, and stunted growth. These same characteristics can be caused by nutrient deficiencies and, without check plots (areas not sprayed with the herbicide), it can be challenging to tell them apart. The manager could consider several factors when assessing the possibility of herbicide damage. First, does the area of damage match that of a recent herbicide application or, if not, does the damage occur in a manner that might indicate the influence of wind-associated drift or water-associated flooding that could have brought herbicide into the area? Second, does the timing of the injury match an earlier preemergent or postemergent herbicide application? For example, if the damage shows up in late July, but the last herbicide application was a preemergent application before sowing, then herbicide damage is unlikely. Third, do the physical symptoms match possible herbicide effects? Individual herbicides and classes of herbicides affect plants in different ways. Associating plant symptoms with the mode of action of a class of chemicals or a specific compound can be instrumental in diagnosis. Finally, does the intensity of the damage seem to vary by soil characteristics? Damage from postemergent herbicides like glyphosate, for example, are typically found across an entire application area and not related to changes in soil moisture, fertility, or organic matter content. In summary, diagnosing herbicide damage can be a complex matching of plant symptoms, application timing, product, site characteristics, crop species, application method, and other factors. The services of an expert may be required.

Table 6.3*—Midsummer foliar nutrient levels in hardwood seedlings.*

Element	Unit	Low	Medium	High
N	%	1.0	2.0	3.0
P	%	0.12	0.2	0.3
K	%	0.6	1.2	2.4
Ca	%	0.3	0.5	0.8
Mg	%	0.1	0.15	0.3
S	%	0.06	0.1	0.2
Na	%	0.01	<0.05	0.15
Al	ppm	200	<400	2,000
Fe	ppm	100	400	2,000
Mn	ppm	100	300	1,000
Zn	ppm	30	60	100
B	ppm	15	25	60
Cu	ppm	2	8	15

ppm = parts per million.

Once it is apparent that the crop is showing signs of nutrient deficiency, a tissue analysis will help achieve proper diagnosis. Previous soil analyses may be used or current soil samples may help in diagnosis, but at this point a tissue sample will more accurately indicate which nutrient is deficient. The sample should be WHOLE leaves taken from individual seedlings in the affected area, about 2 ounces (56 grams) of green sample per tree. The number of leaves will vary depending upon size.

Select leaf samples from affected parts of the seedling. The location of the leaf sample is important, as some elements are not mobile in the plant: Iron is a good example, where older leaves may contain low but adequate levels of iron, while new leaves may be deficient. A general leaf sample from all parts of the individual seedling may indicate adequate average iron levels, leading to an inaccurate diagnosis. If, on the other hand, the entire seedling seems to be affected, then leaf samples should be taken using "typical" leaves.

Table 6.3 provides general guidelines for hardwood leaf nutrient contents. While providing estimated values for low, medium, and high nutrient levels, these values should be used in conjunction with previous or current soil tests and seedling morphological development to make an assessment of seedling nutrition. Good photographs of nutrient deficiency symptoms in nursery-grown hardwood seedlings are generally not available. Erdmann et al. (1979) and Hacskaylo et al. (1969) have photographs derived from nutrient omission studies with seedlings of a variety of hardwood species.

References

Brady, N.C.; Weil, R.R. 2000. Elements of the nature and properties of soils. Upper Saddle River, NJ: Prentice-Hall Inc.

Burns, R.M.; Honkala, B.H., tech. coords. 1990. Silvics of North America: 2. Hardwoods. Agric. Handb. 654. Washington, DC: U.S. Department of Agriculture, Forest Service. 877 p.

Cole, D.W.; Rapp, M. 1981. Elemental cycling in forest ecosystems. In: Reichle, D.E., ed. Dynamic properties of forest ecosystems. New York: Cambridge University Press: 341–375.

Darusman, L.R.; Stone, D.A.; Whitney, D.A. [et al.]. 1991. Soil properties after twenty years of fertilization with different nitrogen sources. Soil Science Society of America Journal. 55: 1097–1100.

Davey, C.B. 1994. Soil fertility and management for culturing hardwood seedlings. In: Landis, T.D.; Dumroese, R.K., tech. coords. Proceedings, Forest and Conservation Nursery Associations. Gen. Tech. Rep. RM-GTR-257. Fort Collins, CO: U.S. Department of Agriculture, Forest Service, Rocky Mountain Forest and Range Experiment Station: 38–49.

Davey, C.B. 2005. Hardwood seedling nutrition. In: Dumroese, R.K.; Riley, L.E.; Landis, T.D., tech. coords. National proceedings, Forest and Conservation Nursery Associations. RMRS-P-35. Fort Collins, CO: U.S. Department of Agriculture, Forest Service, Rocky Mountain Research Station.

dos Santos, H.Z. 2006. Morphological and nutritional development of three species of nursery-grown hardwood seedlings in Tennessee. Auburn, AL: School of Forestry & Wildlife Sciences, Auburn University. M.S. thesis,

Deines, J. 1973. The effect of fertilization on the growth and development of 1-0 sycamore (*Platanus occidentalis* L.), sweetgum (*Liquidambar styraciflua* L.), and green ash (*Fraxinus pennsylvanica* Marsh.) seedlings. Raleigh, NC: North Carolina State University. 80 p. M.S. thesis.

Erdmann, G.G.; Metzger, F.T.; Oberg, R.R. 1979. Macronutrient deficiency symptoms in seedlings of four northern hardwoods. Gen. Tech. Rep. NC-53. U.S. Department of Agriculture, Forest Service, North Central Forest Experiment Station. 36 p. https://www.nrs.fs.fed.us/pubs/gtr/gtr_nc53.pdf

Goldy. R. 2013. Knowing nutrient mobility is helpful in diagnosing plant nutrient deficiencies. College of Agriculture and Natural Resources. Michigan State University Extension.

Hacskaylo, J.; Finn, R.F.; Vimmerstedt, J.P. 1969. Deficiency symptoms of some forest trees. Research Bulletin 1015. Wooster, OH: Ohio Agricultural Research and Development Center.

Kopittke, P.M.; Menzies, N. W. 2007. A review of the use of the basic cation saturation ratio and the "ideal" soil. Soil Science Society of America Journal. 71: 259-265.

Londo, A.J.; Kushla, J.D.; Carter, R.C. 2006. Soil pH and tree species suitability in the South. Southern Regional Extension Forestry SREF-FM-002.

Magdoff. F.; Van Es, H. 2009. Building soils for better crops: sustainable soil management. Handbook Series Book 10. Washington, DC: U.S. Department of Agriculture, National Institute of Food and Agriculture, Sustainable Agriculture Research & Education Program.

May, J.T. 1984. Nutrients and fertilization. In: Lantz, C. The southern pine nursery handbook. Atlanta, GA: U.S. Department of Agriculture, Forest Service Southern Region: 1–38.

Reich, P.B.; Oleksyn, J.; Modrzynshi, J. [et al]. 2005. Linking litter calcium, earthworms and soil properties: a common garden test with 14 tree species. Ecology Letters 8: 811–181.

Schulte, E.E.; Kelling, K.A. 1985. Soil calcium to magnesium ratios–should you be concerned? University of Wisconsin Extension Bulletin G2986.

South, D.B. 1975. The determination of nursery practices for the production of quality sweetgum (*Liquidambar styraciflua* L.) and sycamore (*Platanus occidentalis* L.) planting stock. Raleigh, NC: North Carolina State University. M.S,. thesis.

Stone, J.M. 1980. Hardwood seedling production: what are the fertility requirements? In: Proceedings of The North American Forest Tree Nursery Soils Workshop. U.S. Department of Agriculture, Forest Service, and Canadian Forestry Service.

Tisdale, S.L.; Werner, W.L.; Beaton, J.D.; Havlin, J.L. 1993. Soil fertility and fertilizers. Upper Saddle River, NJ: Prentice-Hall Inc.

Villarubia, J.M. 1980. Effect of nitrogen rate and source on growth and performance of *Liquidambar styraciflua* (sweetgum) and *Fraxinus pennsylvanica* (green ash) seedlings in a Virginia nursery. Raleigh, NC: North Carolina State University. 91 p. Ph.D. dissertation.

Weatherly, C. 2018. ArborGen Inc. Bluff City, AR. personal communication.

ELDERBERRY

Hardwood Seedling Growth and Development and the Impact of Pruning and Environmental Stresses

7

T. Starkey
Tom Starkey is retired from Southern Forest Nursery Management Cooperative, Auburn University, Auburn, AL

Outline

Facing Page: *Beautiful elderberry seedlings during irrigation. (Photo by Greg Hoss.)*

Introduction

The environment and genetics control the growth and development of all hardwood and conifer seedlings. While a nursery manager has no ability to manipulate the genetics of the seedling once a seedlot is chosen, a manager can manipulate the phenotypic expression of seedling genetics by utilizing different cultural management tools. These tools can modify the seedling environment to a limited extent and influence seedling development to achieve a specific seedling morphology and/or physiology. When applied at the correct time and in the correct manner, cultural activities such as irrigation, fertilization, weed control, and pest control have significant effect upon seedling growth and development. This chapter discusses the typical seedling growth and development pattern, the "target seedling" concept, the effect of pruning on seedling development, and the potential effects of abiotic stresses.

Seedling Growth Phases

The Growth Curve

When seedling growth is measured and plotted over a nursery season, the growth line will typically take the form of an "S-shape" curve (fig. 7.1). Any number of morphological parameters follow this pattern: height, root-collar diameter, root weight, shoot weight, and probably any other morphological growth parameter. Each parameter may not follow the same time reference, but they will typically follow the S-shape development pattern. For example, root growth and shoot growth are not always synchronized, with one happening faster than the other for brief periods of time.

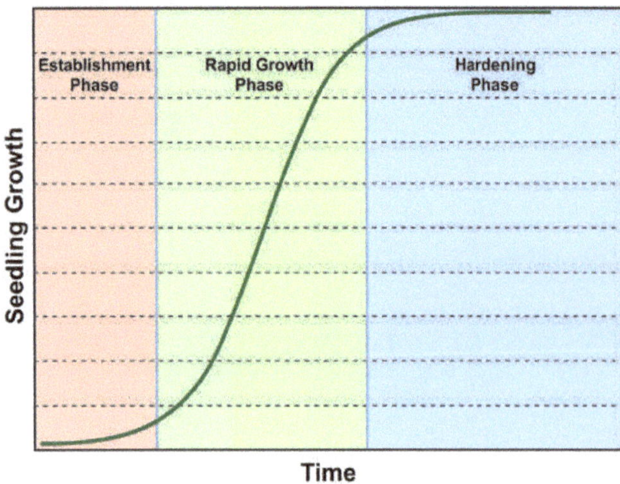

Figure 7.1—*Three phases of seedling growth on an S-shaped growth curve.*

Three different phases of growth can be used to describe the S-shaped curve; the establishment phase, the rapid growth phase and the hardening phase (Landis et al. 1998). The duration of each phase may vary, depending upon such factors as species, sowing date, environmental conditions, amount of fertilization, and other cultural practices. Although the characteristic shape of the growth curve is generally accepted, this exact shape is rarely seen in reality. Nevertheless, the three growth phases are always present, although the duration of the phases and the shape of the curve may vary. The nursery manager needs to understand these phases and their duration, because the timing and impact of cultural activities will vary within each growth phase.

Establishment Phase

This phase begins with the sowing of the seed and ends with the development of the first true leaves. In hardwoods, the establishment phase may last 6 to 12 weeks (Jacobs and Wilkinson 2009), depending on time of sowing and species. This phase is critically important since it establishes the seedling in the nursery bed or container. Failure to establish the seedling results in an empty space in the nursery bed or an empty cavity in a container, allowing weeds to grow. Temperature and moisture are important during this phase in order to facilitate germination and prevent disease (Landis et al. 1998). It may appear from monitoring top growth that little is happening during this growth phase. In reality, rapid root growth is occurring in both hardwood and conifers.

Rapid Growth Phase

Both stem and leaf biomass begin to increase rapidly during this phase and become the bulk of total seedling biomass. The rapid growth phase begins with the appearance of true leaves and continues at an accelerated or exponential rate of growth and ends in the fall as growth begins to slow due to the cooler weather and/or cultural practices of the nursery manager to reduce fertilization and/or irrigation. This is the period when seedlings add significant biomass and require adequate supplies of nutrients and water for proper development. Stress during this phase may stop or slow the growth of the seedling, resulting in reduced growth or, in some cases, cessation of all top growth. It is important that during this growth phase the seedlings be protected from stresses such as high temperatures, drought, or nutrient limitations. Typically, the duration of the rapid growth phase is greater than the other two and extends through the late spring and summer months in the Southern Region.

Hardening Phase

In the hardening phase, seedling growth begins to slow down naturally during the late summer and early fall with the advent of cooler temperatures and shorter days. Deciduous seedlings will lose their leaves in late fall/early winter. However, in late August and September and while seedlings are still photosynthesizing, a nursery manager must make the determination if the seedlings have reached their target size. If the target size has been achieved, a nursery manager may begin to reduce fertilization and adjust irrigation cycles to promote less frequent but deeper irrigation (see chapter 11c). This prevents the seedling from exceeding the target size and physiologically stresses the seedling to reduce transplant shock and better prepare it for outplanting (Jacobs 2011). Although top growth may be shutting down, this is a period of continued root and diameter growth albeit at a reducing rate until the leaves of the hardwoods die or fall off. On the other hand, if a species has not reached target size by late August/September, a nursery manager will need to "push" that species with additional fertilization into the fall.

The hardening phase, whether it occurs before or at the same time as natural leaf fall, gradually conditions the seedling for optimum performance after outplanting. During the rapid growth phase, the seedling shoot can be very fleshy and succulent. Any cultural manipulations to achieve hardening should be a gradual preparation of seedling physical and physiological characteristics for outplanting. This is particularly important if individual seedlots must be "pushed" to achieve target size before leaf fall. The reductions in photoperiod and lower fall temperatures, along with cultural activities such as reducing irrigation to induce moisture stress and changing the fertilization rates, will properly harden seedlings when done over a period of time (Landis et al. 1998, Jacobs and Wilkinson 2009, Jacobs and Landis 2009, Jacobs 2003).

Utilizing Growth Curves in Nurseries

The use of growth curves and data collected from history plots (chapter 10) allows the nursery manager to determine if the current seedling crop development is ahead or behind that of previous years. Any given parameter of seedling growth is plotted on the Y-axis, while time is plotted on the X-axis of a graph. Although any number of seedling growth parameters can be followed over time, the more commonly applied parameters are seedling height, in either inches or centimeters, and root-collar diameter, expressed most commonly in millimeters. Time units on the X-axis may be either the number of days from sowing or actual calendar date.

The data collected from history plots over several growing seasons can be used to generate a target growth curve. Growth curves will vary from year to year, according to changes in the natural environment and the influence of cultural practices. A theoretical growth curve can be generated by averaging the data over multiple years for any one species. When seedling measurements are made at any point during the growing season, they should be compared to growth curves generated using data from previous years to determine if the current seedling growth is on target. Based on the results, fertility and/or irrigation practices can then be altered to bring the growth in line with targeted levels.

The "Target" Hardwood Seedling

The Target Seedling Concept

The concept of a target seedling has been defined as "targeting specific physiological and morphological characteristics that can be linked with reforestation success" (Rose and Haase 1995). The concept of a target seedling began in the late 1970s and early 1980s and became more popular following a symposium on the subject in 1990 (Rose et al. 1990, Rose and Haase 1995, Landis 2003). At that time, nursery managers and researchers grew more interested in seedling quality and acknowledged that a quality seedling is made up of both morphological and physiological characteristics. In addition, and perhaps more importantly, the evolution of the target seedling concept recognized the need for communication between nursery managers and regeneration foresters regarding the ideal seedling qualities needed to maximize seedling survival and development on planting sites (Rose and Haase 1995). Even so, it may not be feasible to implement cultural practices specific to a single species to achieve the morphological seedling characteristics requested by individual customers, unless the request is for a particularly large order.

Matching seedling quality to specific site conditions is not common with reforestation seedlings in the Southern Region. In the central hardwood region, however, providing seedlings to match site conditions has been done (Jacobs 2011). Research has shown that improving root morphology for outplanting on droughty sites can increase survival (Jacobs et al. 2005, Jacobs et al. 2009). Nutrient-loaded seedlings and the use of container hardwood stock have proven to be successful on mine reclamation sites (Davis and Jacobs 2004, Birge et al. 2006, Salifu 2009). Providing tall container-grown hardwoods to reduce deer browse has prompted interest in the central region (Morrissey et al. 2010). This last technique may have application in the Southern Region, where a nursery manger can withhold top clipping on a portion of the seedlings to provide taller, more competitive seedlings.

Morphological Targets for Hardwood Seedlings

The most frequently measured morphological traits for hardwood seedlings include height, root mass, and root-collar diameter (caliper) (Jacobs and Wilkinson 2009). Other less-common traits that have been considered include leaf weight, number of branches, and bud size or appearance, which are more frequently employed by researchers than by growers (Rose and Haase 1995). Target seedling traits utilized today are, for the most part, determined by either State or Federal organizations.

Many States and/or regional organizations have established hardwood seedling specifications for their geographic area. These specifications are generally set by either a State organization, such as the forestry commission, or by a Federal Government entity, such as the U.S. Army Corp of Engineers. For example, the following are the 2017 specifications for "large stock plantings" of the Corp of Engineers Rock Island District of Mississippi.

- 5/8 inch (in) (9.5 millimeters [mm]) caliper at 6 in (15 centimeters [cm]) above the ground.
- A minimum of 4 feet (ft) (1.2 meters [m]) tall.
- Local ecotype seed should be used from the progeny where the trees are going to be planted.

In this case, "large stock plantings" are container hardwood seedlings produced in 1- or 3-gallon (gal) (3.7 liter [L] or 11.3 L) pots or unpruned bareroot seedlings, both of which may surpass 4 ft. Taller seedlings are often desired when planting in areas of heavy deer browse or bottom lands prone to flooding. By requiring a "local ecotype seed," the guidelines specify that the seed source (i.e., genetics) used for seedling production must match the environmental conditions of the planting site.

However, specifications for hardwood planting stock can vary by organization as well as by State and region. The following are hardwood planting stock criteria established by USDA's Natural Resources Conservation Service for the State of Arkansas (2013).

- A minimum root collar diameter of 1/4 in (6 mm) above the swell is required for all oak species and desired for all other hardwood species. Nonoak species may be smaller so long as all other specifications are met.
- A minimum tap root length of 6 in (15 cm) below the root collar.
- The ratio of the length of the shoot to the length of the tap root should be from 1.5 to 2.5, unless top pruned at the seedling nursery. Seedlings top pruned at the seedling nursery are acceptable. No top pruning should be done at the planting site. Tops should be proportional to the tap root length; e.g., 9 to 15 in (23 to 38 cm) above the root collar for a 6 in (15 cm) root.
- Healthy first-order laterals and fibrous roots must be present.
- Roots must be moist, not moldy, with NO over-abundance of lenticels, and not discolored (inside or out). The outside of the roots should not be black, the cambium cannot be discolored, and the internal part should be white or creamy in color.

The Alabama Forest Commission (2011) provides the following hardwood specification guidelines: "Seedlings are perishable; keep seedling roots moist at all times. Plant only dormant seedlings and plant promptly after being received. Discard seedlings that are obviously small, diseased, dried out or damaged. Acceptable hardwood seedlings for planting should be a minimum of 18 in (46 cm) tall and 3/8 in (9.5 mm) in root collar diameter."

Other planting guidelines, such as no root pruning of seedlings after they leave the nursery, vary from State to State. Although reforestation foresters are beginning to realize that allowing onsite root pruning by tree planters may reduce survival and initial establishment, some States are reluctant to take a firm stand on root pruning or remove outdated online information allowing root pruning. The specifications in these examples indicate that height and root collar diameter are the most common morphological parameters utilized. Root collar diameter (RCD) is considered the single best indicator of seedling quality, since it is correlated with other morphological parameters such as height, seedling dry weight, root biomass, and field performance (Mexal and Landis 1990, Rose and Haase 1995). Hardwood seedlings with larger root collars, regardless of height, perform better on outplanting (Webb 1966, Jacobs 2011, McNabb and VanderSchaaf 2005).

Height, by itself, is a poor indicator of seedling quality. However, when combined with other morphological parameters, the usefulness of height improves. For example, the height/diameter (mm/mm) ratio can provide a relative indication of how spindly a seedling may be. For example, comparing a seedling with an RCD of 10 mm (0.4

in) and a height of 500 mm (20 in) to one with an RCD of 10 mm (0.4 mm) and a height of 300 mm (12 in) would have a height/diameter ratio of 50 for the first and 30 for the second. The seedling with the height/diameter ratio of 50 would be spindlier than the seedling with the height/diameter ratio of 30. In areas where seedling height may be desired to get above brush competition, a tall seedling with a large root collar (and large root system) would be more desirable (Rose and Haase 1995) than a tall seedling with a smaller RCD and smaller root system.

Tap root length is another commonly mentioned morphological parameter in hardwood seedling specifications. This is an important parameter since many hardwoods can have rather extensive root systems which require careful tap root undercutting at the nursery prior to seedling lifting and shipment. Root volume/mass has been recognized as an important factor in seedling outplanting survival. Although root volume/mass is not generally measured by nurseries due to its difficulty, managers recognize the importance of a fibrous root system for survival. A 6 in (15 cm) tap root, although important to get the roots deep in the soil, says nothing about the root mass or fibrosity (Rose and Haase 1995). To calculate and express the root biomass in an easier way, the Southern Forest Nursery Management Cooperative uses the root/weight ratio, which is defined as the weight of the root system compared to the total seedling weight expressed as a percentage. For example, a root/weight ratio of 30 percent means that 30 percent of the total weight of the seedling is in the root system. The root/weight ratio is easier to calculate and understand compared to calculation based on volume. Although research has established root/weight ratio guidelines for conifers, acceptable ranges of root/weight ratios for hardwoods have yet to be defined.

Monitoring Seedling Nutrient Levels

Work remains on how to use the physiological characteristics to develop target seedling parameters for hardwoods. Even so, nursery managers should consider the development of specific nutrient levels. In conifers and species that retain their foliage, a poor nutrient level may appear in the seedling crop as chlorosis. However, with hardwoods, which typically change color in the fall and then lose their leaves in early winter, the presence of a nutrient problem in the crop will not be evident to a nursery manager or customer. Since good nutrition is vital to seedling establishment and rapid spring growth (Jacobs et al. 2004, Jacobs et al. 2005), nursery managers should consider collecting foliar analysis before color change and leaf fall. The data can be used as part of the history plot information to target nutrient levels for specific hardwoods and may help explain survival or establishment difficulties.

The idea of exponential nutrient loading—that is, gradually increasing seedling nutrition levels over the growing season, before outplanting, on mine reclamation and other nutrient-poor soils—has been done with conifers (Jacobs 2011). Some outplanting trials with hardwoods show the applicability of this concept on these special sites (Birge et al. 2006, Salifu and Jacobs 2006, Salifu et al. 2008, 2009a, 2009b).

Impact of Seedbed Density on Seedling Morphology

The density at which hardwood seedlings are grown affects all aspects of seedling morphology, more so than any other cultural decision a nursery manager may make. Seeding density has a direct and visible effect on stem caliper, as caliper generally decreases as density increases. Producing a large-caliper seedling is important because increasing seedling root biomass has been associated with increased field survival and growth for some species (Jacobs et al. 2005, Weigal and Johnson 1998). Growing each species at the proper bed density can directly increase the number of permanent roots. However, accurate seed testing data are often lacking, and the decision as to what density to sow hardwoods relies heavily on the nursery manager's experience with that species. This can make growing hardwoods a challenge. One nursery manager recently reported that, based upon poor seed bed densities of a particular species the previous year, he decided to increase the seed density the following year. He commented, "This was a bad mistake, since it appeared that every seed germinated." Seedling quality that season suffered due to excessive seedling density.

Although the relationship between density and caliper is consistent, the relationship of density with height is complex and variable (Mexal and Landis 1990). Hardwood seedlings are grown at lower densities than conifers because their branching structure and leaf size require more space. Although there is a general consensus that increasing density results in a decrease in hardwood caliper (Schultz and Thompson 1990), no consistent relationship between density and height can be found in the research literature.

The number and size of first-order laterals appear to be useful indicators of survival and early growth for hardwoods (Gould et al. 2009, Schultz and Thompson 1990, 1996). These researchers stated that a "competitive" northern red oak seedling should have at least five permanent first-order laterals. Other species require eight or more first-order laterals for good field survival (Schultz et al. 1990). Nursery practices that encourage root development, such as undercutting and root-wrenching, are important to developing a large fibrous root system (Weigal and Johnson 1998).

Growth Manipulation Through Pruning

Uses of Root and Top Pruning

The decision to adopt a nursery practice should ultimately be based on whether it increases survival and growth after outplanting. In a survey of southern nurseries, Vanderveer (2005) received a range of responses as to what cultural manipulations were used to grow hardwoods for the reforestation market. Responses indicated some nurseries always top pruned while others never top pruned. Some nurseries always laterally pruned, while others did not even own a lateral pruner. The survey indicated the decision to use cultural practices such as top pruning, undercutting, lateral pruning, and root wrenching was based most commonly on customer specifications. Hardwood seedlings are typically sold to either the horticultural or reforestation market. Those nurseries that grow seedlings for the horticultural market must produce a larger seedling with more rigid specifications than nurseries that provide seedlings for reforestation. Most of the hardwoods sold for reforestation are used for wetland mitigation or wildlife food plots and are grown in nurseries that also grow conifers for reforestation. The implementation of certain cultural practices to increase survival and growth after outplanting was not specifically reported in Vanderveer's 2005 survey.

It is this author's experience that most nurseries currently top prune, lateral prune, and undercut, while not all root wrench. A large part of the decision to adopt any of these options focuses on facilitating the lifting, packing, and shipping process. McNabb (2004) reported that root culturing of hardwoods in southern nurseries was primarily used to control shoot height. Top pruning allows nurseries to more easily handle and ship seedlings. Lateral pruning cuts the lateral roots between drills and facilitates lifting. Undercutting many times is done to meet customer specifications for a tap root length, but it also facilitates the lifting process. Just as these procedures aid in shipping, however, when done at the right time and for the right reasons, they can increase seedling outplanting performance. One nursery manager who regularly root wrenches does so on the belief that it provides a more fibrous root system, in addition to improving soil aeration. This same manager reports that root wrenching in combination with water management between July and September offers the greatest benefit.

Root Pruning

Root pruning primarily includes lateral root pruning, undercutting, and root wrenching (Landis 2008). Table 7.1 provides a comparison of these three common root pruning methods used in the Southern Region. The objectives of root pruning are to encourage the development of lateral roots, control taproot length to facilitate lifting, and provide a seedling that will have a competitive advantage when outplanted. Root manipulation is intended to produce first-order laterals greater than 1 mm, since those less than 1 mm are probably lost in lifting and planting (Schultz and Thompson 1990). Nurseries that use root pruning methods only to aid in lifting should consider their use at other times during the growing season as a method to increase root biomass, which ultimately can increase field survival.

Top Pruning

When surveying nurseries that top pruned hardwood seedlings, South (1996) found that 9 of 13 nursery managers did so on a regular basis. Three reasons were provided for the decision to top prune: (1) to reduce lifting, packing, and shipping costs, (2) to reduce stem dieback after planting, and (3) to increase outplanting survival. Being able to control the height of the seedling by top pruning produces a seedling better suited to the environmental conditions after outplanting in reforestation areas, wetland mitigation, and wildlife food plots. Sufficient research has proven that survival is often increased and shoot:root ratio improved when seedlings are top pruned (South 1996, South 2016). Tall seedlings are not only more difficult to lift and pack and cost more to ship, they also stand a greater chance of going through transplant shock because sufficient roots may not have been lifted to support the top growth.

Top pruning occurs primarily from June to September in the Southern Region where the growing season can be 6 to 7 months long. The frequency of top pruning depends upon how fast the species grows. There does not appear to be a consensus in the literature as to the number of prunings necessary, although twice is most commonly reported. One nursery manager first top prunes when seedlings are between 18 in (46 cm) and 20 in (51 cm) of height, with a second top clipping no later than August, when seedlings are 24 in (61 cm) to 26 in (66 cm). Top pruning is done more frequently with a sickle bar mower than a rotary bush-hog mower, as is used in conifer nurseries. Nursery managers using the sickle bar mower report a cleaner cut. Top pruning hardwoods in the fall after leaf fall does not appear to have any adverse effect on survival and may reduce handling costs, while allowing the root system to continue growing in the nursery (Briscoe 1969, South 1996).

The Management of Abiotic Stresses

Extremes in wind, temperature, and soil moisture are abiotic factors that can affect hardwood seedling growth. The diagnosis of abiotic damage relies on observing patterns of damage to the crop in the nursery or field, damage to individual seedlings, and weather records and cultural practices (Cram 2012). However, the occurrence of an abiotic stress may not always result in visible seedling symptoms, even when resulting in a reduction in seedling growth.

Drought Stress

Drought stress may or may not cause visible symptoms in the nursery, depending on the severity of the stress. Drought stress can occur in the summer when sufficient irrigation to maintain optimum growth is not provided. If the reduction in irrigation is minor and of short duration, seedlings may not suffer. If the irrigation reduction is sustained, however, at a minimum the growth rate will probably be reduced even if there are no visible seedling symptoms. A prolonged reduction in irrigation may result in symptoms where the top-most seedling leaves wilt, followed by tip burn on the edges, starting with the top-most leaves. Premature dropping of the leaves may occur in cases of more severe drought stress.

Heat Stress

Heat injury on southern hardwoods is not commonly reported. One of the primary reasons is that hardwoods are most often sown early in the spring, before high temperatures cause significant injury. If heat injury should occur, the injury would likely be similar to that occurring on conifers. The severity of the injury will depend upon the thickness of the bark at the ground line. Heat lesions generally occur on one side of the seedling stem at the ground line. The lesion may appear as a discoloration or an actual collapse of the stem tissue on one side. When the damage is a lesion resulting from collapsed tissue, it is common for the stem just above the lesion to swell slightly resulting from damage to the phloem tissue and the inability of carbohydrates to flow normally from the leaves to the roots.

Table 7.1*—Comparison of root pruning methods. (Modified from Landis, 2008)*

Term	Function	Cultural objectives	Implement	Timing
Undercutting	1. Cut roots in a horizontal plane. 2. Generally 15-18 cm.	1. Encourage root fibrosity. 2. Reduce shoot growth (make sure height target is achieved). 3. Control tap root growth. 4. Facilitate lifting.	1. Sharp, thin fixed blade or oscillating blade covering full bed width. 2. Frequent sharpening of the blade is important. 3. Tractor must be kept at a constant speed. 4. Keep blade absolutely horizontal.	One or two times during the growing season, or prior to lifting.
Wrenching	1. Induce moisture stress and loosen soil within root zone. 2. Tear or break fine feeder roots.	1. Reduce shoot growth 2. Improve soil physical properties: - Reduce compaction, - increase aeration, - improve drainage.	Sharp fixed blade at an angle (30°) covering full bed width.	Once to several times during the growing season, or prior to lifting.
Lateral root pruning	Cuts roots in vertical plane between rows of seedlings.	1. Encourage root fibrosity 2. Facilitate lifting.	Coulter blades spaced between seedling rows.	Once to several times during the growing season, or prior to lifting.

Freeze injury

Freeze injury occurs when seedlings have not been acclimated to cold temperatures. This can occur in hardwood nurseries when fall-sown seedlings begin to germinate and are subjected to freezing temperatures after germination (Cram 2012) or when spring-sown hardwoods are exposed to an early fall freeze before the seedlings are hardened off. Information regarding the freeze tolerance of hardwood seedlings is far from complete. It is known that conifer families differ in freeze tolerance. In the case of hardwoods, however, even the relative sensitivity to freeze damage among species is unknown. Also, even though freeze injury is not commonly reported on hardwoods, it should not be assumed hardwoods are more tolerant to freeze injury than pines. It may be just a lack of observation. Much of the research on freeze tolerance in hardwoods has been done in the northern region and relates specifically to seedling storage (Wilson and Jacobs 2006).

Reports of freeze injury to hardwoods is less common than to conifers (Lantz 1985, South 2006). The author has personally examined hundreds of reports of freeze injury on conifers in the Southern Region, but none on hardwood seedlings. There may be several reasons why freeze injury on hardwood seedlings is not frequently reported.

1. Nursery managers may believe that freeze-associated leaf damage is generally of little concern since the leaves are going to fall off anyway in late fall/early winter or will resprout.
2. Following an early winter freeze in the nursery, a nursery manager may incorrectly assume seedlings are not injured because at this time of year most hardwood leaves are already losing their color and vigor and are already falling. Attention may be focused on more visible damage to conifers.

Figure 7.3—*A healthy conifer seedling stem (top) compared to a freeze-damaged stem (bottom). (Photo Tom Starkey 2013.)*

Figure 7.2—*Freeze injury in the cambium area of conifer seedling. (Photo by Tom Starkey, 2012.)*

3. The thicker bark on some hardwoods may provide some protection from stem damage which is easier to observe than root damage.
4. Many times freeze injury is noted in conifers as burned needles or needle tips only after outplanting and warm weather begins. Postplanting foliar damage on hardwoods, however, may not be visible because they do not typically have leaves at outplanting. Freeze injury may, therefore, appear as a seedling that is just slow to break bud in the spring. The major impact of freeze injury for both conifers and hardwoods is damage to cambium tissue of the stem and roots, or both. Seedlings may even be killed in the nursery when freeze damage is severe. More commonly, however, freeze injury causes partial mortality of cambial tissue and results in poor outplanting survival and slow growth.

Assuming that identifying freeze injury in hardwoods is similar to that in pines, the identification of such injury is easily diagnosed following a freeze event in the nursery or the field. Temperatures in the mid- to low-20s °F have the greatest impact on conifers, and subfreezing temperatures that are preceded by a warm spell have the greatest impact on seedlings. To diagnose freeze injury, the nursery manager should wait about 2 weeks following a freeze event. Choose seedlings from the outside drills facing the predominant wind direction. On these seedlings scrape the bark off the stem or root to reveal a light brown to khaki-brown discoloration. Figures 7.2 and 7.3 show this discoloration in conifers. Sometimes this brown discoloration is only on one side of the stem or root. In this case, the seedling will live, but establishment will be slow until the seedling is able to outgrow the effect of the freeze. Similar stem discoloration has been reported for citrus (http://www.crec.ifas.ufl.edu/extension/trade_journals/2016/2016_December_freeze.pdf).

Seedling root systems never go dormant in the Southern Region, thus the root systems of conifers and probably hardwoods are more susceptible to freeze injury than the shoots. Applying irrigation (chapter 5) may help reduce freeze injury to the roots. Wet soils provide more insulation to the seedlings and conduct heat better than do dry soils. Moist, compact soils will store more heat during the day and thus be able to transfer heat to the seedling roots at night. (Poling 2007, Striegler 2007, Perry 1988, Powell and Himelrick 2000). When soils are dry, cold air can permeate the air spaces into the soils and reach temperatures below freezing. Many conifer nurseries leave irrigation pipes in the field during the winter to provide moisture if needed, particularly before a dry weather front. Ensuring that the seedbed is moist to wet prior to a dry front passing will provide some freeze protection for roots.

References

Alabama Forestry Commission 2011. Planting hardwood seedlings. PHS050511. 1 p. http://www.forestry.state.al.us/PDFs/ResourceSheets/Timber/Regeneration/Planting_Hardwood_Seedlings.pdf

Birge Z.K.D.; Salifu, K.F.; Jacobs, D.F. 2006. Modified exponential nitrogen loading to promote morphological quality and nutrient storage of bareroot-cultured *Quercus rubra* and *Quercus alba* seedlings. Scandinavian Journal of Forest Research. 21: 306–316.

Briscoe, C.B. 1969. Establishment and early care of sycamore plantations. Res. Pap. SO-50. New Orleans, LA: U.S. Department of Agriculture, Forest Service, Southern Forest Experiment Station. 21 p.

Cram, M.M. 2012. Environmental and mechanical damage. In: Cram, M.M.; Frank, M.S.; Mallams, K.M., tech. coords. Forest nursery pests. Agric. Handb. 680. Washington, DC: U.S. Department of Agriculture, Forest Service: 177–181.

Davis, A.S.; Jacobs, D.F. 2004. First-year survival and growth of northern red oak seedlings planted on former surface coal mines in Indiana. In: Barnhisel R.I., ed. Proceedings of American Society of Mining and Reclamation 21st Annual National Conference and 25th West Virginia Surface Mining Drainage Task Force symposium. American Society of Mining and Reclamation: 480–502.

Gould, P.J.; Harrington, C.A. 2009. Root morphology and growth of bare-root seedlings of Oregon white oak. Tree Planters' Notes. 53(2): 22–28.

Jacobs, D.F. 2003. Nursery production of hardwood seedlings. FNR-212. West Lafayette, IN: U.S. Department of Agriculture, Forest Service, North Central Research Station; and Department of Forestry and Natural Resources, Purdue University, 8 p.

Jacobs, D.F. 2011. Targeting hardwoods. In: Riley, L.E.: Haase, D.L.; Pinto, J.R., tech.coord. National Proceedings: Forest and Conservation Nursery Associations—2010. Proc. RMRS-P-65. Fort Collins, CO: U.S. Department of Agriculture, Forest Service, Rocky Mountain Research Station: 115–120.

Jacobs, D.F.; Landis, T.D. 2009. Hardening. In: Dumroese, R.K.; Luna, T.; Landis, T.D., eds. Nursery manual for native plants: a guide for tribal nurseries. Nursery management. Agric. Handb. 730. Washington, DC.: U.S. Department of Agriculture, Forest Service: 217–228.

Jacobs D.F.; Ross-Davis, A.L.; Davis A.S. 2004. Establishment success of conservation tree plantations in relation to silvicultural practices in Indiana, USA. New Forests. 28: 23–36.

Jacobs, D.F.; Salifu, K.F.; Davis, A.S. 2009. Drought susceptibility and recovery of transplanted *Quercus rubra* seedlings in relation to root system morphology. Annals of Forest Science. 66: 504.

Jacobs, D.F.; Salifu, K.F.; Seifert, J.R. 2005. Relative contribution of initial root and shoot morphology in predicting field performance of hardwood seedlings. New Forests. 30: 235–251.

Jacobs, D.F.; Wilkinson, K.M. 2009. Planning crops and developing propagation protocols. In: Dumroese, R.K.; Luna, T.; Landis, T.D., eds. Nursery manual for native plants: a guide for tribal nurseries. Nursery management. Agric. Handb. 730. Washington, DC: U.S. Department of Agriculture, Forest Service: 33-53.

Landis, T.D. 2003. The target seedling concept—a tool for better communication between nurseries and their customers. In: Riley L.E.; Dumroese R.K.; Landis T.D., tech coord. National Proceedings: Forest and Conservation Nursery Associations.

Landis T.D. 2008. Root culturing in bareroot nurseries. Forest Nursery Notes. 28(1): 9–15.

Landis, T.D.; Tinus, R.W.; McDonald, S.E.; Barnett, J.P. 1998. Seedling growth and development: the container tree nursery manual. Agric. Handb. 674. Washington, DC: U.S. Department of Agriculture, Forest Service. 167 p.

Lantz, C.W. 1985. Freeze damage to southern pine seedlings in the nursery. In: Lantz, C.W., tech. coord. 1984 southern nursery conferences proceedings. Atlanta, GA: U.S. Department of Agriculture, Forest Service, State and Private Forestry: 20–29.

Leach, G.N.; Gresham, H.H.; Webb, A.L. 1986. Seedling grade and nursery seedling density effects on field growth in loblolly pine. Gulf States Operation Res. Note GS-86-03. Champion International Corp. 12 p.

McNabb, K.L. 2001. Hardwood seeding production techniques in the Southern United States. In: Cicarese L., ed. Nursery Production and Stand Establishment of Broad-Leaves to Promote Sustainable Forest Management. IUFRO Group 3.02.00. Operational Methods in the Establishment and Treatment of Stands: 83–88.

McNabb, K.; Vanderschaaf, C. 2005. Growth of graded sweetgum 3 years after root and shoot pruning. New Forests. 29: 313–320.

Mexal, J.G.; Landis, T.D. 1990. Target seedling concepts: height and diameter. In: Rose, R.; Campbell, S.J.; Landis, T.D., eds. Target Seedling Symposium, Combined meeting of the Western Forest Nursery Associations. Gen. Tech. Rep. RM–200. Fort Collins, CO: U.S. Department of Agriculture, Forest Service, Rocky Mountain Forest and Range Experiment Station: 17–35.

Morrissey, R.C.; Jacobs, D.F.; Davis, A.S.; Rathfon, R.A. 2010. Survival and competitiveness of *Quercus rubra* regeneration associated with planting stocktype and harvest opening intensity. New Forests. 40: 273–287.

Perry, K. 1988. Basics of frost and freeze protection for horticultural crops. HortTechnology. 8(1): 10–1.

Poling, E.B. 2007. Overview of active frost, frost/freeze and freeze protection methods. In: Understanding and preventing freeze damage in vineyards workshop proceedings. Columbia, MO: University of Missouri, Columbia: 47–61.

Powell, A.A.; Himelrick, D.G. 2000. Methods of freeze protection for fruit crops. ANR-1057B. Alabama Cooperative Extension Service. 8 p.

Rose, R.; Carlson, W.C.; Morgan, P. 1990. The target seedling concept. In: Roseburg, O.R.; Rose, R.; Campbell, S.J.; Landis, T.D., eds. Proceedings, Combined meeting of the Western Forest Nursery Associations. Gen. Tech. Rep. RM-200. U.S. Department of Agriculture, Forest Service: 1–8 p.

Rose, R.; Haase, D.L. 1995. The target seedling concept: implementing a program. In: Landis, T.D.; Cregg, B., tech coords. National Proceedings of the Forest and Nursery Conservation Association. Gen. Tech. Rep. PNW-GTR-365. Portland, OR: U.S. Department of Agriculture, Forest Service, Pacific Northwest Research Station: 124–130.

Salifu, K.F.; Apostol, K.G.; Jacobs D.F.; Islam, M.A. 2008. Growth, physiology, and nutrient retranslocation in nitrogen-15 fertilized *Quercus rubra* seedlings. Annals of Forest Science. 65: 101.

Salifu K.F.; Islam, M.A.; Jacobs, D.F. 2009. Retranslocation, plant and soil recovery of nitrogen-15 applied to bareroot *Juglans nigra* seedlings. Communications in Soil Science and Plant Analysis. 40: 1408–1417.

Salifu, K.F.; Jacobs, D.F. 2006. Characterizing fertility targets and multi-element interactions for exponential nutrient loading of *Quercus rubra* seedlings. Annals of Forest Science. 63: 231–237.

Salifu, K.F.; Jacobs, D.F.; Birge, Z.K.D. 2009. Nursery nitrogen loading improves field performance of bareroot oak seedlings planted on abandoned mine land. Restoration Ecology. 17: 339–349.

Schultz, R.C.; Thompson, J.R. 1989. Hardwood seedling root development. Ames Forester. Ames, IA: Iowa State University Department of Forestry: 19–21.

Schultz, R.C.; Thompson, J. R. 1990. Nursery practices that improve hardwood seedling root morphology. Forestry Publications: 13.

Schultz, R.C.; Thompson, J.R. 1996. Effect of density control and undercutting on root morphology of 1+0 bare-root hardwood seedlings: five-year field performance of root-graded stock in the central USA. New Forests. 13(1–3): 297–310.

South, D.B. 1996. Top pruning bareroot hardwoods: a review of the literature. Tree Planters' Notes. 47(1): 34–40.

South, D.B. 2006. Freeze injury to southern pine seedlings. Gen. Tech. Rep. SRS-92. Asheville, NC: U.S. Department of Agriculture, Forest Service, Southern Research Station: 441–447.

South, D.B. 2016. Top-pruning of bareroot hardwood seedlings. Tree Planters' Notes. 59(2): 37–48.

Striegler, K.R. 2007. Passive freeze prevention methods. In: Understanding and preventing freeze damage in vineyards workshop proceedings. Columbia, MO: University of Missouri, Columbia: 39–46.

U.S. Army Corp of Engineers. 2017. Tree planting on the Upper Mississippi River. http://www.mvr.usace.army.mil/Missions/Recreation/Mississippi-River-Project/Natural-Resource-Management/Forestry-Management/Tree-Planting/.

U.S. Department of Agriculture (USDA), Natural Resources Conservation Service, Arkansas (NRCS). 2013. Tree establishment for Arkansas code 612. 9 p.

Vanderveer, H.L. 2005. Survey of root and shoot cultural practices for hardwood seedlings. In: Dumroese, R. K.; Riley, L.E.; Landis, T.D., tech. coords. National proceedings: Forest and Conservation Nursery Associations. Proc. RMRS-P-35. Fort Collins, CO: U.S. Department of Agriculture, Forest Service, Rocky Mountain Research Station: 21–23.

Webb, C.D. 1966. Seedling grades in hardwoods. Southeastern Area Forest Nurserymen Conference. https://rngr.net/publications/proceedings/1966/seedling-grade-in-hardwoods.

Weigel, D.; Johnson, P. 1998. Planting white oak in the Ozark highlands: A shelterwood prescription. Technical Brief No. 5. St. Paul, MN: U.S. Department of Agriculture, Forest Service, North Central Forest Experiment Station.

Wilson B.C.; Jacobs, D.F. 2006. Quality assessment of temperate zone deciduous hardwood seedlings. New Forests. 31: 417–433.

Chemical Weed Management in Northern Hardwood Nurseries

8a

J. Wichman and R. Garrett

Jim Wichman retired as nursery program manager, Indiana Division of Forestry

Richard Garrett is nursery manager, Maryland Department of Natural Resources

Outline

Facing Page: *Clean, healthy seedbed. (Photo by Jeanie Redicker.)*

Precautionary Note on Herbicide Use

The following information is a record of herbicides that have been found useful in the past. It is not a recipe for a particular use in a specific nursery. There are many herbicides and many different labels for those herbicides. The information provided herein is a place to start because pesticide labels may change over time. Before using any pesticide product, check with the appropriate State pesticide regulatory authorities to determine if that product is registered in that State, Tribe, or other jurisdiction for the intended application site. The cardinal rule for any pesticide use is to READ AND FOLLOW CAREFULLY ALL LABEL INSTRUCTIONS. The pesticide label is a legal document providing instructions on the proper use of the product, including application rate and labeled species. The label also provides much useful information on safe handling procedures, weeds controlled, and conditions that may adversely affect the activity of the herbicide on weeds or the crop. If the herbicide has a label for ornamental nurseries, it can be used in hardwood nurseries, provided other aspects of the label are followed.

The Timing and Use of Herbicides in Northern Hardwood Nurseries

Use of herbicides is most effective when combined with other cultural practices such as weed sanitation and soil fumigation. The timing of herbicide application depends on many factors. One of the most fundamental considerations is whether the herbicide compound has "preemergent" or "postemergent" herbicidal activity. Preemergent products are applied to the soil where they are taken up by germinating weeds and then slow or terminate essential plant biochemistry so weeds never emerge from the soil, or expire soon after emergence. These compounds remain active in the soil for a period of time depending on soil texture, soil organic matter, rate of application, as well as soil temperature and amount of precipitation. Preemergent herbicides may be used for weed control in hardwood seedling beds because tree seedlings are not seriously damaged due to several factors, such as a large seed size compared with weed seed, tree seed planted below the zone of herbicide activity, tolerance of some species even when exposed to the herbicide, and timing the application to after tree seedling germination is complete. In addition, tree seed is frequently planted in the fall. Typically, preemergent herbicides are applied in the spring, before hardwood seedling emergence, during seedling emergence, or 4 to 6 weeks after seedling emergence, depending on the herbicide. If a preemergent herbicide is applied after hardwood sowing in the fall, the herbicide probably would not effectively control weeds in the spring due to leaching or degradation. Also, fall application would inhibit the establishment of living mulch cover crops used in many nurseries.

A postemergent herbicide, on the other hand, is applied to the weed after it has emerged from the soil and is actively developing. These compounds are typically absorbed into the plant through the leaves. Some postemergent compounds can be sprayed over the top of growing hardwood seedlings. These are primarily herbicides that only control annual and perennial grasses. Other postemergent compounds should not be applied to emerged and growing hardwood seedlings, however, as they are broad-spectrum herbicides that kill both grasses and broadleaves. The nursery manager must be aware of these distinctions.

Preemergent Herbicides Used in Seedbeds

The herbicides discussed below have been used by nursery managers in the Northeastern United States. There may be other formulations of the same chemical that could be advantageous in some situations. An internet search on the chemical name will provide pesticide labels and material data safety sheets (for example, the Crop Data Management Service database http://www.cdms.net/label-database). It is essential to understand the correct timing of application as it relates to both the seedling crop and the weed to be controlled.

Cavalcade 65WDG

Cavalcade 65WDG (prodiamine) is a soil-active preemergent compound labeled for a wide range of hardwood species. This herbicide disrupts cell division and, therefore, interferes with germination. It controls most grasses and broadleaf weeds, but weeds that have emerged prior to application will not be effectively controlled. The label states that the foliage of seedlings may be temporarily injured if this herbicide is applied when the plants are "flushing." The label also states that unless it is certain the foliage of the species to be treated will not be damaged, wait to apply until the foliage has "hardened off" (not actively growing) and wash the herbicide off the foliage with irrigation immediately after application. Some nurseries wait 4 to 6 weeks after seedling germination to apply this herbicide. Unless one has experience with this herbicide, try a small-scale test before treating the entire crop and/or discuss this with a nursery manager who has used this herbicide. It can be applied more than once per season as long as the total does not exceed the amount specified by the label. Irrigate immediately after application to move the herbicide into the soil. Some nursery managers have been applying this before germination in the spring to larger seeded hardwood species. Black cherry (*Prunus serotina* Ehrh.), red osier (*Cornus sericea* L), silky (*Cornus oblique* Raf.) and grey (*Cornus racemosa* Lam.) dogwood, sassafras (*Sassafras albidum* Presl.) , persimmon (*Diospyros virginiana* L.), American plum (*Prunus Americana* Marsh.), and black locust (*Robinia pseudoacacia* L.) all readily germinate through the low application rate as listed on the label. Oaks and walnut also tolerate it.

Pendulum 2G or Pendulum AquaCap

Pendulum 2G and Pendulum AquaCap (pendimethalin) are soil-active preemergent compounds that can be applied to a wide range of hardwood species. Pendimethalin disrupts cell division and therefore interferes with germination. It controls many grasses and broadleaf weeds, but weeds that have emerged prior to application will not be effectively controlled. The label states: "Do not apply during bud swell, bud break, or at time of first flush of new growth." The label refers to use on established plants. It can be reapplied one additional time during the growing season. Irrigation is necessary to incorporate into the soil following application.

SureGuard

SureGuard (flumioxazin) is a soil-active and mostly preemergent compound that can be applied to some hardwood species. It inhibits chlorophyll biosynthesis and controls many grasses and broadleaf weeds. The label states, "Do not apply to trees less than one year old," and "Application to green foliage or green bark may cause unacceptable damage."

This herbicide is most effective when applied preemergent to weeds but has some postemergent activity on small emerged weeds. If applied postemergent to the crop, apply before tree seedlings break bud. Irrigation is necessary following application to incorporate into the soil. This herbicide is not widely used in northern hardwood nurseries, therefore try it in small test plots or consult a nursery manager with experience in its use.

Lontrel

Lontrel (clopyralid) is a soil-active preemergent compound that has been used in some nurseries when species of clover (*Trifolium* spp.) or medic (*Medicago* spp.) are a weed problem because of their resistance to soil fumigants. However, the label states that postemergent applications be directed to avoid the foliage of most hardwood species. Nursery managers who have used this product recommend the lower application rates. Clopyralid may carryover in the soil from one year to the next, possibly resulting in damage to a subsequent legume crop such as black locust, Kentucky coffee tree (*Gymnocladus dioicus*, L., K. Koch), redbud (*Cercis canadensis* L.), or soybeans as a cover crop. This herbicide is not widely used in this region so small test plots should be installed as a precaution.

Postemergent Herbicides Used in Seedbeds

Fusilade DX

Fusilade DX (fluazifop-p-butyl) is a postemergent compound with little or no soil activity and can be applied over the top to most hardwood species to control annual and perennial grasses. While it acts on meristematic tissue in roots and stems of grasses, it does not control broadleaf weeds. Since Fusilade DX does not have soil activity, it only controls grass weeds that have emerged at the time of application. Use in hardwood nurseries can be inferred under the "Nonbearing Crop" section of the label. The label states the following: "Nonbearing crops not listed should be screened for phytotoxicity prior to widespread use."

Envoy Plus

Envoy Plus (clethodim) is a postemergent herbicide that controls annual and perennial grasses, much like Fusilade DX, and acts on meristematic tissues in roots and stems. The label lists many hardwood tree species. Like Fusilade DX, it does not have soil activity and only controls grasses to which it is applied. Grasses that emerge after application are not controlled.

Herbicides Used To Control a Cover Crop Planted as a Living Mulch

Typically, the living mulch crop is planted with the tree seed in the fall. Wheat and rye are frequently used, as their seed germinates quickly in the fall to form a living mulch that reduces soil erosion, frost heave, seed predation, and damage from extreme winter cold. This mulch crop must be killed in late winter before the seedling crop begins to emerge. The herbicides discussed below are applied to the foliage of the cover crop and do not have soil activity. Some nurseries have used oats in the place of wheat or rye. Oats are killed by winter cold, not requiring the use of an herbicide. Oats may, however, be killed too soon by cold weather in the fall and not provide the crop protection desired.

Roundup Pro

Roundup (glyphosate) is a systemic (moves within the plant) postemergent herbicide that is applied in late winter to the foliage of the cover crop. It will kill any weed that has germinated over winter, whether grass or broadleaf, including the cover crop. Activity is slow under the cool late winter conditions, therefore it is essential to apply several weeks before seedlings begin to emerge.

Gramoxone SL 2.0

Gramoxone SL 2.0 (paraquat dichloride) can be applied in late winter as described above, but is not systemic and only kills the foliage that is contacted. Activity is very rapid, usually within a few days, killing both broadleaf and grass weeds. This herbicide must be applied before any crop seedlings have emerged or it will kill the foliage of emerged seedlings. If the growing point of the emerged seedlings is above ground, it may kill the seedlings.

Fusilade DX or Envoy Plus

Fusilade DX (fluazifop-p-butyl) or Envoy Plus (clethodim) can be used to kill wheat or rye living mulch if the seedling crop emerges before glyphosate or paraquat can be applied.

Herbicides Used in Cover Crops and Green Manure Crops

Weed control in cover crops as part of a weed sanitation program is another important way herbicides are used in the nursery. In this situation, refer to the parts of the label applicable to the cover crop or to noncrop uses. However, if the cover crop is harvested and sold as an agricultural commodity, follow the part of the label applicable to that crop. One goal of weed sanitation is to minimize the quantity of weed seed that is carried over in the soil from the cover crop to the nursery crop.

Roundup Pro

Roundup (glyphosate) is a broad-spectrum herbicide that controls most grasses and broadleaf weeds. A commonly used strategy is to use corn or soybean varieties that are Roundup Ready (genetically modified to tolerate glyphosate). In this case, glyphosate can be applied over the top of the cover crop and weeds to eliminate most grasses and broadleaf weeds without damaging the cover crop. Glyphosate is not soil active so it only controls the weeds present at the time of application. Often the cover crop is planted at densities significantly higher than normally used in field crop production, thereby quickly producing a canopy to inhibit the germination of weeds after the crop becomes too tall for additional glyphosate applications. For cover crops where Roundup Ready varieties are not available, such as wheat and sorghum, other herbicides can be used, depending on weed species and growth stage of weed or crop.

Valor EZ

Valor EZ (flumioxazin) is the agriculture version of Sureguard and does a very good job of preemergent weed control when soybeans are used as a cover crop. Since nurseries have a low tolerance for weeds, a preemergent application at planting is well worth the investment, especially since Roundup has some resistance issues.

Harmony Extra SG

Harmony Extra SG (thifensulfuron-methyl) is a selective spring-applied postemergent herbicide used in a wheat crop to control many weeds that have germinated since the crop was planted the previous fall.

2,4-D Amine 4

2,4-D amine 4 (dimethylamine salt of 2,4 dichlorophenoxy-acetic acid) is a selective postemergence herbicide used to control broadleaf weeds in cover crops such as sorghum or corn. This herbicide selectively controls broadleaf weeds without significantly damaging the grass cover crop or grass weeds.

Basagran

Basagran (sodium salt of bentazon) is a selective postemergence herbicide used to control broadleaf weeds and sedges in corn, sorghum, and soybean cover crops.

Other Products

The application of herbicides that are labeled for use in an agricultural crop grown as a cover crop, or used in noncrop areas such as bed-ends, can help reduce weed seed production. This may be particularly important where weed seed may be washed, wind blown, or transported on equipment into seedling production areas. For example, Lontrel applied to bed-ends can help keep clover populations from establishing and subsequently being carried into production areas. One must be cautious, however, of herbicide carry-over if the area will later be used as a seed bed. The local farm supply business or the County Extension Agent may be able to suggest herbicides to meet specific needs.

Weed Management in Southern Bareroot Hardwood Nurseries

8b

D.B. South

David B. South is emeritus professor, School of Forestry and Wildlife Sciences, Auburn University, AL

Outline

Facing Page: *Controlling nutsedge on fallow ground by treating emerged plants with glyphosate. (Photo by David South.)*

Introduction

The hardwood nursery manager's primary objective is to produce morphologically improved stock as economically as possible. Morphologically improved hardwood seedlings have a minimum root-collar diameter of 10 millimeters (mm); are grown at low seedbed densities; have a higher probability of survival; have a higher root/weight ratio (root dry weight/seedling dry weight), often due to top-pruning; and have a greater root growth potential than smaller stock. Weeds can be a major obstacle to this goal since they compete with seedlings for light, water, and nutrients. In addition, handweeders often pull up seedlings while weeding, reducing revenue from seedling sales. In some cases, weed populations will stunt seedlings and will cause large variations in seedling size at lifting.

To maintain a relatively weed-free nursery, most hardwood nursery managers implement a comprehensive, year-round weed control program. In the past, some seedbeds required more than 3,800 hours of handweeding per hectare (Abrahamson 1987). Today, many managers use an integrated weed management (IWM) program (Walker and Buchanan 1982), which includes sanitation, soil fumigation, and herbicide applications to keep weed populations low and minimize handweeding. As a result, several hardwood nurseries now require less than 60 hours of handweeding per hectare.

Weed Identification

To achieve good weed control, weed species must be accurately identified, especially when troublesome species are present. For example, some herbicides will suppress yellow nutsedge (*Cyperus esculentus* L.) but have little effect on purple nutsedge (*Cyperus rotundus* L.), even though the two species appear similar. Several online sites are available for identifying common weeds and extension weed specialists should be able to identify rare species. Table 8b.1 lists some of the more common weeds in southern nurseries, with their scientific names.

Table 8b.1*—Typical weed species in southern hardwood nurseries.*

Common name	Scientific name
Grasses	
Bermudagrass	*Cynodon dactylon* (L.) Pers.
Crowfootgrass	*Daclyloctenium aegyptium* (L.) Ritcher
Hairy crabgrass	*Digitaria sanguianlis* (L.) Scop.
Sourgrass	*Digitaria insularis* (L.) Mez ex Ekman
Barnyardgrass	*Echinochioa crus-galli* (L.) Beauv.
Goosegrass	*Elusine indica* (L.) Gaertn.
Sedges	
Flathead sedge	*Cyperus compressus* L.
Yellow nutsedge	*Cyperus esculentus* L.
Common nut sedge	*Cyperus compressus* L.
Broadleaves	
Prostrate pigweed	*Amaranthus bitoides* S. Wats.
Redroot pigweed	*Ameranthus retrofelus* L.
Spiney amaranth	*Amaranthus spinosus* L.
Sicklepod	*Cassis obtusifolia* L.
Eclipta	*Eclipta alba* (L.) Hassk.
Dogfennel	*Euportorium capillifolium* (Lam.) Small
Spurge	*Chamaesyce maculata* (L.) Small
Tall morningglory	*Ipomoea purpurea* (L.) Roth
Carpetweed	*Mollugo verticillata* L.
White clover	*Trifolium repens* L.

Sanitation

Preventing weeds from going to seed in the nursery is an important sanitation practice, since weed populations in future years greatly depend upon the number of seed produced during the current season. If one yellow nutsedge plant is allowed to mature, it can produce more than 2,400 seeds. A mature purslane plant (*Portulaca oleracea* L.) can produce over 52,000 seeds, and a single redroot pigweed (*Ameranthus retrofelus* L.) can produce 117,000 seeds or more (Stevens 1932). The importance of preventing a single weed from maturing and producing seed in the nursery cannot be overemphasized. A severe infestation of nutsedge can quickly result from failure to control even a single plant. For example, one tuber of purple nutsedge produced 1,168 plants and 2,324 tubers after 6 months (Ishii et al. 1971). Weeds must be prevented from going to seed not only in the seedbeds, but also on the riserlines, fencerows, cover-crop areas, and fallow areas (Wichman 1982).

Irrigation Water

Irrigation water can be a major source of introduced weeds when the water is from a lake, pond, or river. Screens installed at the intake pipe can help filter out large-seeded weeds. Although the screens may require frequent cleaning, it is easier to remove the weed seeds from the screens than to remove weeds from seedbeds. When irrigating from ponds, it is best to keep the pond edges free of weeds. When installing a new nursery, a deep well is preferred over surface water sources.

Cover-Crop Seeds

Sowing weed seeds along with cover-crop seeds can be minimized by always using certified seed. At one nursery, the use of cheap, uncertified seed resulted in a large infestation of morning glory (*Ipomoea* spp.). Regulations require certified seed to be free of primary noxious weeds and to contain only small amounts of common weeds. The percentage of common weeds must be shown on the certification tag. It is best to buy seeds with the lowest percentage of common weeds.

Machinery

Weed seeds, rhizomes, and tubers are easily introduced by machinery. Frequent washings reduce the amount of weeds introduced by soil carried on tillage equipment, tractors, and vehicle tires. Weed seeds are often spread by combines during the harvest of cover crops. For this reason, it is better to leave cover crops unharvested unless combines are carefully cleaned before and after use.

Some weeds spread slowly by vegetative means alone. For example, nutsedge would spread less than 3 meters (m) (10 feet [ft]) per year without help from nursery workers and their cultivation equipment (Klingman and Ashton 1975). For this reason, make a special effort to avoid spreading nutsedge. Map infested seedbeds in the summer to help identify areas in which to avoid soil movement (thus spreading nuts) in the winter after lifting. Lift nutsedge-free areas first to avoid spreading tubers to noninfested fields. Time taken to prevent mechanical dissemination of nutsedge tubers will be repaid several-fold in the ease of eliminating nutsedge from a nursery.

Wind

Wind will constantly introduce weed seeds, but the impact may be reduced by planting windbreaks between the nursery and adjacent weed sources. Windbreaks will also help to protect the nursery from high winds that blow mulch off beds, blow plastic off fumigated soil, and cause excessive drying of the beds.

Mulches

In the past, the use of straw mulches after sowing was a major source of introduced weeds (Bland 1973, Mullin 1965, South 1976). For example, pine straw mulch increased time spent on handweeding by 260 to 500 hours per hectare at some nurseries (Bland 1973, South 1976). The expense and introduction of weed seed has reduced use of straw mulches over time. Several managers were using pine straw in 1980 (Boyer and South 1984), but today few use it due to the expense. New bark or sawdust mulches are relatively weed free (Stringfield 2005), but old, stockpiled supplies are often contaminated with weed seed. Several hardwood managers apply weedfree soil stabilizers after sowing. Most of these managers will forgo using mulch, and therefore will apply additional irrigation.

Figure 8b.1*—When nursery managers adopt an effective integrated weed management program, the amount of handweeding can be kept to a minimum. Handweeding is most effective when weeds are small, before they go to seed. Weeding takes less time when the soil is moist and the weed has a small root system. (Photo by David South.)*

Organic Amendments

In some cases, using organic amendments will introduce weed seeds. In one nursery, rush (Juncus spp.) was introduced when an organic amendment was donated to the nursery. Yard litter and leaves collected by municipalities can contain many types of weed seeds. The value of these "free" amendments will depend on the increase in cost of subsequent weed control. Composting can help reduce the viability of many weed seeds, but some will likely remain viable.

Handweeding

Frequent weeding can be an important IWM tool. Handweeding is best conducted when the soil is moist and weeds are small (fig. 8b.1). Weeding small plants has two advantages: the weeds are often removed before they go to seed, and the weeds are easier to remove when the roots are small. In many cases, the total weeding cost is less than if weeding is delayed until the weeds are large and hard to remove.

The use of seasonal labor varies with each nursery. When using contract labor, the cost of 100 hours of handweeding might exceed $4,900 per hectare. Therefore, the use of herbicides depends, in part, on the cost of handweeding. At some nurseries, herbicides are used and minimal handweeding is required, while other managers rely on handweeding and, except for soil fumigants, do not apply herbicides to hardwood seedbeds. With an effective IWM program, hardwood seedbeds may require less than 60 hours of handweeding per hectare (South 2009).

Mechanical Cultivation

Mechanical cultivation for weed control between seedling rows is feasible when the spacing between rows is 30 cm (12 in) or wider (Barham 1980, Stanley 1970). Several types of seedbed and alleyway cultivators are available (Lowman et al. 1992). For example, a "brush-hoe" can be effective in reducing weeds in hardwood seedbeds (South 1988), although it has some drawbacks. To obtain a specified level of weed control requires a precise adjustment to ensure a proper working depth (Weber 1994). Weeds within the row remain uninjured. Any small error in alignment can damage hardwood seedling roots or shoots. In 2006, only 2 hardwood managers, out of 26, were using mechanical weed control between seedling rows (South 2009).

Living Mulch

The "living mulch" concept was used by the Virginia Department of Forestry during the 1980s. Rye (*Secale cereale* L.) seed were drilled into the sections immediately before sowing hardwoods in the fall. The "living mulch" protected the fall-sown seedbeds from injury by wind, rain, and frost. This system was also effective for fall-sown hardwoods in Illinois and Indiana (Stauder 1994, Wichman 1994). Nursery managers in Georgia and Tennessee currently sow wheat (*Triticum aestivum* L.), rye, or oats (*Avena sativa* L.) on prepared beds before fall sowing acorns (Ensminger 2002). The living mulch is then sprayed with an herbicide in February, prior to emergence of oak seedlings. This system offers several advantages, including retarding weed growth.

Fall Sowing

Fall-sown hardwoods, such as red oaks (*Quercus* spp.) and black walnut (*Juglans nigra* L.), typically have fewer weeds the following year than spring-sown crops. This reduction in weeds is due to application of herbicides sooner in the spring and the fact that fall-sown crops typically achieve full canopy closure and shade out weeds sooner than spring-sown crops (fig. 8b.2).

Soil Fumigation

Effective soil fumigation with methyl bromide is a cornerstone of a successful IWM plan at many nurseries. Several

***Figure 8b.2**—Weed control is typically easier when hardwoods are sown in the fall or winter because the canopy closes sooner in the spring and the resulting shade reduces growth of various weed species. (Photo by David South.)*

nursery managers contend that soil fumigation is more important when growing hardwoods because, when compared with conifers, fewer effective, registered herbicides exist (Murray 2009). It is relatively easy to justify soil fumigation because it typically costs less than 6 percent of the wholesale value of the hardwood crop. For this reason, most managers in the South fumigate the soil prior to each hardwood seedling crop. Although dazomet is used in northern hardwood nurseries (Schroeder and Alspach 1995, Storandt 2002), hardwood managers in the South have traditionally relied on a combination of methyl bromide and chloropicrin to reduce weed, nematode, and fungi populations.

In the future, methyl bromide will continue to be produced by oceans, fires, and certain plants and fungi. It is possible, however, that production in the United States will decline due to regulations (Enebak et al. 2013). If this occurs, some managers will likely switch to alternative fumigants, such as chloropicrin and dazomet, that have relatively low efficacy on weeds. Although dazomet can control certain soilborne pests, it is not effective in controlling nutsedge (Carey 1995; Carey and South 1999; Fraedrich and Dwinell 2003). If the use of effective soil fumigants declines, nursery managers will need to increase herbicide use to control weeds in fallow fields or cover crops.

Herbicide Use

The Weed Science Society of America (WSSA) sorts herbicides into 27 groups according to their chemical structure and activity. About one-third of these groups are used operationally in bareroot hardwood nurseries (table 8b.2). Herbicides in the cyclohexanedione family (WSSA group 1) and dinitroanaline family (WSSA group 3) are commonly used in hardwood seedbeds.

Herbicides can be grouped into selective (not generally harmful to hardwood seedlings) or nonselective (should not contact bark and foliage). Glyphosate is typically a nonselective herbicide (kills both weeds and hardwoods) while sethoxydim is a selective herbicide (kills only grasses) (South and Gjerstad 1982). It is important to know the specific crop/weed system involved. For example, the herbicide clopyralid is a selective herbicide for black walnut but it is nonselective when applied to black locust (*Robinia pseudoacacia* L.).

The terms preemergence or postemergence are used to describe when the herbicide is applied. For example, preemergence herbicides, such as napropamide, kill germinating weeds before they emerge through the soil surface. Some preemergence herbicides can be applied after emergence of the hardwood crop but before the emergence of the weed. Postemergence herbicides, on the other hand, are applied after the weeds emerge. When discussing herbicides, it is important to clarify if the application is to be made after the crop emerges and before the weeds emerge (e.g., pendimethalin, a preemergence herbicide) or after weeds emerge but before the hardwoods emerge (e.g., glyphosate, a postemergence herbicide).

Herbicide Applications in Cover Crops

The number of mature weeds in this year's cover crop will determine the amount of weed seeds present in next year's seedbeds. Some cover crops grow quickly and shade out the soil, thus reducing germination and growth of weeds. These cover crops are preferred over those that are sown at low densities and allow light to reach the soil. In the South, most herbicides used in cover crops will have no effect on seedling growth the following year. This is especially true when the herbicide is applied before July 1. Check with nursery experts, however, to ensure that carryover from one season to the next will not be a problem. Some herbicide labels include information on the number of months required before sowing sensitive crops.

Cover-crop rotation provides an excellent opportunity to control weeds that are resistant to herbicides used in seedbeds. For example, if only diphenylether herbicides (WSSA group 14) were continually used on an area, resistant weed species such as prostrate spurge (*Euphorbia maculat*e L.) could rapidly increase. However, by using an herbicide from a different herbicide family in the cover-crop area, the spread of troublesome weeds could be checked. Recommendations for using herbicides in cover crops vary, depending on the region and weed species to be controlled. The local extension service can provide specific recommendations on herbicides and use rates. Some genetically modified cover crops have a glyphosate-resistant gene that some managers use as part of an IWM program to reduce nutsedge in cover crops.

Herbicide Applications on Fallow Land

Weed control with herbicides is much easier on fallow ground (fig. 8b.3) than it is on hardwood seedling beds because: (1) a greater number of herbicides may be applied to fallow ground; (2) injury from drift is less likely; (3) multiple applications can be made; (4) timing of the application is not restricted to stage of hardwood growth; and (5) it is easier to see the weeds. For troublesome weeds like nutsedge, multiple applications of glyphosate on fallow ground is the preferred method to reduce the number of tubers in the soil (Fraedrich et al. 2003). At some nurseries, more glyphosate is used in fallow fields than is used in bareroot seedbeds (Juntunen 2001).

***Table 8b.2**—Common names and trade names of selected herbicides used in southern hardwood nurseries.*

Common name	Product names	Comment	WSSA group	REI* hours
		Soil fumigant		
Chloropicrin	Various	Good nutsedge control	n/a	>120
Dazomet	Basamid	Poor nutsedge control	27	>120
Methyl bromide	Various	Excellent nutsedge control	n/a	>120
		After sowing for oaks, walnut, hickory		
Oxyfluorfen	Goal, Galigan, Goaltender	Field-grown	14	24
		Very selective grass herbicides		
Clethodim	Clethodim, Select, Shadow	Grass control only	1	24
Fluazifop	Fusilade	Grass control only	1	12
Fluazifop	Segment, Sethoxydim	Grass control only	1	12
		Herbicides with some selectivity when applied over established hardwoods		
Dcpa	Dacthal	Found in groundwater	3	12
Dithiopyr	Dimension	Established plants only	3	12
Oryzalin	Surflan	May cause galls	3	24
Pendimethalin	Pendulum (Aquacap)	May cause galls	3	24
Prodiamine	Barricade, Resolute	May cause galls	3	12
Trifluralin	Trifluralin HF	Certain labels only	3	12
Clopyralid	Lontrel	Will injure legumes	4	12
Oxyfluorfen	Goaltender	Field-grown	14	24
S-metolachlor	Pennant	Active on sedge	15	24
Napropamide	Devrinol	Some grass control	15	12
		Granular herbicides – can be applied over transplanted stock		
Flumioxazin	Broadstar	Apply to dry leaves Do not apply to bedding plants	14	12
Indaziflam	Marengo	Apply to dry leaves	29	12
Oxadiazon	Ronstar	Apply to dry leaves	14	12
Prodiamine	Barricade, Resolute	May cause galls	3	12
Oxyfluorfen + pendimethalin	OH2	Apply to dry leaves	14 3	24
Dimethanamid + pendimethalin	Freehand	May cause galls	15 3	24
		Granular herbicides – cannot be applied to seedbeds due to label restrictions		
Dichlobenil	Casoron	4 weeks after transplanting	20	12
Pronamide	Pronamide	Not for use on 1-0 stock	3	24
		Nonselective herbicides – applications must be directed away from seedlings		
Glyphosate	Roundup	Use shielded applicator	9	4
Pelargonic acid	Scythe	Use shielded applicator	27	12
Sulfosulfuron	Certainty	Avoid contact with leaves	2	12

WSSA = Weed Science Society of America
*REI: Restricted-entry intervals for agricultural uses. Check the AGRICULTURAL USE REQUIREMENTS section of the label for required REI.

Figure 8b.3—An effective way to control nutsedge on fallow ground is to treat emerged plants with glyphosate. Some managers treat nutsedge two or three times from June to September to reduce the population of tubers in the soil. (Photo by David South, 2012.)

Herbicide Applications on Riserlines and Fencerows

It is important to control weeds on riserlines and fencerows, not only to prevent weeds from producing seed, but also to reduce the cover available for small rodents. Some managers apply a tank mix of two or three preemergence herbicides to riserlines at the time of sowing to prevent weeds from maturing and going to seed. Other managers wait for weeds to develop and then apply a postemergence herbicide to kill emerged weeds. This type of application is often done with a shield designed to reduce drift to the hardwood crop (fig. 8b.4). Several types of shields can be used to reduce the potential of drift when applying herbicides to riserlines (Kees 2008). The number of herbicides that may be applied on riserlines is more than the number the U.S. Environmental Protection Agency (EPA) allows to be applied to tree seedlings. To reduce the risk of injury, managers should avoid applying herbicides that are very water soluble (which will move into adjacent seedbeds) or very persistent in the soil.

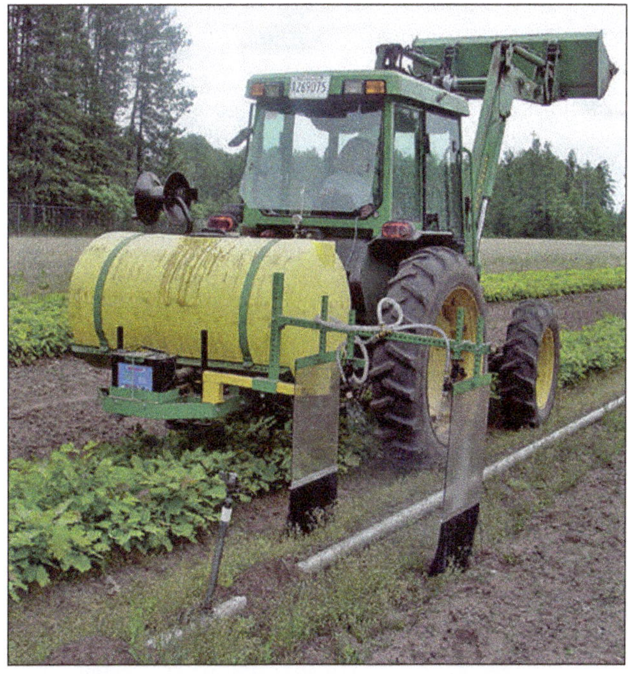

Figure 8b.4—Controlling weeds adjacent to seedbeds is an important part of an integrated weed management program. Some managers prefer to apply preemergence herbicides to irrigation lines at time of sowing hardwoods, and others wait to treat emerged weeds with postemergence herbicides that have no soil activity. (Photo by Christine Makuck, USDA Forest Service, 2001.)

Herbicide Applications in Seedbeds

At time of sowing. Some hardwood nursery managers do not apply herbicides at time of sowing since they typically sow on recently fumigated fields. However, because fumigated soils can easily be contaminated with wind-blown seed, other managers apply herbicides at time of sowing (Jacob 2009, Murray 2009). Several preemergence herbicides can be applied at sowing to large-seeded species like oaks, black walnut, pecan (*Carya illinoinensis* L.), and hickory (*Carya* spp.). In contrast, only a few preemergence herbicides may be applied to small-seeded species like American sycamore (*Platanus occidentalis* L.). Managers who apply herbicides at time of sowing, in general, have less weeding times than those who rely solely on soil fumigants.

Oxyflurofen is labeled for use on field-grown deciduous trees and has been used operationally as a preemergence herbicide (applied just after sowing) on large-seeded hardwoods (Jacob 2009, Murray 2009). It should be applied before seeds germinate because contact with the herbicide can injure newly emerged tissues. Once oxyflurofen is applied to the soil, large-seeded hardwoods can usually penetrate the herbicide barrier without much damage.

After the first true leaves have formed. Herbicide selectivity is based on physiological or morphological differences between crop and weed. For example, a physiological difference between broadleaves and grasses is the basis of selectivity for clethodim, sethoxydim, and fluziflop-butyl. As a result, these postemergence herbicides typically do not cause injury to hardwoods after their first true leaves have formed. Preemergence herbicides (like prodiamine and pendimethalin) are active mainly on seed germination. These herbicides can also be applied once hardwood seedlings have germinated and have developed a few true leaves. The herbicide prodiamine is toxic to small hardwood seed such as sycamore if applied at time of seeding, but when applied after the seedlings are 5 centimeters (cm) (2 inches [in]) or taller, the chance of injury is greatly reduced. Although these herbicides will not control emerged weeds, they will help keep subsequent weed seed from germinating (South 1984a). Several nursery managers in the South successfully use this technique.

Some foliar-acting postemergence herbicides (like clopyralid) are selective and will affect the foliage of some weeds without harming certain hardwoods (Lawrie and Clay 1994; South 2000; Jacob 2009). Clopyralid, however, does have activity on legumes and therefore will injure eastern redbud (*Cercis canadensis* L.) and black locust. Injury has also been observed on black alder (*Alnus glutinosa* L.), hackberry (*Celtis occidentalis* L.), and dogwood (*Cornus florida* L.).

Granular Herbicide Formulations

The WSSA defines granularas "a dry formulation consisting of discrete particles generally less than 10 mm^3 (.0006 in^3) and designed to be applied without a liquid carrier." Granular herbicides are often used in horticultural nurseries and a number of granular herbicides are labeled for use on hardwoods. However, the cost of using granular herbicides is greater than for liquid formulations. The per-hectare cost to treat with granular herbicides could exceed $300, which may be 8 to 10 times the cost of applying the same active ingredient sold as a liquid formulation.

An advantage of granular herbicides is that when hardwood leaves are dry, the granules drop to the ground and do not affect the foliage (fig. 8b.5). When applied to dry foliage, herbicide granules of oxyfluorfen and oxadiazon may be less phytotoxic to foliage than liquid formulations (which may contain inert ingredients such as naphthalene). In cases where granules are lodged in the foliage, a sufficient amount of irrigation soon after treatment will reduce the chance of phototoxicity. For this reason, a wide variety of species are listed on granular herbicide labels. Granules of flumioxazin, oxyfluorfen, or oxadiazon could cause some temporary necrosis if they are allowed to remain on leaves.

Granular herbicides are not applied at time of sowing, but are applied after the hardwoods have developed true leaves. Although effective weed control can be obtained with granular herbicides (Reeder et al. 1991), most nursery managers choose not to use granular formulations due to the added expense and because application is easier when herbicides are sprayed.

Managers should be aware that "water dispersible granules" (WDGs) do not fit the WSSA definition even though they are called "granules." Therefore, do not treat WDG formulations

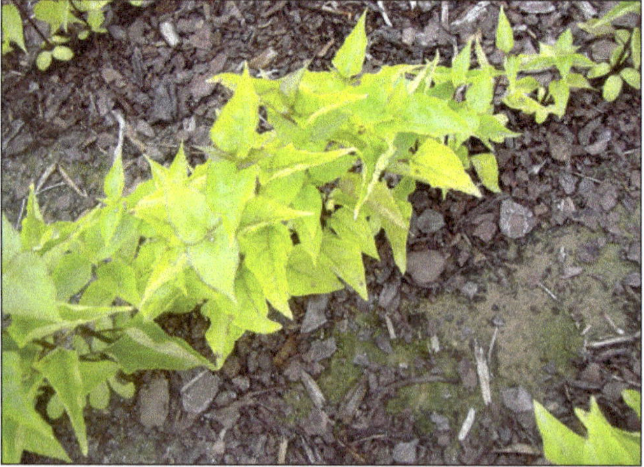

***Figure 8b.5**—Although granular herbicides are typically more expensive, they often are less phytotoxic than liquid formulations. Granular herbicides should be applied to dry foliage, which allows most of the granules to roll off the foliage. Those that remain lodged in the foliage could be shaken off by dragging a cloth or bar over the foliage. (Photo by David South, 2007.)*

as though they were true granular formulations. WDG formulations should be mixed with water and applied as a liquid spray. Carefully follow label directions when applying WDG formulations.

Directed Herbicide Application Using Shields

One way to provide selectivity is to ensure the herbicide does not come in contact with the hardwood foliage. This can be done with careful directed applications by hand or by using shields when applying herbicides between drill rows (fig. 8b.6). To reduce the potential for injury, direct most foliar-active herbicides away from the crop and toward the weeds.

Some nursery managers apply glyphosate "as needed" to control troublesome perennial weeds between rows using shielded sprayers (South and Carey 2005, Stallard 2005, Windell 2006). Glyphosate is a foliar-applied, nonselective herbicide with no soil activity. Glyphosate is bound tightly to soil particles and is unlikely to move offsite. The relatively slow absorption of glyphosate into foliage causes efficacy to be reduced by rains within a couple of hours of application.

Herbicide Injury

Although many factors can injure seedlings, herbicides are often the first to be blamed. For example, herbicides have been blamed for injury caused by fertilizer. To reduce chances of a misdiagnosis, nursery managers should leave a few untreated areas in the seedbeds (i.e., check plots). The size of the check plot can be relatively small. These check plots are not only useful for diagnosing herbicide injury (fig. 8b.7), but also provide a useful demonstration of what seedbeds would look like without the use of herbicides.

In some cases, herbicide injury will be minor and ephemeral. In fact, some herbicides might initially cause injury but eventually produce stock that is larger than untreated controls with no injury symptoms (Reeder et al. 1994). Therefore, most hardwood managers are more concerned with treatments that cause an "economic" injury to their crop than one that causes a "cosmetic" injury to leaves, especially when hardwoods drop their leaves before lifting.

Economic injury occurs when an herbicide treatment reduces crop value (e.g., when the number of shippable

Figure 8b.6—*This photograph shows an example of a shielded herbicide applicator designed for hardwood seedbeds. The advantage of this model is that it can be operated by one person. (Photo by David South, 2010.)*

Figure 8b.7—*Use of untreated check plots can help to properly identify herbicide injury. Seedlings on both seedbeds experienced sandblasting during a May storm. Seedlings on the bed on the left were injured by sand that carried an herbicide, while those on the right were blasted with soil that did not contain an herbicide. In this case, injury was temporary and seedlings were fully recovered by July. (Photo by David South, 2010.)*

seedlings produced per seedbed is reduced). The problem is determining which herbicides reduce seed germination prior to operational use. In some cases, herbicide trials are designed in such a manner that even a 50-percent reduction in crop value would not be classified as "significant" injury (Garrett et al. 1991, South 1992). The low power of these experimental designs is due primarily to the high level of variability in many hardwood seedbeds.

Herbicide injury can result when the label instructions or precautions are not followed. An improperly calibrated herbicide sprayer may result in decreased uniformity and increased risk of injury. Also, consult with nursery experts to learn the latest information on an herbicide. For example, some managers have observed injury to dogwood when a certain herbicide in WSSA group 1 was applied to newly emerged seedlings. These injuries occurred because one brand contained 65-percent solvent naphtha and 7-percent naphthalene (which can injure new foliage when applied under high temperatures). Consultation with an expert might have prevented injury if the product recommended contained low amounts of naphtha and naphthalene.

Hardwoods occasionally have been injured when environmental conditions are right and the herbicide "lifts-off" the soil within water vapor and then drifts over newly emerged hardwood seedlings (South 1984b), a process known as co-distillation. This type of injury may occur soon after seedbeds have been treated with oxyfluorfen on warm, sunny days. The injury is usually just cosmetic—the new leaves turn brown. Fortunately, the affected seedlings typically recover and grow normally.

The use of dinitroaniline herbicides (WSSA group 3) has injured certain hardwood species at a few nurseries (Derr and Salihu 1996, Hood and Klett 1992, South 1992, Warren and Skroch 1991). In some cases, herbicide galls formed on the stem near the groundline (Altland 2005, South 2009). For example, sugarberry (*Celtis laevigata* Willd.) was injured after prodiamine and pendimethalin (fig. 8b.8) were applied. A postemergence application (after both weed and crop emergence) of oryzalin has caused injury and stem breakage on American sycamore, river birch (*Betula nigra* L.), yellow poplar (*Liriodendron tulipifera* L.), redbud, elm (*Ulmus* spp.), buttonbush (*Cephalanthus* spp.), plum (*Prunus* spp.), and black willow (*Salix nigra* L.).

In some cases, herbicide injury occurs when an herbicide applied to fallow ground carries over to the next year. For example, injury occurred when certain herbicides in the imidazolinone family were used the previous year on fallow land. A number of factors determine the length of

***Figure 8b.8**—Some hardwood species are more tolerant of herbicides than others. For example, sugarberry (*Celtis laevigata Willd.*) can be injured by certain dinitroanaline herbicides. (Photo by Chase Weatherby, ArborGen, 2008.)*

time that an herbicide remains biologically active in the soil. In the South, most herbicides in WSSA groups 1, 3, and 15 do not persist long enough to affect hardwoods sown the next year. In regions where soils are cooler (e.g., Saskatchewan), however, herbicide carryover is more likely. This difference is primarily because the rate of microbial decomposition is slower in Saskatchewan than in Alabama or Georgia.

Herbicide injury will sometimes occur after a wind storm. For example, herbicide injury to sawtooth oak (*Quercus acutissima* L.), swamp chestnut oak (*Quercus michauxii* Nutt.), and persimmon (*Diospyros virginiana* L.) was noticed at 2 days after seedlings were sandblasted (Skidmore 1966) with high winds. The herbicide (in this case, oxyfluorfen), was carried with the soil and the abrasions allowed the herbicide to enter the stem and foliage. Although oak seedlings in check plots were also sandblasted (fig. 8b.7), they were not injured because the sand did not contain the herbicide. Use of a soil stabilizer would have reduced the amount of sandblasting and this would subsequently have reduced this type of injury.

In some situations, injury to adjacent seedbeds has occurred when dazomet or metham sodium was applied without a tarp (Buzzo 2003, Scholtes 1989, Starkey 2011). To reduce the potential for injury to adjacent crops, a plastic tarp is recommended when fumigating with these compounds. Some contractors now only use a plastic tarp when fumigating with metham sodium.

Purchase liquid fertilizers in returnable totes only from a reputable dealer. Reputable dealers either do not refill herbicide totes with fertilizer solutions or they ensure the totes are thoroughly cleaned before they are refilled. At one nursery, injury resulted when a fertilizer dealer did not thoroughly clean out a tote that had previously contained triclopyr.

Economics

Some nursery managers base their weed management decisions on securing economic profits and on maintaining good reputations for producing high-quality nursery stock. Their justifications for using herbicides include keeping seed efficiency high (South 1987) and production costs low. Managers operating as nonprofit entities look to achieve target production goals within a given budget. Both types of operations can benefit by using an effective IWM program to reduce handweeding costs.

The easiest way to justify the use of herbicides is to compare the cost of treatment with the cost of handweeding. For example, at a nursery where hand labor costs $15 per hour, an herbicide application that costs $30 per nursery hectare would be justified if it reduced handweeding by 2 hours or more. Thus, when seedbeds require 100 hours of handweeding ($1,500 total) to remove small grasses, 10 applications of herbicides ($300) could reduce weed-control costs by as much as $1,200 (assuming the use of herbicides eliminated the need for handweeding the grass).

Another method to justify herbicide use is to determine how many seedlings are lost to weed competition and to handweeding. If a nursery loses $0.30 every time a seedling is inadvertently pulled up by a weeder, then saving 100 seedlings could justify an herbicide treatment that cost $30. Therefore, even in rare cases in which use of herbicides does not reduce the annual cost of weed control, their use could still be justified when seedling sales are increased. An examination of a hardwood nursery budget might reveal that herbicide treatments amount to less than 0.5 percent of the retail value of the crop (table 8b.3). Therefore, use of herbicides may be justified when seedling production is increased by just 0.5 percent. This would be equivalent to selling 502,500 seedlings instead of 500,000 seedlings per hectare.

Conclusions

Because of the numerous species involved, a single herbicide regime (e.g., South 1992) is unlikely to be effective for all hardwood species. Weed species, hardwood species, soil types, and labor costs vary with the nursery; therefore, weed management regimes vary. The most effective IWM programs, however, include a rigorous sanitation program and judicious use of efficacious herbicides.

***Table 8b.3**—Example of weed management costs in hardwood nurseries. Data assumes 444,600 seedlings per hectare and a price of $0.30/seedling.*

Weed management practice	Active ingredient kg/ha	$ Per thousand seedlings	Percentage of total crop value
Herbicides in seedbeds	2.24	$0.50	0.2%
Herbicides on fallow ground	–	$0.70	0.2%
Handweeding – $15 per hour	–	$2.08	0.7%
Soil fumigation	392	$17.22	5.7%
Total		**$20.50**	**6.8%**

kg/ha = kilograms per hectare.

Acknowledgment

The Auburn University Southern Forest Nursery Management Cooperative supported the development and writing of this report.

References

Abrahamson, L.P. 1987. Forest tree nursery herbicide studies at the Oklahoma forest regeneration center. In: Landis, T.D., tech. coord. National proceedings, Intermountain Forest Nursery Association. Gen. Tech. Rep. RM-151. Fort Collins, CO: U.S. Department of Agriculture, Forest Service, Rocky Mountain Forest and Range Experiment Station: 49–57.

Altland, J.E. 2005. Weed control in nursery field production. Extension Service Report EM8899-E. Eugene, OR: Oregon State University. http://oregonstate.edu/dept/nursery-weeds/feature_articles/em8899.pdf. (August 2015).

Barham, R.O. 1980. Handweeding times reduced in hardwood seedbeds by a modified rolling cultivator. Tree Planters' Notes. 31(4): 30–32.

Bland, W.A. 1973. Study to evaluate the effects and costs of mulching materials in loblolly pine seedbeds. Forestry Note No. 3. Raleigh, NC: North Carolina Forest Service.

Boyer, J.N.; South, D.B. 1984. Forest nursery practices in the South. Southern Journal of Applied Forestry. 8(2): 67–75.

Buzzo, R.J. 2003. Phytotoxicity with metam sodium. In: Riley L.E., Dumroese R.K., Landis, T.D., tech. coords. National proceedings: Forest and Conservation Nursery Associations. Proceedings RMRS-P-28. Ogden, UT: U.S. Department of Agriculture, Forest Service, Rocky Mountain Research Station: 79–83.

Carey, W.A. 1995. Chemical alternatives to methyl bromide. In: Landis, T.D.; Dumroese, R.K., tech. coords. National proceedings: Forest and Conservation Nursery Associations. Gen. Tech. Rep. RM-257. Fort Collins, CO: U.S. Department of Agriculture, Forest Service, Rocky Mountain Research Station: 4–11.

Carey, W.A.; South, D.B. 1999. Effect of chloropicrin, vapam, and herbicides for the control of purple nutsedge in southern pine nurseries. In: Landis, T.D.; Barnett, J.P., tech. coords. National proceedings: Forest and Conservation Nursery Associations. Gen. Tech. Rep. SRS-25. Asheville, NC: U.S. Department of Agriculture, Southern Research Station: 39–40.

Derr, J.F.; Salihu, S. 1996. Preemergence herbicide effects on nursery crop root and shoot growth. Journal of Environmental Horticulture. 14(4): 210–213.

Enebak, S.A.; Jackson, D.P.; Starkey, T.E.; Quicke, M. 2013. Evaluation of methyl bromide alternatives on loblolly pine production and seedling quality over three growing seasons at the Pine Hill Nursery in Camden, Alabama. Journal of Horticulture and Forestry. 5(3): 41–47.

Ensminger, P. 2002. Nursery practices in Tennessee. In: Dumrose, R.K.; Riley, L.E.; Landis, T.D., tech. coords. National proceedings: Forest and Conservation Nursery Associations. Proceedings RMRS-P-24. Ogden, UT: U.S. Department of Agriculture, Rocky Mountain Research Station: 281–283.

Fraedrich, S.W.; Dwindell, L.D. 2003. An evaluation of dazomet incorporation methods on soilborne organisms and pine seedling production in southern nurseries. Southern Journal of Applied Forestry. 27(1): 41–51.

Fraedrich, S.W.; Dwindell, L.D.; Cram M.M. 2003. Broadcast applications of glyphosate control nutsedge at a south Georgia forest tree nursery. Southern Journal of Applied Forestry. 27(3): 176–179.

Garrett, H.E.; Stenberg, R.C.; Cox, G.S. [et al.]. 1991. A case for herbicidal weed control in forest nurseries. In: Kaufman, J.E.; Westerdahl, H.E., eds. Chemical Vegetation Management. Athens, GA: Plant Growth Regulator Society of America: 83–101.

Hood, L.R.; Klett, J.E. 1992. Preemergent weed control in container-grown herbaceous and woody plants. Journal of Environmental Horticulture. 10(1): 8–11.

Ishii, K.; Yamagi, K.; Manabe, T. 1971. Development and chemical control of purple nutsedge in the forest nursery. Weed Research, Japan. 12: 45–49.

Jacob, R. 2009. Hardwood weed control: Iowa Department of Natural Resources Forestry, Iowa State Nursery. In: Dumroese, R.K.; Riley, L.E., tech. coords. National proceedings: Forest and Conservation Nursery Associations. Proceedings RMRS-P-58. Fort Collins, CO: U.S. Department of Agriculture, Rocky Mountain Research Station: 76–78.

Juntunen, M.L. 2001. Use of pesticides in Finnish forest nurseries in 1996. Silva Fennica. 35(2): 147–157.

Kees, G. 2008. Herbicide shield for spraying irrigation pipelines. Tech Tip 0824–2343–MTDC. Missoula, MT: U.S. Department of Agriculture, Forest Service, Missoula Technology and Development Center. 4 p. http://www.fs.fed.us/t-d/pubs/pdfpubs/pdf08242343/pdf08242343dpi300.pdf. (August 2015).

Klingman, G.C.; Ashton, F.M. 1975. Weed science: Principles and practices. New York: John Wiley and Sons. 431 p.

Lawrie, J.; Clay, D.V. 1994. Tolerance of 2-year-old forestry trees to five herbicides. Forestry. 67(4): 287–295.

Lowman, B.J.; Landis, T.D.; Zensen, F.; Holland, B.J. 1992. Bareroot nursery equipment catalog. MTDC Project Report No. 9224-2839-MTDC. Missoula, MT: U.S. Department of Agriculture, Forest Service, Missoula Technology and Development Center. 198 p.

Mullin, R.E. 1965. Effects of mulches on nursery seedbeds of white spruce. The Forestry Chronicle. 41(4): 454–465.

Murray, A. 2009. Successes and failures in controlling weeds in hardwood seedbeds at the Arkansas Forestry Commission Baucum Forest Nursery. In: Dumroese, R.K.; Riley, L.E., tech. coords. National proceedings: Forest and Conservation Nursery Associations. Proceedings RMRS-P-58. Fort Collins, CO: U.S. Department of Agriculture, Rocky Mountain Research Station: 74–75.

Reeder, J.A.; Gilliam, C.H.; Wehtje, G.R.; South, D.B. 1991. The effects of selected herbicides on propagation of chestnut oaks in containers. Combined Proceedings of the International Plant Propagators' Society. 41: 325–329.

Reeder, J.A.; Gilliam, C.H.; Wehtje, G.R. [et al.]. 1994. Evaluation of selected herbicides on field-grown woody ornamentals. Journal of Environmental Horticulture. 12(4): 236–240.

Scholtes, J.R.1989. Soil fumigation at J. Herbert Stone Nursery. In: Landis, T.D., tech. coord. National proceedings: Intermountain Forest Nursery Association. Gen. Tech. Rep. RM-184. Fort Collins, CO: U.S. Department of Agriculture, Pacific Northwest Research Station: 35–37.

Schroeder, W.R.; Alspach, L.K. 1995. Herbicide program at the PFRA shelterbelt centre. In: Landis, T.D., Cregg, B., tech. coord. National proceedings: Forest and Conservation Nursery Associations. Gen. Tech. Rep. PNW-365. Portland, OR: U.S. Department of Agriculture, Pacific Northwest Research Station: 80–83.

Skidmore, E.L. 1966. Wind and sandblast injury to seedling green beans. Agronomy Journal. 58: 311–315.

South, D. 1976. Pine straw mulch increases weeds in forest tree nurseries. Highlights of Agricultural Research. Auburn, AL: Auburn University, Agricultural Experiment Station. 23(4): 15.

South, D.B. 1984a. Chemical weed control in southern hardwood nurseries. Southern Journal of Applied Forestry. 8(1): 16–22.

South, D.B. 1984b. Response of loblolly pine and sweetgum seedlings to oxyfluorfen. Canadian Journal of Forest Research. 14(4): 610–604.

South, D.B. 1987. Economic aspects of nursery seed efficiency. Southern Journal of Applied Forestry. 11(2): 106–109.

South, D.B. 1988. Mechanical weed control for the forest nursery. Georgia Forestry Commission Research Report. 1: 1–9.

South, D.B. 1992. Prodiamine: a herbicide for pine and hardwood nurseries. Southern Journal of Applied Forestry. 16(3): 142–146.

South, D.B. 2000. Tolerance of southern pine seedlings to clopyralid. Southern Journal of Applied Forestry. 24(1): 51–56.

South, D.B. 2009. A century of progress in weed control in hardwood seedbeds. In: Dumroese, R.K.; Riley, L.E., tech. coords. National proceedings: Forest and Conservation Nursery Associations. Proceedings RMRS-P-58. Fort Collins, CO: U.S. Department of Agriculture, Rocky Mountain Research Station: 80–84.

South, D.B.; Carey, W.A. 2005. Weed control in bareroot hardwood nurseries. In: Dumroese, R.K.; Riley, L.E.; Landis, T.D., tech. coords. National proceedings: Forest and Conservation Nursery Associations. Proceedings RMRS-P-35. Fort Collins, CO: U.S. Department of Agriculture, Rocky Mountain Research Station: 34–38.

South, D.B.; Gjerstad, D.H. 1982. Postemergence control of grasses with selective herbicides in pine and hardwood seedbeds. Tree Planters' Notes. 33(1): 24–28.

Stallard, D.H. 2005. Using shielded sprayers to control weeds in nursery beds. In: Dumroese, R.K.; Riley, L.E.; Landis, T.D., tech. coords. National proceedings: Forest and Conservation Nursery Associations. Proceedings RMRS-P-35. Fort Collins, CO: U.S. Department of Agriculture, Rocky Mountain Research Station: 24–25.

Stanley, H. 1970. Hardwood weed control. In: Jones, L., tech coord. Proceedings, Southeastern Nurserymen's Conferences. Atlanta, GA: U.S. Department of Agriculture, Forest Service, Southeastern Area: 60–61.

Starkey, T.E. 2011. The history and future of methyl bromide alternatives in the Southern United States. In: Haase, D.L.; Pinto, J.R.; Riley, L.E., tech. coords. National proceedings: Forest and Conservation Nursery Associations. Proceedings RMRS-P-68. Fort Collins, CO: U.S. Department of Agriculture, Rocky Mountain Research Station: 31–35.

Stauder, A.F. 1994. The use of green overwinter mulch in the Illinois State Nursery program. In: Landis, T.D., tech. coord. National proceedings, Northeastern and Intermountain Forest and Conservation Nursery Association. Gen. Tech. Rep. RM-243. Fort Collins, CO: U.S. Department of Agriculture, Rocky Mountain Forest and Range Experiment Station: 51–53.

Stevens, O.A. 1932. The number and weight of seeds produced by weeds. American Journal of Botany. 19(9): 784–794.

Storandt, J. 2002. Red oak propagation at the Griffith State Nursery, Wisconsin Rapids, Wisconsin. In: Dumrose, R.K.; Riley, L.E.; Landis T.D., tech. coords. National proceedings: Forest and Conservation Nursery Associations. Proceedings RMRS-P-24. Ogden, UT; U.S. Department of Agriculture, Rocky Mountain Research Station: 120–121.

Stringfield, D. 2005. Weed management. In: Dumroese, R.K.; Riley, L.E.; Landis, T.D., tech. coords. National proceedings: Forest and Conservation Nursery Associations. Proceedings RMRS-P-35. Fort Collins, CO: U.S. Department of Agriculture, Rocky Mountain Research Station: 39–40.

Walker, R.H.; Buchanan, G.A. 1982. Crop manipulation in integrated weed management systems. Weed Science. 30 (Suppl. 1): 17–24.

Warren, S.L.; Skroch, W.A. 1991. Evaluation of six herbicides for potential use in tree seedbeds. Journal of Environmental Horticulture. 9(3):160–163.

Weber, H. 1994. Mechanical weed control with a row brush hoe. Acta Horticulturae. 372: 253– 260.

Wichman, J.R. 1982. Weed sanitation program at the Vallonia Nursery. Tree Planters' Notes. 33(4): 35–36.

Wichman, J.R. 1994. Use of wheat as a living mulch to replace hydromulch for fall sown seedbeds. In: Landis, T.D., tech. coord. National Proceedings, Northeastern and Intermountain Forest and Conservation Nursery Association. Gen. Tech. Rep. RM-243. Fort Collins, CO: U.S. Department of Agriculture, Rocky Mountain Forest and Range Experiment Station: 55–56.

Windell, K. 2006. Shielded herbicide sprayer for hardwood nursery seedling beds. Tech. Rep. 0624-2827-MTDC. Missoula, MT: U.S. Department of Agriculture, Missoula Technology and Development Center. 18 p. http://www.fs.fed.us/t-d/pubs/pdfpubs/pdf06242827/pdf06242827dpi300.pdf. (August 2015).

Pest Management of Bareroot Hardwood Seedlings

9

S.A. Enebak

Scott A. Enebak is professor and associate dean for instruction, School of Forestry and Wildlife Sciences, Auburn University, Auburn, AL

Outline

Facing Page: *Leaf spots on* Quercus *spp. indicating localized fungal infections. (Photo by Scott Enebak.)*

Disease Management

Root Diseases

Damping-off. A number of soilborne fungi, present in nursery soil, are capable of inciting disease in bareroot hardwood seedlings. The term "damping-off" describes the rapid and sudden mortality of young germinates prior to the lignification and hardening of the seedling stem, resulting in the seedling collapsing. Preemergence damping-off occurs before the seedling emerges from the soil and occurs when the fungi infect the seed or radical before the stem emerges from the soil. Preemergence damping-off appears to the manager as reduced or slower germination than what is expected of a particular seed source. In contrast, postemergence damping-off is mortality of the seedling after the young germinate has emerged from the soil (fig. 9.1). The seed/hypocotyls/seedling could have been infected at any time postsowing, but at least the seedling was able to emerge from the soil. As a general rule, smaller seeded species are more susceptible than larger seeded species to damping-off. Depending on the timing of infection and tree species, and because of their relative size, seedlings may not even "damp-off," but die, turn brown, and remain standing. This type of damping-off could be considered a seedling blight (the rapid and sudden death of a seedling) or could also be considered root rot, if later in the growing season.

The fungal genera responsible for damping-off include *Fusarium* spp., *Rhizoctonia* spp., *Cylindrocladium* spp., *Pythium* spp., and *Phytophthora* spp. These fungi are generally opportunistic saprophytes that feed on dead and decaying plant material and, under certain conditions, are capable of infecting seed, hypocotyls, roots and stems of hardwood seedlings. Infection by these soilborne fungi may result in mortality in the nursery, poor seedling quality (culls), or reduced survival after outplanting. Preemergent and postemergence damping-off will appear in nurseries as an expanding circle, either across or along a seedling bed as the fungi move through the soil infecting and killing seed/seedlings within the soil. Many times, infection is masked during cool periods but suddenly appears when temperatures increase and the seedling, its root system compromised by the fungal infection, cannot translocate enough moisture to remain turgid and damps-off.

Figure 9.1*—Postemergence damping-off of hardwood seedlings due to soilborne fungi. (Photo by Scott Enebak.)*

Both cultural and chemical methods can be used to minimize the effects of these fungi on seedling production. These fungi are usually present in low numbers and can survive in the soil in plant debris or, as in the case of *Rhizoctonia* and *Cylindrocladium*, in dormant spores that remain viable for years. Their effect on seedling mortality tends to increase when seedbeds are used continuously without rotations of cover crops, so crop rotation should be a part of the nursery's management plan. Excessive moisture and cool temperatures cause fungi to build up in large numbers, as cool, wet soil promotes fungi and slows seedling growth. Soils high in clay content or that drain poorly and retain moisture longer favor the damping-off fungi, especially the water molds *Pythium* and *Phytophthora*. Sowing hardwood seed in raised seedling beds and fields that drain excess water away from seedling roots will go a long way to controlling the fungi that infect seedling roots. Also, the addition of nitrogen early in the season favors soilborne fungi, so minimizing fertilizer until the seed has germinated will decrease the amount of damping-off that occurs early in the season. The soil pH also influences fungal behavior, with pH above 6 favoring the pathogen's growth at the expense of seedling performance. Nurseries that can maintain high levels of organic matter (greater than 3 percent) will find that damping-off is reduced due to the effects of the antagonistic, beneficial soilborne fungi that use organic matter as a food source and will outcompete the soilborne pathogens responsible for damping-off. In addition, damping-off is favored by organic materials that decrease soil pH and organic matter that increases the carbon nitrogen ratio.

While these cultural methods have been shown to be effective in minimizing damping-off, by far the most common and effective step in controlling damping-off diseases is the use of a soil sterilent prior to sowing. Historically, this has been either a fall or spring soil fumigation with combinations of methyl bromide and chloropicrin (98:2, 67:33, 80:20) at 350 to 400 pounds of active ingredient per acre (lb ai/ac) (388 to 444 kilograms of active ingredient per hectare [kg ai/ha]) or dazomet (350 to 400 lb ai/acre, 388-444 kg ai/ha). These compounds generally eliminate most of the soilborne fungi, weeds, insects, and nematodes within the soil profile, rendering the area semi-sterile. With the gradual phase-out of methyl bromide as a soil sterilent, compounds with 100-percent chloropicrin (table 9.1) have shown to be as effective as methyl bromide combinations in disease control, but are weak in weed control (South and Enebak 2005). Spring fumigation, followed by a spring sowing, will have less damping-off than any other option. For those nurseries that use some type of soil fumigation, hardwood seedlings should always be sown in first-year fumigation soil to reap the benefits of the reduced weed, insect, fungal, and nematode pressure.

Unlike soil fumigants that are presowing, there are fungicides that can be applied as a soil drench during the growing season, if necessary. These treatments will work only for a few targeted damping-off pathogens, which will need to be identified before treating the area. Damping-off caused by a specific soilborne pathogen can be controlled using the fungicides listed in table 9.2.

Root rot. Later in the growing season, the same soilborne fungi responsible for damping-off are capable of causing root rot, which may result in seedling stunting, mortality, or poor survival after outplanting. Depending on the fungus involved, the disease may be either *Cylindrocladium* root rot or *Phytophthora* root rot, as a number of species within each fungal genera can be responsible. Many hardwood species can be infected by these three fungi, including sweetgum (*Liquidambar styraciflua* L.), yellow poplar (*Liriodendron tulipifera* L.), black walnut (*Juglans nigra* L.), dogwood (*Cornus florida* L.), eastern redbud (*Cercis canadensis* L.), chinquapin (*Castanea* spp.), and many oak species (*Quercus* spp.). In addition to root decay, the fungi can be spread by rain and soil splash, resulting in stem lesions and foliage blights.

Table 9.1—*Soil fumigants used to treat nursery soils prior to sowing.*

Soil fumigant	Percent compound
Methyl bromide /chloropicrin	67/33 or 80/20
Chloropicrin	100%
Chloropicrin +	80% & 20% solvent
Dazomet	100%
Chloropicrin & 1, 3-dichloropropene	60% & 40%
Metam / potassium sodium	
Methyl iodide / chloropicrin	98/2 or 67/33
Dimethyl disulfide (DMDS) / chloropicrin	79/21

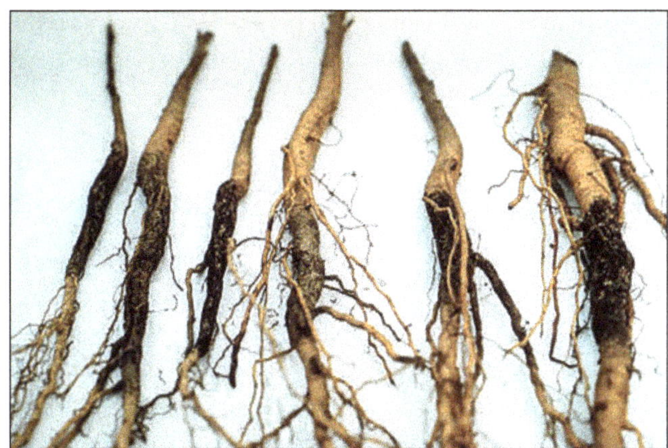

Figure 9.2—*Dark-stained roots indicative of root-rot caused by* Cylindrocladium *spp. (Photo by Scott Enebak.)*

Identification of these diseases on hardwood seedlings is based on the dark blackening of the roots or stems typically has longitudinal swellings and cracks along the infected area (fig. 9.2). Seedling mortality caused by root rot will appear as an expanding circle, either across or along a seedling bed, as the fungi move from seedling to seedling. The same cultural techniques can be used to control these fungi as are used to minimize damping-off: good soil drainage, proper soil pH, and high organic matter. If root rot does occur, then soil drenches of the

Table 9.2—*Fungicides to control damping-off and root rot soilborne pathogens.*

Soilborne fungi	Compound	Fungicide
Pythium spp and *Phytophthora* spp	Aliette	Aluminum tris (o-ethyl phosphonate)
	Sudue Maxx	Mefenoxam
	Pageant	Pycraclostrobin & boscalid
	Banrot	Thiophanate-methyl & etridiazole
	Captan	Captan
	Terraclor 75 wp	Pentachloronitrobenzene (pcnb)
Fusarium spp and *Rhizoctonia* spp	Cleary's 3336	Thiophanate methyl
	OHP 6672	Thiophanate methyl
	Banrot	Thiophanate-methyl & etridiazole
	T-Methyl	Thiophanate-methyl
	Pageant	Pycraclostrobin & boscalid
Cylindrocladium spp	Cleary's 3336	Thiophanate methyl
	Omega 50°F	Fluazinam
	Terraguard 50W	Triflumizole

infected area have been shown to be effective in stopping the continued spread of the disease. Culling and destroying infected seedling material from the nursery beds will decrease inoculum later in the season and future crops.

Foliage Diseases

A multitude of leaf diseases occur on hardwood seedlings, most of them caused by fungi within the large fungal group *Ascomycota.* Fungi growing on leaf surfaces can be a concern because they reduce the area for plant photosynthesis and growth. Reduced vigor makes trees more susceptible to attack by insects and other fungi and appear unhealthy. Foliage pathogens are considered weak pathogens and generally do not kill trees, but can do so under extreme conditions. *Anthracncose,* as a rule, are the most severe pathogens on hardwoods and result in tree mortality, especially dogwood and sycamore anthracnose. Some foliage diseases are host-specific, having evolved to infect only one or two hosts. Some foliage diseases are not host-specific and can occur on any number of hardwood species, resulting in symptoms that include localized necrotic leaf spots to total death of the leaf. Severe infections may result in terminal growth reduction and mortality of smaller hardwood species. Hardwoods are less susceptible to foliage diseases than conifers; hardwoods have the ability to refoliate, whereas conifers will die once leafless. The fungi responsible for foliage diseases are spread via wind and rain, and infection occurs when specific temperature, moisture, and humidity requirements are met, along with a suitable host tissue. The fungi typically over-winter in the infected leaves that have been cast onto the nursery soil. Eliminating the leaves at the end of the growing season and/or rotating a nonhardwood crop in heavily infected areas will decrease disease incidence in future crops.

Powdery mildew. Seven fungal genera are responsible for powdery mildews on hardwood seedlings: *Erisyphe, Phyllactinia, Microsphaera, Podosphera, Sphaerotheca, Cystotheca,* and *Unicula.* All of them are obligate plant fungal parasites in that they do not live outside their specific host. Unlike most other fungal pathogens, powdery mildews do not require moisture for infection to occur. These fungi are host-specific and there are genotypes within a tree species that can be either resistant or susceptible to infection. Susceptible hardwood species include *Acer* spp., *Carya* spp., *Cornus* spp., *Juglans* spp., *Populus* spp., *Plantanus* spp., *Quercus* spp., and *Ulmus* spp. Superficial mycelia cover the plant surface giving it a blotchy, powdery, white, gray or tan appearance (fig. 9.3). Close examination of the leaf surface will reveal small black fruiting structures (cleistothecia) that are used to identify the fungus to species. Damage caused by powdery mildew is typically minor, with leaf surfaces becoming blistered and distorted. Severe infections may result in terminal growth reduction and mortality of smaller hardwood species. In some cases, nursery managers have used powdery mildew as a natural top clipping to maintain seedling height. A number of fungicides are available that can control this common and widespread fungal disease and can be applied at the first sign of infection and carried throughout the growing season (table 9.3).

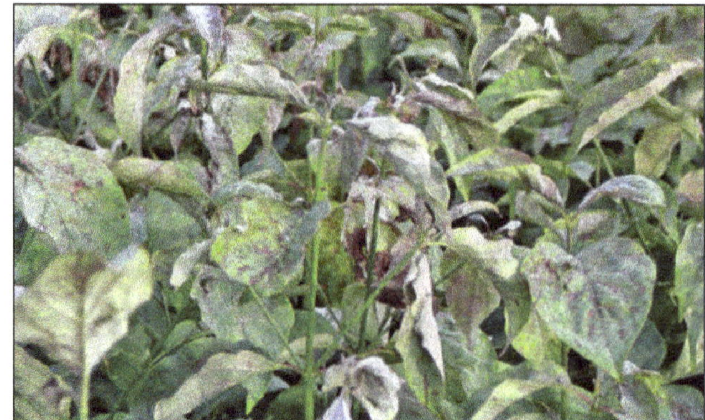

Figure 9.3*—Powdery mildew growing on the leaf surface giving the seedling a white, gray or tan appearance. (Photo by Scott Enebak, Auburn University, 2004).*

Anthracnose. A number of hardwood species are susceptible to anthracnose diseases, which is a name given to fungi that cause a characteristic lesion, necrosis, and incomplete leaf/twig/branch development on hardwood

Table 9.3*—Fungicides to control powdery mildews, anthracnose, leaf spot, and rust foliage diseases on hardwood seedlings.*

Disease	Compound	Fungicide
Powdery mildew	Aliette	Aluminum tris (o-ethyl phosphonate)
	Sudue Maxx	Mefenoxam
	Pageant	Pycraclostrobin & boscalid
	Banrot	Thiophanate-methyl & etridiazole
	Captan	Captan
Anthracnose	Cleary's 3336	Chlorothalonil
	OHP 6672	Mancozeb
	Banrot	Mancozeb
Leaf spots/blights	Cleary's 3336	Thiophanate-methyl
	Bravo 720	Chlorothalonil
	Topsin M	Thiophanate-methyl
	Captan	Captan
Leaf rusts	Bayleton	Triadimefon

seedlings, resulting in defoliation, cankers, and dieback of seedlings. Like powdery mildews, a number of pathogens are responsible for these symptoms on seedlings, which include fungi in the genera: *Apiognomonia, Asteroma, Colletotrichum, Cryptocline, Gnomonia, Gnomoniella, Discella, Discula* and *Monostichella.* With numerous fungal genera responsible for infection, there are many hardwood species that serve as hosts to the pathogens. These include seedlings in the genera *Acer* spp., *Betula* spp., *Carya* spp., *Fraxinus* spp., *Quercus* spp., *Tilia* spp., *Ulmus* spp., and other commonly grown hardwood species. Some of the more sensitive species include sycamore (*Plantanus occidentalis* L.), black walnut (*Juglans nigra* L.), and *Quercus* in the white oak group. Symptoms on infected leaves depend on the tree species, but begin as tiny dead spots, becoming large and irregular. Dead areas turn brown, black, or purple and may merge until the whole leaf dies (fig. 9.4). Seedlings infected in the early spring resemble leaves damaged by frost. If they are not killed by the fungi, young leaves may become distorted by the unequal growth in healthy and infected parts. When severely infected, trees may lose their leaves, but if defoliation occurs in spring, seedlings may produce a second crop of leaves. The disease is most severe when growing conditions in the spring are cool and moist. The fungi tend to be more active when temperatures remain below 10 °C (50 °F) for a period of 72 hours, which favors spore production. In contrast, temperatures above 16 °C (61 °F) do not favor the development of the disease and, depending on the weather conditions, there may be multiple periods of infection over the growing season. The fungi responsible for anthracnose diseases overwinter in leaves and cankers on small twigs and spores and spread via wind, rain, and irrigation. Multiple and severe infections can weaken infected hardwood seedlings, predisposing them to other fungi and insects.

Since the fungi overwinter in soil debris, sowing hardwood seed in newly fumigated soil will reduce the chances of carryover from the previous year's crop. Removal and destruction of infected material will also decrease the amount of inoculum present in the area. Timely application of fungicides registered for use on anthracnose pathogens is one method to decrease seedling culls and increase seedling growth and appearance. A number of fungicides are labeled for use in nurseries and should be alternated to avoid developing pesticide resistance (table 3).

Leaf spots, blights, and rusts. A number of other fungi are capable of infecting various hardwood species that result in spots, blights, blotches, blisters, or rusts. Unlike anthracnose diseases, leaf spot diseases are characterized by well-defined necrotic leaf lesions (fig. 9.5). Seedling species and fungi determine the shape, size, and color of the spot, which may be limited by the venation. Necrotic spots may be bordered by yellow or purple margins. Some of the hardwood species more sensitive to leaf spot diseases include *Populus* spp. and *Quercus* spp., both of which have a number of fungal diseases specific to them. Most of these hardwood diseases are not serious unless the infection occurs early in the growing season, when young or smaller seedling species are defoliated. Severe infection may result in complete defoliation, resulting in seedling mortality or poor-quality seedlings that may not be shippable. While there are some fungicides labeled for use on foliage diseases, managers need to positively identify the causal agent before treating. Generally, these types of foliage diseases are cosmetic and treatment to control them is not warranted (table 9.3).

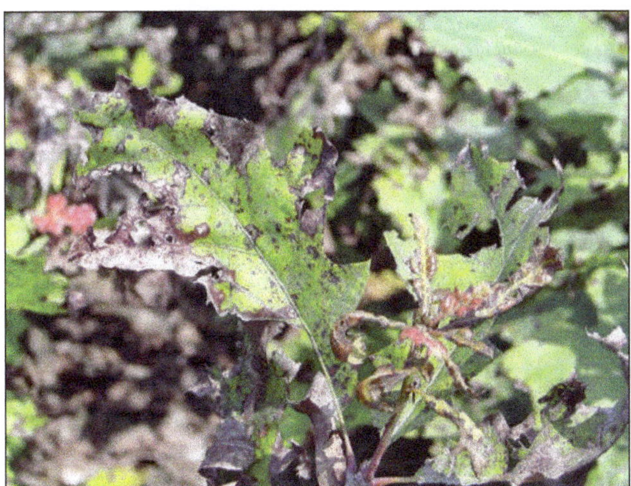

Figure 9.4*—Symptoms of anthracnose infection on hardwood seedlings. Severe infection may result in complete defoliation of the seedling and stem dieback. (Photo by Scott Enebak, Auburn University, 2004.)*

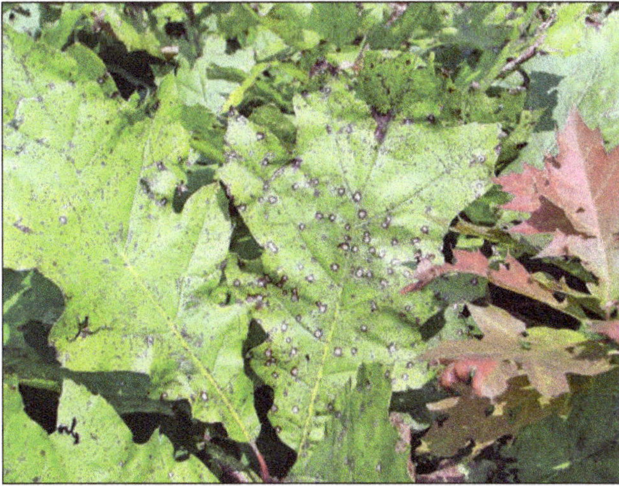

Figure 9.5*—Leaf spots on* Quercus *spp. indicating localized fungal infections. (Photo by Scott Enebak, Auburn University, 2004.)*

Nematode and Insect Management

Nematodes

Hardwood seedlings are particularly susceptible to parasitic nematodes. Continuous cultivation of the same species within an area is conducive to the buildup of nematode populations that, if not controlled, can result in significant seedling mortality. Nematodes are found throughout North America and certain nematodes have a wide host range and feed on many hardwood hosts, while other nematodes have a limited host range in their feeding habits. Nurseries with sandy, well-drained soils tend to have more nematode problems than heavier soils (e.g., more silts and clays). The nematodes most damaging to hardwood seedling crops are the root knot nematode (*Meloidogyne* spp.), the lance nematode (*Hoplolaimus* spp.), the lesion nematode (*Pratylenchus* spp.), the stunt nematode (*Tylenchorhynchus* spp.), the stubby-root nematode (*Trichodorus* spp.), and the dagger nematode (*Xiphinema* spp.).

The response of hardwood seedlings to infestation by nematodes varies with the seedling-nematode combination. The aboveground symptoms are similar to root diseases, as the nematodes' feeding activities interfere with normal root/shoot physiology. Generally, infected seedlings are stunted, lack vigor, and have foliage that is reduced in size and number, eventually becoming chlorotic (resembling nutrient deficiency) despite adequate soil fertility. In periods of high heat and low moisture, seedlings with nematode problems may wilt due to lack of turgor pressure. Symptomatic seedlings will appear in small circular patches that enlarge over the growing season and coalesce with other infestations. Belowground symptoms of the roots depend on the nematode species. Root-knot nematodes cause galls to form, with a proliferation of roots near the galls. Stubby and stunt nematode feeding activity results in root discoloration, surface lesions, and stunting of the lateral root systems. Dagger nematodes cause galls at the root apex and distortion of the lateral roots. Lesion and lance nematodes result in necrosis of the root cortex that appears like root decay of the feeder roots and creates wounds for soilborne pathogens (e.g., *Fusarium* spp., *Pythium* spp., etc.) that are only a problem on seedlings when nematodes are present.

Culturally, selection of a nonhost cover crop and using proper crop rotations will go a long way to keep nematode species and numbers below threshold levels. Certain crops like corn and sorghum can increase nematode populations, whereas cover crops like pearl and brown-top millet decrease nematodes (Cram and Fraedrich 2005). In addition to crop rotation, hardwood seedlings should be sown only in first-year fumigated soil. Broad-spectrum preplant soil fumigants that include combinations of methyl bromide, chloropicrin, or 1,3-dichloropropene have been shown to be the most effective in reducing nematode populations (table 9.1) when used prior to sowing. Nematodes cannot be eliminated from soil, but proper rotations and soil fumigations can reduce nematodes to levels that will not affect seedling production.

Piercing and Sucking Insects

There are many insects associated with hardwood seedling production, and they vary in the activities that are detrimental to hardwood seedling health. One large group of insects are those that use their mouthparts to pierce into seedling tissues (leaves, stems, buds) and remove (suck) the cellular contents as part of their feeding activities. In addition to removing sugars and photosynthates from the tree, some insects inject materials that are detrimental to the hardwood seedling health. These include growth hormones, viruses, bacteria, and toxins that may appear weeks to months after the insect has fed and moved on. Often the insect pest may be long gone but the damage is already done. Hundreds of different insects feed on hardwood species, with some more host-specific than others. This section breaks them down into three large, artificial groups, based on their feeding habits and movements.

Leafhoppers. Leafhoppers are small insects, usually less than 13 millimeters (mm) (1/2 inch [in]) long and can be either brightly colored or drab, but are usually patterned with stripes. They are wedge-shaped and tend to "hop" around the seedling when disturbed. They use their piercing/sucking mouthparts to feed on the leaves and stems of many hardwood species grown in the Eastern United States. With many leafhopper species, their feeding introduces viruses that can block conductive tissue and alter leaf physiology. Cupping, curling, and leaf distortions are common when populations are high. These insects tend to come and go, so a watchful eye is necessary, along with an active insecticide spray program that includes systemic insecticides for control (table 9.4).

Aphids. Aphids are small (2 to 5 mm), soft-bodied insects that have a tremendous capacity for reproduction (fig. 9.6). They can be identified by their characteristic pear-shaped body and tube-like projections from the rear of the abdomen. They have a complex life cycle that

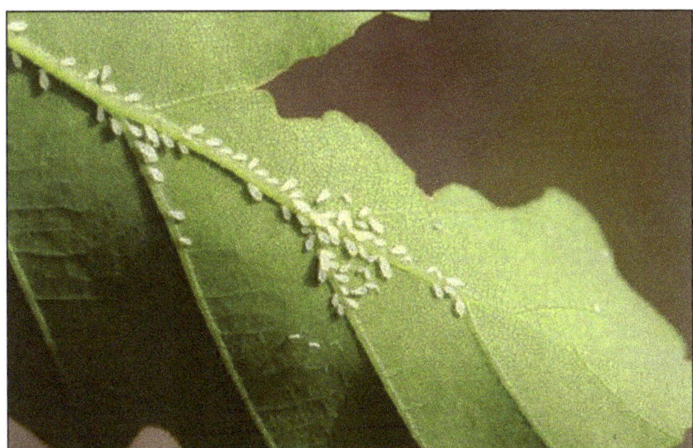

Figure 9.6—Aphids feeding on the underside of leaves may cause cupping, curling or even stem dieback if populations are high enough. (Photo by Scott Enebak.)

includes flight and flightless forms and they can reproduce without males. A single female can quickly become hundreds in a short period of time. They vary in color, ranging from green to black, and feed on the undersides of leaves and seedling stems, often congregating in family groups. Like leafhoppers, they feed on hardwood seedling tissue, remove nutrients from the seedling, and can introduce viruses that alter leaf hormone physiology. One unique feature of aphids is the production of honeydew, a sticky substance excreted from their bodies which is high in sugar content and attractive to ants. The ants will "farm" the aphids and go to great lengths to protect the aphids from other insect predators. Aphids tend to be more sessile and move less than either leafhoppers or plant hoppers, and thus they tend to be noticed more often. An active insecticide spray program that includes both contact and systemic insecticides will minimize the effects of these insects on hardwood seedling production.

Scale insects. Of the piercing and sucking insects, scale insects are the least mobile and, therefore, the least problematic of this group on hardwood seedling production. Most of their life cycle is spent as a wingless, legless female covered with a waxy or resinous secretion (fig. 9.7). They are loosely divided into three groups: mealy bugs, soft scales, and armored scales, based on the type of scale the insect produces while attached to the seedling. They have piercing/sucking mouthparts and, once established, will sit on a seedling stem and feed for the duration of their life. The waxy coating or scale the insect produces protects the insect from predators and insecticide applications that rely on contact exposure. One symptom that may appear when either aphids or scale insects are present is the development of sooty molds. These black to brown fungi do not hurt the seedling, but are living off the insects' honeydew and result in leaf curling, cupping, or defoliation. Systemic insecticides generally are best for piercing/sucking

Table 9.4—Insecticides to control insects on hardwood seedlings. (Photo by Scott Enebak.)

Disease	Compound	Fungicide
Leafhoppers/Plant hoppers	Sevin	Carbaryl
	Diazinon	Diazinon
	Talstar	Bifenthrin
	Astro	Permethrin
Aphids	Safer soap	Insecticidal soap
	Orthene	Acephate
	Astro	Permethrin
Scales	Sevin	Carbaryl
	Astro	Permethrin
	Safer soap	Insecticidal soap
	Malathion	Malathion
Spider mites	Safer soap	Insecticidal soap
	Talstar	Bifenthrin
	Malathion	Malathion
May, June, and Japanese beetles	Sevin	Carbaryl
	Malathion	Malathion
	Astro	Permethrin
	Orthene	Acephate
Grasshoppers	Diazinon	Diazinon
	Astro	Permethrin
	Pounce	Permethrin
	Orthene	Acephate
Caterpillars	Sevin	Carbaryl
	Astro	Permethrin
	Pounce	Permethrin
	Orthene	Acephate
Leaf-tiers, rollers, and miners	Orthene	Permethrin
	Pounce	Permethrin
	Astro	Permethrin
White grubs	Dursban	Chlorpyrifos
Cutworms	Astro	Permethrin
	Pounce	Permethrin
	Orthene	Acephate
	Dursban	Chlorpyrifos

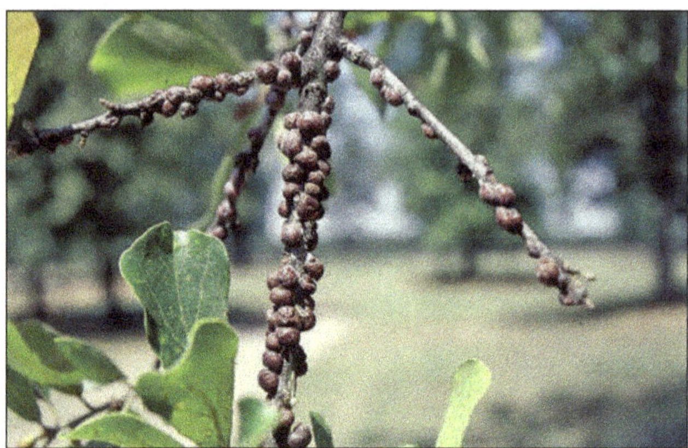

Figure 9.7—Scale insects feeding on a water oak seedling stem. (Photo by Scott Enebak.)

insects (table 9.4).

Spider mites. Spider mites are small (1 to 3 mm) noninsects (Arachnida) that occur in many of the same habitats occupied by insects. They are oval in shape with two body parts, have no wings, and are easily transported by wind. A small hand lens is needed to identify this insect. The two most important species of mites on hardwood seedlings is the two-spotted spider mite (*Tetranychus urticae*) and the European red mite (*Panomychus ulumi*). Spider mites feed on the underside of leaves, stems, and buds, removing nutrients from seedlings in a similar way to aphids and scales. Extensive outbreaks of the spider mite usually have mats of webbing that protect and shelter the mite colony as they feed. Leaves with large populations of mites turn yellow, then brown, and can result in leaf curling and premature defoliation. Stunting and deformation of small-statured hardwood tree species is also possible. Controlling either mite species requires compounds specific for mites, because many "insecticides" are ineffective for this purpose.

Leaf Feeding Insects

There are hundreds of insect species that have mandibles they use to bite, chew, and digest hardwood plant tissue for food. To make things simple, they have been broken down into groups with similar damage, life habits, and control methods: beetles, grasshoppers, caterpillars, leaf-tiers, leaf-rollers, and leaf-miners.

May, June, Japanese, blister beetles and borers. The adult stage of white grub larvae (discussed later) feed on the leaves, stems, and buds of hardwood seedlings. There are hundreds of beetle species in many genera that feed on all hardwood species. Some beetles are host-specific, like May and June beetles (*Phyllophaga* spp.) that tend to favor *Quercus* spp., and the cottonwood leaf beetle that feeds only on *Populus deltoids* (L.). In contrast, others like the Japanese beetle (*Popillia japonica*) will feed on hundreds of different hardwood species. The insects, depending on the species, range in color from brown to black, and can have spots, stripes, or metallic shine (fig. 9.8). The beetles range from 2 to 4 centimeters (cm) (3/4 to 1 1/2 in) length and can fly great distances. The feeding activities of the adults are capable of damaging the stem and defoliating hardwood seedlings. Damage to the stems may result in top dieback or infection by fungi. Damage to the leaves can range from marginal, interveinal, to complete skeletonizing of the leaves. Severe outbreaks may result in defoliation that can reduce seedling growth resulting in stunting and poor appearance that may need to be culled. Nursery beds near *Quercus* spp., bodies of water, and lights tend to have increased incidence compared with areas away from those nursery borders. The beetles can appear suddenly and quickly damage seedlings. An active insect monitoring program should be part of a nursery's daily activities. Insects can be controlled with timely applications of foliar insecticides that can provide either contact, stomach, or systemic activity (table 9.4).

Grasshoppers. Insects similar to the beetles in their feeding activities and damage include those in the order *Orthoptera* in the genus *Melanoplus*. Many different grasshopper species within this genus have large wings and can fly great distances to nurseries and feed upon the foliage of susceptible hardwood seedlings. The population of this insect varies greatly from year to year and is closely tied to the temperatures and moisture. Severe outbreaks are typically preceded by several years of hot, dry summers and warm winters. In contrast, cool, wet winters interfere with the insect's life cycle, decreasing its numbers and its potential risk on hardwood seedlings. An active insect monitoring program that examines hardwood foliage for the presence or sign of feeding damage will keep managers alert to the potential for treatment. To con-

Figure 9.8—Adult stage of white grubs in the genus Phyllophaga *feed on hardwood stems and foliage. The larval stage of this insect feeds on seedling root systems causing stunting and mortality. (Photo by Scott Enebak.)*

firm damage caused by grasshopper feeding, look for ragged feeding damage on the stem or the foliage that may have a shredded appearance. Grasshoppers can be controlled with contact, stomach, or systemic insecticides (table 9.4).

Caterpillars. Caterpillars are the immature (larval) stage of moths and butterflies in the order Lepidoptera. Generally, moths are drab colored and active at night, while butterflies are colorful and active during the day. Both have species within their respective groups where adults will lay their eggs on emerging hardwood seedlings and the subsequent larvae (caterpillars) will feed on the foliage of seedlings during the growing season. One of the more detrimental larvae on hardwood trees is the gypsy moth; it has defoliated and killed thousands of acres of forests throughout the Eastern United States. Fortunately, their life cycle is such that the gypsy moth is not an issue in hardwood nurseries. There are, however, a few notable caterpillars that can become established in hardwood seedling beds. These include caterpillars in the genus *Anisota* with the common names of spiny, orange-striped, and pink-striped oakworms. These larvae feed on many *Quercus* species as well as *Carya* and *Betula*. Other less common larvae that occur in hardwood seedling beds include the variable oakleaf caterpillar and the green-striped maple worm. These larva feed on *Quercus*, Acer and *Ulmus* species. Like other hardwood seedling insects, a monitoring program that examines hardwood foliage for their presence or signs of foliage feeding damage will keep managers alert to the potential for treatment. Most of these caterpillars can be controlled with contact, stomach, or systemic insecticides (table 9.4).

Leaf-tiers, leaf-rollers, and leaf-miners. Within the Lepidopera order is a subset of caterpillars that feed on the foliage of hardwood seedlings either within a tent-like structure formed by the insect (leaf-rollers or leaf-tiers) or within the upper and lower leaf surface (leaf miners). Leaf-tiers bind two or more leaves together with strands of silk where it then feeds, rests, and hides from predators within the leaves (fig. 9.9). A leaf-roller folds or rolls one leaf and binds it with silk strands that it produces. Like the leaf-tier, the larva of the leaf-roller will feed, rest, and hide from predators within the rolled leaf. Leaf-miners are small larva that feed between the upper and lower surface of leaves that create mines, blotches, or leaf deformities. Holding the leaf up to the light will reveal small larva through the semi-transparent damaged areas. While there are many different leaf-tiers found in North America, one of the most common leaf-tiers is *Croesia semippurpurana*, a small green larva that prefers *Quercus* spp. A few common leaf-rollers include *Archips semiferanus*, *A. argyrosplilus*, and *Choristoneura fractivittanna* that feed mostly on *Quercus* spp. but will feed on other hardwood seedlings as well. There are many different species of leaf-mining insects associated with hardwood species and include the solitary oak leaf-miner (*Camararia hamadryadella*), the gregarious oak leaf-miner (*C. cincinnatiella*), the elm leaf-miner (*Fenusa ulmi*), and the birch leaf-miner (*F. pusilla*). These are specialized insects that, because of their unique feeding habits (between the upper and lower epidermal leaf cells), tend to be host-specific. Damage usually results in necrotic, brown leaf tissue that may be cast if severe enough. Like other hardwood defoliating insects, the leaf-miners, leaf-tiers, and leaf-rollers can be controlled with timely applications of foliar insecticides that can be either contact, stomach, or systemic (table 9.4).

Figure 9.9*—A number of insects in the order* Lepidoptera *(butterflies and moths) will roll or tie up leaves and feed within the leaf nest. (Photo by Scott Enebak.)*

The effects of these insects on seedling health, vigor, and survival are relative to the number of insects and the size

Figure 9.10*—White grub larvae are always "C-shaped" and feed on their sides. With a 2- to 3-year life cycle, these insects are capable of killing seedlings through root feeding activity. (Photo by Scott Enebak.)*

of the seedling. Many leaf-miners on a small seedling are more detrimental than a similar number of insects on a larger seedling. While no one likes the appearance of foliage insects on their seedlings, when the seedlings drop their leaves in the fall, the evidence of foliage damage disappears. Thus, in many cases, treating the nursery for foliage insects is more for the nursery managers' comfort than to stop actual damage to the seedlings.

Root Feeding Insects

White grubs. White grubs consist of over 100 different species within the genera *Diplotaxis, Dichelonyx, Serica,* and *Catalpa* and are found throughout North America. They are most severe in newly established nurseries, 2 to 3 years after soil fumigation, and on agricultural sites being converted to forests. The larva are always "C-shaped," generally white, and are found near seedling roots upon which they feed (fig. 9.10). All hardwood species are susceptible. Root systems will appear sparse and have symptoms of chewing and gouging of lateral and tap roots. Seedling foliage will turn yellow, then brown, and cause stunting and seedling mortality. Infested areas will appear stunted in patches within and across a nursery bed as the larva feed and move through the soil. As few as one white grub per square foot is capable of causing significant seedling damage. Adults of the larval stage are May, June, green, and Japanese Beetles. Their life cycle is 2 to 3 years in the soil, with damage increasing each successive year post fumigation, due to increasing relative larva numbers and size of the larva. Adults feed on *Quercus* spp., thus nursery areas surrounded by oaks have increased incidence and damage due to the larval stage. Because adult beetles are attracted to light and are lazy fliers (less than 100 yards), sowing seedlings away from mature oaks near the nursery will go a long way to minimizing the effect of white grubs on seedling damage. By far, the most effective method for control is soil fumigation with broad-spectrum preplant soil fumigants prior to sowing. Combinations of methyl bromide, chloropicrin, or 1,3-dichloropropene have been shown to be the most effective in reducing white grub populations (table 9.1). Spot treatment with granular or soil drenches of insecticides is also effective for control (table 9.4).

Cutworms. Another soil-inhabiting insect that feeds upon hardwood seedlings are the cutworms in the genus *Noctiduae*. These small (1/4 in) (6 mm) worms or larva can be dull gray, brown, black, striped, or spotted, are found throughout the Eastern United States, and can destroy thousands of hardwood seedlings in a week. They are stout, soft-bodied, smooth, and tend to curl up in a ball when

***Figure 9.11**—Cutworms feed on small succulent hardwood seedling stems and cotyledons early in the growing season. (Photo by Scott Enebak.)*

disturbed (fig. 9.11). The larvae hide during the day and emerge at night to feed upon the young succulent stems, cotyledons, leaves, and roots of hardwood seedlings. They tend to cut the cotyledons/leaves from the stem, leaving just a small stub of a seedling stem remaining, thus their name: cutworms. Because of their size, smaller seeded hardwoods are more susceptible to their feeding activities than larger seeded species, and they are more problematic during the early periods of germination than later in the season. As with white grubs, broad-spectrum preplant soil fumigants have been shown to be the most effective in reducing cutworm levels (table 9.1). Monitoring nursery beds early in the season for their damage and spot treating with granular or liquid insecticides are recommended (table 9.4).

Animal Damage Management

Seed from mature hardwoods and small seedlings in the forest environment are a normal and natural source of nutrition for numerous mammals (mice, voles, deer, and rabbits) and birds in the wild. Acorns are a favorite for squirrels and deer, pecans are crow magnets, and rabbits prefer succulent flowering dogwood seedlings. However, when these same seed and seedlings are planted in rows for human use (reforestation), animals are just doing what is natural for them—looking for something to eat (food)—and interfering with a manager's objective of selling trees. Unlike diseases and insects that tend to be random and arbitrary, animals and birds are searching for seed and seedlings; it is all they do, all the time, and they will never stop trying.

Deer

One of the more troublesome mammals is the white-tailed deer (*Odocoileus virginianus*), which has seen populations reach damaging levels throughout its range due to harvest restrictions and modified land use (Russell et al. 2001). The effect of browse damage on hardwood seedlings depends on the amount of browse, the season of browse, and the relative seedling size. Smaller seedlings are more susceptible to damage than larger seedlings. With respect to *Quercus* spp., deer browse that occurs during the growing season is more detrimental than deer browse during the dormant season (Woolery and Jacobs 2010). To reduce deer damage, numerous odor and taste repellants have been developed; unfortunately, no standard method to test repellent effectiveness has been adopted. Currently, there are three types of repellents: area, contact, and systemic. Area repellents act by odor and include things such as soap bars, blood meal, feather meal, and even human hair balls. Contact repellents are sprayed or dusted onto the foliage of hardwood seedlings to protect against browse. These include compounds such as hot sauce, Ro-Pel®, and Hinder®. Systemics are compounds that are applied to the growing area and are taken up by the plant, making them unpalatable to deer feeding. Their ease of use also mitigates the problems of washing away or retreating that is required with contact repellents. A systematic analysis of deer repellent products by Hani and Conover reported that Deer-Away Big Game Repellent® and predator odors were more effective than all other repellents tested (El Hani and Conover 1997). However, while there were differences in effectiveness and cost of application, even the best deer repellent did not reduce browse to zero. So, if any damage is unacceptable, then another method must be employed.

Scare tactics are steps taken to frighten deer away from nursery beds that would reduce damage caused by their feeding or migrating activities. These include motion-sensing pyrotechnics, noise, light, and irrigation. While good in theory, pyrotechnics (fireworks, gunfire, propane cannons) tend to annoy neighbors in urban settings, and studies have shown that deer get used to the disturbance and over time gradually ignore the noise. Thus, scare tactics could work in situations where short-term control is needed.

Short of deer repellents and scare tactics, by far the most effective method to minimize deer damage is a well-built fence. Deer can breach fences by going over, through, or under, but studies have shown that an 8-foot (ft) (2.4-meter [m]) fence surrounding nursery beds sown to hardwood seedlings would keep 99 percent of the deer out (USDA 2007). Of the 23 nurseries reporting on methods to control deer, all that had put in a deer exclosure fence mentioned it being "by far the absolute best monies we ever spent." In many situations, the entire nursery does not need to be fenced, only the portion that is used to sow hardwoods and allow for a complete crop rotation (conifer, cover crop, etc.) within that area. Access gates into the area need to be the same height of the fence and must be secured during the growing season. As one nursery manager noted, "You don't want a bunch of deer enclosed in the hardwood seedling beds, either."

Birds

Seed predation by birds on certain hardwood species can result in complete failure of the seedling crop to poor stocking levels due to seedling culls. Minimizing bird predation of hardwood seed can be done via physical, scare tactics, poisons, and repellants. Many different bird species are involved with seed predation, depending on the hardwood seed. Crows (*Corvus* spp.), common grackles (*Quiscalus* spp.), mourning doves (*Zenaida* spp.), turkeys (*Meleagris* spp.), and the common blackbird (*Turdus* spp.) are the most common seed predators found in hardwood nurseries. Like a deer fence, a netting constructed over hardwood seedbeds after sowing reduces predation to zero. This method is costly in both labor and materials to construct and then remove later in the growing season. Tactics using shotguns, predator calls, and scarecrows have some success but, like deer, birds eventually become accustomed to their use and ignore all tactics to frighten them away, feeding on the seed at will.

Poisons (avicides) are available, but their restrictions by State and Federal laws, as well as their lack of selectivity for killing bird species, keeps their use in controlling hardwood seed predation to only the most severe cases. One step below poisons is the use of seed repellents (table 9.5). As a standard practice in conifer bareroot nurseries, seed is pretreated with thiram prior to sowing. This works both as a fungicide to control damping-off and as a mammal and bird repellent. Despite its effectiveness on conifers, few (1 out of 84) hardwood nurseries use thiram as a seed treatment to control damping-off (South and Carey 2008). A seed predation trial conducted by the Southern Forest Nursery Management Cooperative in 2010 reported that seed color was the most important factor in determining whether or not seed was eaten (Starkey et al. 2010). Simply coating seed with a clay powder reduced seed predation over all other treatments tested. Other trials on seed predation noted that both seed size and mulch type affected seed predation by birds. Generally, the larger the seed, the more seed predation and the smaller the seed, the less seed predation. The addition of mulches on seedbeds decreased seed predation as seed size increased, but increased seed mortality of small seed. Thus, manipulating the appearance of the seedbeds with the use of seed treatments and mulches can reduce seed predation. Similar to deer repellents, there are a myriad of products available for discouraging bird predation. The efficacy of some of these products in hardwood seeding beds has not been tested, but some possible seed treatments to control bird predation can be found in table 9.5.

***Table 9.5**—Bird and mammal repellents used on hardwood seed and foliage to deter seed and seedling predation.*

Predation	Compound	Active Ingredient
Seed/foliage	Defiant	Thiram 75%
	Flight control	9,10 Anthraquinone
	Deer-away big game repellent	36% Putrescent whole egg solids
Seed	Chlorpyrifos	Tchlorpyrifos
	Kaolin clay	Kaolin clay

Small Mammals

Small mammals such as rabbits, mice, moles, and gophers can damage hardwood seedling production either by seed predation (mice, moles, squirrels, and chipmunks), seedling feeding (mice, rabbits, and gophers) or tunneling activities (gophers, mice, and voles). Eliminating their habitat near seedling beds will go a long way to keep the mammals away from the nursery and out of the seedling beds. Mowing the grass and keeping fence rows clean of trees removes the areas that would allow small mammals a place to rest and hide from predators and away from seedling beds. Similar to bird predation, small mammals' feeding activities can significantly affect seeding production. Seed treatment with thiram has been shown to deter seed predation from small mammals and the use of thiram as a spray will deter rabbit and deer from feeding on seedlings. Bait stations that attract small mammals to food treated with poison have also been shown to be effective, as well as trapping (gophers) and using firearms with a permit.

References

Cram, M.M.; Fraedrich, S.W. 2005. Management options for control of a stunt and needle nematode in southern forest nurseries. In: Dumroese, R.K.; Riley, L.E.; Landis, T.D., tech. coords. 2005. National proceedings: Forest and Conservation Nursery Associations. Proceedings RMRS-P-35. Fort Collins, CO: U.S. Department of Agriculture, Forest Service, Rocky Mountain Research Station.

El Hani, A.; Conover, M.R. 1997. Comparative analysis of deer repellents. In: Mason, J.R., ed. Repellents in wildlife management. Fort Collins, CO: U.S. Department of Agriculture, National Wildlife Research Center: 147–155.

Russell, F.L.; Zippin, D.P.; Fowler, N.L. 2001. Effects of white-tailed deer (*Odocoileus virginianus*) on plants, plant populations and communities: a review. American Midland Naturalist. 146: 1–26.

Starkey, T.E.; Quicke, M.; Enebak, S.A. 2010. The efficacy of commercial repellents to deter seed predation. Southern Forest Nursery Management Cooperative, Auburn University. 6 p.

South, D.B.; Carey, W.A. 2008. Use of pesticides in bareroot hardwood seedbeds in the Southern United States. Tree Planters' Notes. 53: 57–62.

South, D.B.; Enebak, S.A. 2005. Integrated pest management practices in southern pine nurseries. New Forests. 31: 1–19.

U.S. Department of Agriculture (USDA), National Wildlife Research Center (NWRC). 2007 Research Update. Summer 2007. p 10.

Woolery, P.O.; Jacobs, D.F. 2011. Photosynthetic assimilation and carbohydrate allocation of *Quercus rubra* seedlings in response to simulated herbivory. Annuals of Forest Science. DOI: 10.1007/s13595-011-0064-4.

Inventory Methods

Inventory Methods

10

T. Starkey

Tom Starkey is retired from Southern Forest Nursery Management Cooperative, Auburn University, Auburn, AL

Outline

Facing Page: *Inventory methods photo collage. (Photos by Chris Rosier.)*

Introduction

The Value of an Inventory

An inventory is a complete listing of the goods and stock produced by a company, including a value of these goods. It does not matter whether the company sells toothpaste, cars, aspirin, or tree seedlings. The ultimate goal is the same and involves several factors: (1) making a reliable estimate of the number of goods produced, (2) making an estimate of the marketability or quality of the goods produced, and (3) making these estimates within certain economic constraints.

Those working in the forest seedling nursery industry realize there are stumbling blocks to accurate inventories. The first stumbling block is that it is impossible to count (inventory) every seedling in the nursery. Nursery managers must settle for an estimate. How close this estimate is to the true number of seedlings varies by species grown and how much time (money) managers are willing to invest in the inventory. The second stumbling block is that seedlings are not of uniform quality. There is a range of acceptable seedling quality within every nursery bed. During the inventory process, the number of marketable seedlings must be estimated.

Why is an accurate inventory necessary? First and foremost, an accurate inventory is needed so those selling the seedlings know how many can be sold. A nursery manager growing 1,000,000 hardwoods should not be satisfied with a sampling error of 10 percent. This means there could be a surplus or a shortage of 100,000 seedlings at the end of the season. If hardwoods were selling for $250 per thousand seedlings, the nursery would either lose $25,000 by underestimating the true number of sellable seedlings or the nursery may need to return $25,000 to customers because it oversold the true number of seedlings.

An inventory is deemed accurate when, at the end of the season, the number of seedlings reported in the fall inventory closely approximates the number of seedlings sold by the sales team, plus any unsold seedlings. The ability to achieve accurate inventories have always been an issue of discussion between nursery managers growing hardwood seedlings and administrative accounting personnel. Pine inventories are generally much more accurate than hardwood inventories. The difference is due to the large amount of variation associated with hardwood seedlings compared to pine seedlings. It is probably safe to say that because of this variability, the accuracy of hardwood inventories will seldom be as good as pine inventories.

Types of Inventories

There are various types of inventories performed in forest seedling nurseries (Rosier 2015). The first is an inventory of seed in storage and is generally only done in nurseries with long-term seed storage. The second type of inventory is conducted the first few weeks after sowing to determine sowing efficiency and detect any early problems in seed germination. The spring and fall seedling inventories are the third type. The fourth type of inventory is a history plot to track seed germination and/or the growth of seedlings during the season. The fifth and last type of inventory is the packing inventory, which is done at the time of shipping, to determine quantity and quality of seedlings shipped to customers.

This chapter focuses on seedling inventories conducted in the spring and fall as well as history plots. In the Southeastern United States, the spring inventory is usually conducted in June or July, after germination is complete. The primary purpose of the spring inventory is to provide nursery administration with an estimate of the number of potentially sellable seedlings by species and seedlot. Since at this point it is not possible to determine the actual number of cull seedlings (those that will not reach sellable quality standards), nurseries will use past experience to estimate a certain percent loss during the growing season. The spring inventory also provides valuable information as to seedling density and total linear bed feet of each seedlot or species. In addition, problems due to washout or poor germination should be noted at this time, as they will provide valuable information that can increase the efficiency of the fall seedling inventory.

The most important inventory is the fall seedling inventory, usually conducted in September. It provides an estimate of the number of shippable seedlings per linear bed foot. Very seldom do the spring and fall inventories match. The fall inventory also will estimate the number of seedling considered as culls, which usually result from variances in height, root collar diameter (RCD), stem form, or other abnormalities or diseases. Providing a reliable estimate of the number of shippable seedlings is a little more difficult due to the fact that the seedlings may continue to grow until they lose their leaves. Nurseries will routinely estimate that the final RCD of a pine seedlot will increase by 0.5 to 1.0 millimeters (mm) between the time of inventory and lifting. However, for hardwoods, nurseries do not commonly allow for a similar increase in RCD between the fall inventory and lifting, since most hardwood species stop growth in the fall before conifers.

Variation Within Inventories

The objective of all inventories is not to measure every seedling in the nursery—this would be impossible and/or cost prohibitive. Rather, samples taken at multiple locations within the nursery are averaged to provide an estimate of the true number of seedlings in the nursery.

Variation in seedling numbers and quality is inherent to every nursery bed. For example, if you were to pull and measure every seedling in a 1-foot (ft) (30-centimeter [cm]) swath across a nursery bed in 3 locations, you would quickly observe the following variation:

1. The total number of seedlings will vary in the 3 locations sampled.
2. The number of seedlings in each of the drills across a counting frame will vary.
3. The seedling size (both RCD and height) across a nursery bed within a counting frame will vary.
4. The number of seedlings per square foot will vary.

Sources of variation frequently common to both hardwood and conifer nursery beds may include washed out areas due to irrigation or heavy rains and areas of loss due to insect or disease problems.

Sources of Hardwood Seedling Variation

The variation in hardwood seedlings is substantially greater than is found with conifer seedlings. Some of the common sources of within hardwood production variation are listed below:

- Since nearly all hardwood seed originates from open-pollinated, wild-collected trees, the genetic and resulting phenotypic variation can be substantial.
- Very seldom do nursery managers have seed germination data as they do with conifers. Therefore, planting densities are based generally upon previous years' germination, which can vary from year to year.
- It is not uncommon for one seedlot at a nursery to be composed of seed collected over a wide geographic area resulting in germination variation.
- Even when the seed is sized for sowing the calculation of seeds per pound needed to calibrate the sower is much more variable than with conifers.
- The stratification methodology used by the nursery can interact with the maturity of the seed at the time of collection and result in germination variation.
- Nursery managers have reported that the type of planter used can affect seedbed densities, resulting in additional sources of variation. It is very important that the person responsible for the sowing can actually see the seed being sown to assure the sowing machine is functioning properly.
- Hardwood species that require endomycorrhizae must have uniform distribution of the endomycorrhizae within the seedbed.
- Animal and bird predation can result in seedbed variation.

These sources of variation can result in the following seedbed variation:

- Erratic germination of seed.
- Rapidly germinating seed shading out slower germinating seed, resulting in RCD and height variation.
- Varying number of seed per bed drill.
- Areas of seed bed with either no seed germination or erratic growth of germinates.

When seedbed densities are not consistent within a seedlot, resulting in erratic growth, a bareroot hardwood nursery inventory requires many more sample plots to achieve the same degree of sampling accuracy as a bareroot conifer nursery. All of the above-mentioned sources of variation must be taken into consideration when formulating an inventory plan.

Inventory Tools

Although methods of recording or calculating actual inventories may vary, all nurseries use what is called a "counting frame." This tool, made from either metal or polyvinyl (PVC), is used to standardize the area of the nursery bed being inventoried. Since all nursery beds are 4 ft (1.2 meters [m]) across, all counting frames are 4 ft (1.2 m) long (or slightly larger) to sample across the bed. The width of the frame varies among nurseries. Frames may be 12, 9, or 6 inches (in) (30.5, 23, or 15 centimeters [cm]) wide, with the 12-in (30.5-cm) being most common in both hardwood and pine inventories. It is important that only one size be used by a nursery.

Counting frames are used to calculate the number of seedlings per square foot. When a 12-in (30.5-cm) frame is used, the total number of seedlings counted within the 4-ft (1.2-m) frame is divided by 4 to provide seedlings per square foot. When a 9-in (23-cm) frame is used, the total number of seedlings within the 4-ft (1.2-m) frame is divided by 3. When a 6-in (15-cm) frame is used, the

Table 10.1—Calculations using different size counting frames.

Width of a 4-foot counting frame (in)	Total number of seedlings counted within frame	Appropriate counting frame divisor	Seedlings per square foot
12	80	4	20
9	60	3	20
6	40	2	20
12	75	4	18.75
9	43	3	14.33
6	27	2	13.50

ft = feet. in = inches.

total number of seedlings within the 4-ft (1.2-m) frame is divided by 2 (table 10.1). With the large amount of variation associated with hardwood inventories, a 12-in (30.5-cm) counting frame is recommended.

Some hardwood species have large canopies, which may make it difficult to place the counting frame over the nursery bed. One modification that can be made with PVC counting frames is to have an end that can be removed. With the end removed, the frame is slid across the bed at the ground line and the removable end replaced. Care must be taken that long sides of the frame remain parallel as it is placed on the ground and slid across the nursery bed before the removable end is attached.

When a counting frame is placed over seedlings and pushed down to the soil, the sides of frame frequently bend seedlings over. These are called border seedlings. It is important that all employees involved in the inventory be made aware of how to count these border seedlings. If the ground line of the seedling originates within the counting frame, it should be included in the frame count. However, if the top of seedling is bent over into the interior section of the frame, but the seedling originates outside the frame, it should not be included in the frame count.

Typically, nursery inventories involve several crews assigned to specific areas. Each crew, generally two or three people, has a counting frame and a method of recording the counts (either manually or on a data recorder). With a two-person crew, each person is responsible for counting seedling drills within half the 4 ft (1.2 m) bed. With a three-person crew, the third person generally is responsible for locating the plots and recording the counts.

Sampling Designs

Four sampling designs are commonly discussed when determining how to inventory a nursery (May 1984, Barton and Clements 1961, Duffield 1963, Mullin 1964, Mullin et al. 1955, Ware et al. 1967): random sample, stratified random sample, systematic sample, and stratified systematic sample.

Each of these designs has limitations in its use in a nursery situation.

Random Sample

It is generally assumed that random sampling is better than nonrandom sampling, which may introduce bias into the inventory. This method might work if a nursery only grew one seedlot of one species and seedlings were very uniform. However, all nurseries grow multiple species and frequently multiple seedlots within each species. (For the purposes of this chapter, a "seedlot" is understood to be the smallest uniquely identified population from the same genetic source.) The total number of seedlings in each seedlot may vary. In this case, a truly random sample presents some problems. For example, one seedlot (A) may account for 30 percent of the total hardwoods; the second seedlot (B), 5 percent; the third seedlot (C), 42 percent; the fourth seedlot (D), 17 percent; and the fifth seedlot (E), 6 percent of the total hardwoods.

If a manager decides that 50 samples (plots) are to be taken across the nursery, the location of any of these plots is decided randomly. For example, if the total length of all the bed rows is 6,000 feet, 50 numbers between 1 and 6,000 would be generated. These would be the location of the 50 plots. One problem with this method may be that the seedlots with fewer seedlings (B and E) may not have any plots fall within those seedlots. Another problem by using a strictly random approach is that seedlots with the larger number of seedlings may have a disproportional number of plots. For example, seedlot A and C may have 40 of the total number of plots, leaving just 10 plots for the other seedlots.

Stratified Random Sampling

In this sampling design, all areas of the nursery are divided into units called "strata." Each stratum must be more uniform within than compared to the neighboring stratum. Each seedlot within a nursery would make up individual strata, since each seedlot is more similar then neighboring seedlots. Once the strata are identified, sample plots within each stratum are taken. This sampling design achieves better sampling accuracy than a random sampling design.

The efficiency of this sampling design can further be increased by identifying additional stratum within a strata. For example, a strata consisting of one seedlot may not be uniform because of areas where stand density is low due to poor germination. Another example may be a nursery unit of a single seedlot but further divided into stratum representing large and small seed. The efficiency of the sampling design can be increased by creating substrata that include these areas of low stand density or seed size.

Systematic Sampling

As the name implies, when using systematic sampling within a nursery, sampling units are not chosen at random but are located at fixed intervals. Sometimes the location of the starting point may be chosen at random and then every sampling point after that fixed at a designated interval. A very simple example of a systematic sampling design is to locate sample plots in the third and seventh riser in every fourth bed.

This sampling design is simple to administer and can be done by unskilled workers and results in fewer mistakes. However, a nursery inventory requires all seedlots be sampled, which could be a problem with this method. Also, this sampling design is not favored by statisticians due to its lack of randomness (Mullin 1964, Freese 1962).

Stratified Systematic Sampling

The random, stratified, and systematic sampling designs discussed above all have advantages and disadvantages. Most nurseries in the Southern United States have chosen to combine some of the advantages of the above methods into a fourth design called the stratified systematic sampling, in an effort to increase sampling efficiency (May 1984).

The key to this method is the stratification of the various seedlots within the nursery. First, seedlots are located on a nursery map and designated as strata to be sampled. Areas of nonuniform seedling density within seedlots may also be identified as strata to be sampled. Sampling can begin once all areas of the nursery with seedlings have been assigned to one and only one strata. At this point, there are two approaches commonly used to determine where to locate individual sample plots.

The first approach is to start in the first bed of the first stratum and place a sample plot every "X number" of feet or every "X number" of irrigation risers. The second approach is to start in the first bed of the first stratum and randomly determine "X number" of sampling points within each bed. The number of sampling points per nursery bed is predetermined and based primarily upon previous experience with adjustments made due to seedlot size.

Number and Location of Plots Needed

The number of plots recommended for sampling hardwood seedlings varies between nurseries and even between nurseries within the same ownership. There are various statistical procedures available (May 1984) to determine the number of plots needed, such as using a sample size formula, a specified error limit, or a graphic approach based on historic plot numbers used at the nursery. Current inventory data recorders handle this process automatically. Based on a survey of growers, the most common method currently used is to start with a fixed number of plots based on the nursery manager's experience with that seedlot. This minimum number may or may not be adjusted, depending upon whether a sampling efficiency is calculated. One nursery surveyed that grows fewer than 500,000 hardwoods will start with 4 to 5 samples per seedlot and increase this number as needed. Another nursery growing more than 500,000 hardwoods specifies 8 to 10 plots per seedlot, with a minimum of 3 plots per nursery bed per seedlot, and adjusted as needed. The actual sample plot location may be random or fixed. One nursery using fixed distances between plots in its conifer inventory follows the same practice when sampling the hardwoods. This nursery recommends that all plot locations be evenly spaced across the nursery seedlot. The precise spacing between sampling plots per seedlot is calculated by dividing the total linear bed length in feet by the total number of samples needed. Limits are specified that no plot should be within 40 ft (12.2 m) of another plot or more than 200 ft (61 m) from another. The starting point of first sample is randomly chosen so that it falls within the first 15 ft (4.6 m) of the seedlot.

Data To Be Recorded

In the spring inventory, the total number of living seedlings is reported. This number, minus a nursery cull factor, is used to determine the number of seedling available for sale. Since the ultimate goal of the fall seedling inventory is to determine the number of shippable seedlings, nursery workers conducting the inventory must have a clear understanding of the target specifications for each species. This is a monumental task since it is not uncommon for each State or counties within a State to have specific minimum quality standards. All specifications would include a minimum RCD and minimum height. Any stem abnormalities such as low stem forking or galls would also be important. At the fall inventory, these morphological variables would determine whether a hardwood seedling would be shippable or a cull. Although numerous other variables from previously collected history plots or independent seedling quality evaluations (Wilson and Jacobs 2006) may be considered, they are not normally part of the fall inventory.

Only two items are normally recorded for each sample plot during the fall inventory: the number of seedlings that meet or exceed specifications and the number of culls. One nursery reported that nursery workers will carry calipers to measure seedlings if they are not sure whether a seedling is a cull or shippable. Another nursery may measure the height and RCD on three seedlings within each plot. The nursery manager will then be able to estimate the number shippable seedlings per linear bed foot when all subplots are totaled.

Data Analysis and Determination of the Need for More Sample Plots

The data collected from the field is entered—either by hand or from an electronic data logger—into a computer spreadsheet, such as MS Excel, for analysis. Two approaches can be used to determine if additional plots are required to be within the desired level of accuracy, which is most commonly 5 percent.

The following analysis should be done on each stratum separately to determine if additional plots are needed before combining stratum for a single seedlot.

Method 1

1. Seedling counts are calculated from the inventory to provide an estimate of the number of plantable seedlings per linear bed foot.
2. For each plot, the coefficient of variation (CV) is calculated either by formula or by dividing sample standard deviation by the sample mean and multiplying by 100. The coefficient of variation is expressed as a percent and is a good tool for comparing samples that have different size means. The larger the CV the greater amount of variation. Large amounts of variation from plot to plot are undesirable and will give a large coefficient of variation.
3. The observed level of precision of the mean estimate is calculated by taking the square root of the following equation: $((4*CV^2)/n)$ where n is the number of samples taken.
4. If observed precision is less than 5, no additional plots are required. If it is more than 5, additional plots are required. If observed precision is very large, consideration should be given to further stratifying the plot so that areas within the strata are more similar to one another than to areas outside the strata. The number of additional plots needed can either be determined by trial and error or by solving the following equation for n: $n = ((4*CV^2)/25)$ where $25 = (\pm 5\%^2)$ (Rosier 2015).

Method 2

1. Seedling counts are calculated to provide an estimate of the number of plantable seedlings per linear bed foot.
2. A determination is made as to how wide of a confidence interval (usually 95-percent) about the sample mean you desire. In other words, for the seedling density per sample plot, you may desire that the average sample mean be ± 2 seedlings per linear bed foot.
3. For each plot, a 95-percent confidence interval is calculated. If the confidence interval is within the ± 2 seedlings per linear bed foot, no additional plots are needed. If it is greater than the desired limit, additional plots should be taken.
4. This calculation of the confidence interval can be done in Excel either with the formula function or using the Data Analysis function choosing Data Summary.

Once the degree of desired accuracy has been achieved, the number of seedlings per linear bed foot for the stratum within seedlots can be calculated and combined for the total seedlot.

Another similar method to determine the required sample size can be found in van Belle (2002), chapter 2; this provides an example for calculating sample size using the coefficient of variation.

It is important at this point to distinguish how lifting of conifers differ from lifting of hardwoods. When a conifer nursery lifts 10 linear bed feet (3 m), all seedlings are generally placed into the box or bag. When a hardwood nursery lifts 10 linear bed feet (3 m), only the shippable seedlings are lifted and placed into a bag, leaving the culls in the field. Due to the large amount of variation associated with hardwood inventories, it is not uncommon for a nursery to revise its estimate of the number of shippable seedlings per linear foot during the lifting season. Following the fall inventory, the nursery manager has an estimate of the number of hardwood seedlings per linear foot prior to lifting. After the first few larger orders are lifted, the nursery manager should compare how many bed feet were actually lifted versus how many were estimated to be lifted based on the fall inventory. If these numbers differ substantially, additional sample plots should be added and the new seedling estimate per linear bed foot recalculated. Before adjusting the inventory numbers, however, the nursery managers should determine if the nursery beds lifted are representative of the remaining beds for that seedlot. Although this evaluation procedure is valid for conifers, it is more frequently done for hardwoods because of the increased variation within the seedbed.

Life History Plots

Many nurseries use history plots to provide valuable information for management decisions and tracking seedling development (Belcher 1964). As the name implies, life history plots track various aspects of seedling development and growth over the life of the seedlings. History plots were initially developed as a means of both tracking seedling growth during the season and providing seedling counts for inventories (Belcher 1972). Today, history plots are used primarily as a decision-making tool for information on the current seedling crop, although information from previous years should also be utilized to make decisions most effectively.

Types of History Plots

Nursery history plots can either be permanently established plots that are remeasured or random plots that are relocated at each measurement interval. In either case, history plots have two objectives. First, nearly all nurseries use history plots to monitor germination following sowing. The rate of seed germination is generally tracked over several weeks in permanently established plots within each seedlot. Once germination is complete, the plots are either abandoned or utilized in the next type of history plot.

The second type of history plot is one that monitors seedling growth throughout the growing season. The type of data collected can be as minimal as recording just RCD or more extensive, including multiple parameters such as RCD, height, root development, and seedling nutrition using foliar nutrient analysis (Wilson et al. 2006). Information may be recorded by tracking all seedlings within the designated area, a set number of random seedlings within the area, or specific seedlings within the area. One cautionary regarding the use of permanent plots is that repeated measurements of the same seedlings over the course of a growing season may result in seedlings with a smaller RCD than comparable seedlings outside the plot.

Plot Establishment

Whether history plots are used to monitor germination, follow seedling development, or both, plots should be established immediately after sowing the seed using either a random or systematic procedure. The most common method to establish plot location is to place a counting frame across the seedling bed and the four corners marked with either pin flags or long nails. Twine is used to connect the four corners and establish the plot perimeter. Seed or seedlings that may lie directly on the perimeter are frequently removed so as to better define which seeds or seedlings are within the plot and will be measured.

Measuring History Plots

When only seed germination is of concern, weekly measurements that begin at germination and continue to full germ are the standard. If, during the period of counting, any seed germinates and then dies or fails to properly send down a root radical, that seed should be removed from the area, noted in the data sheet, and then added to all subsequent counts in order to calculate total germination (May 1984, Belcher 1964).

If the history plots are being used to monitor seedling growth, nursery staff who will be recording the data must be properly trained on how to use calipers to measure RCD. Training should include the proper positioning of the calipers on the stem of the seedling and the proper operation of the calipers. Many calipers have two sets of jaws (arms) for measuring items internally or externally. The external jaws are used to measure RCD. The external jaws of many brands are very narrow at the tip of the reference arms and much flatter behind the narrow tip. In order to avoid squeezing the stem too hard using the narrow tip and damaging the seedling, the flatter portion of the arms should be used. The arms should just touch the stem to obtain a proper reading.

History Plot Data Use

There are two primary issues to be addressed when history plots are used to monitor seedling development. First, the nursery manager needs to know if the growth of the current seedling crop is ahead or behind that of previous years. Second, the nursery manager seeks to compare the quality of the current seedling crop to that of previous years. Similar seedling quality data must be available from previous years to address these basic issues and grouped together to generate a generalized growth curve. The relationship of RCD to seedling age is a good example. History plots that monitor seedling quality can be specific to a seedlot that is sown year after year, or more generalized to represent a grouping of similar seedlots. For example, a generalized growth curve for oaks would not be helpful because of the growth differences among hardwoods. Growth curves specific to a species or closely related species would provide better information.

Although growth curves related to RCD and height are the most frequently used, any seedling parameter that is measured routinely can be included. At any point during the growing season when seedling measurements are made, they should be compared to the growth curves generated from previous years' data to determine if the current seedling growth is on target, ahead of, or behind previous years. Based on the results, fertilization or irrigation can be altered to bring the growth in line with previous years.

Important Statistical Terms

Listed below are the definition of some statistical terms that are used in nursery inventories and data summaries.

Measures of Central Tendencies:

Mean. The sum of all the values in the data set divided by the number of values. Used interchangeably with the average of the values.

Median. When all the values of a data set are listed in numerical order, the median is the value at the middle of the list.

Measures of Dispersion (Variability):

Coefficient of variation. A measure of the spread of data points in a data series around the mean. It is calculated by dividing the standard deviation by the mean. Large values indicate that variation is high, which is undesirable.

Confidence interval. Expresses the probability the sample mean will fall between two set values. The confidence interval can take any number of probabilities, with the most common being 95 or 99 percent.

Standard deviation. A measure of the spread of a set of data from its mean. It is calculated as the square root of variance (defined below) divided by the number of samples (usually using the degrees of freedom, so the number of samples -1, denoted as n-1).

Standard error of the mean. A measure of the variation among sample means, and calculated as the standard deviation divided by the square root of the number of individuals in the sample, or "n."

Variance. The spread between numbers in a data set. Variance measures how far each number in the dataset is from the mean. Variance is calculated by taking the differences between each number in the dataset and the mean, squaring the differences (to make them positive).

References

Barton, W.W.; Clements, C.M. 1961. A systematic sampling nursery inventory procedure. Tree Planters' Notes. 46: 19–25.

Belcher, E.W. 1964. The use of history plots in the nursery. Tree Planters' Notes. 64: 27–31.

Belcher, E.W. 1972. Life history plots and inventories. Proceedings Southeast Area for Tree Nurserymen's Conference. 157: 159.

Duffield, J.W. 1963. Inventory procedure for small or specialized forest nurseries. Tree Planters' Notes. 58: 22–25.

Freese, F. 1962. Elementary forest sampling. Agric. Handb. 232. Washington, DC: U.S. Department of Agriculture, Forest Service. 91 p.

May, J.T. 1984. Inventory system. In: Lantz, C.W., ed. Southern pine nursery handbook. U.S. Department of Agriculture, Forest Service, Southern Region. 11 p.

Mullin, R.E. 1964. Comparison of sampling methods of nursery stock. Tree Planters' Notes 67: 3–8.

Mullin, R.E.; Morrison, L.M.; Schweitzer, T.T. 1955. Inventory of nursery stock. Res. Rep. 33. Ontario, Canada: Ontario Department of Lands and Forest. 64 p.

Rosier, C. 2015. Inventory methods. 2015 Forest Nursery Short Course. Auburn University, AL: Auburn University.

van Belle, G. 2002. Statistical rules of thumb. New York: John Wiley & Sons, Inc.

Ware, K.D.; Grebasch, G.; Hamilton, D.A. 1967. Sampling design and computer processing for efficient nursery inventories. Proceedings, Northeast Area Nurserymen's Conference: 27–42.

Wilson B.C.; Jacobs, D.F. 2006. Quality assessment of temperate zone deciduous hardwood seedlings. New Forests. 31: 417–433.

Bareroot Hardwood Seedling Lifting, Packing, and Storage at the Wilson State Nursery in Southern Wisconsin

11a

J.M. Vande Hey

Joseph M. Vande Hey is reforestation team leader and nursery superintendent, Wisconsin Department of Natural Resources F.G. Wilson State Nursery, Boscobel, WI

Outline

Facing Page: *Lifting and packing. (Photo by R. Overton.)*

Brief Description of Nursery Location and Crop

The Wilson State Nursery is located in Grant County in southwest Wisconsin in the Wisconsin River Valley. The soil is a deep Sparta loamy fine sand. There are about 70 acres of nursery beds under irrigation. The nursery annually distributes 2 to 8 million seedlings from a crop that consists of 35 to 40 species of Wisconsin native conifers, hardwoods, and shrubs. Stock is grown as 1-, 2-, and/or 3-year-old seedlings. Hardwoods generally make up about one-third of the annual distribution. Seedlings are used for reforestation/afforestation, conservation, and wildlife habitat. The minimum order size is a packet containing 300 tree seedlings, 500 wildlife shrubs, or 1,000 tree seedlings. Multiple species may be ordered to make up the 500 wildlife shrubs or 1,000 tree seedlings, with individual species requested in increments of 100.

Timing of Lifting and Outplanting

Hardwoods are primarily spring lifted, although if the projected workload is greater than what can be completed in the spring, then some hardwoods are lifted in the fall.

Spring Lifting

Spring lifting generally begins in mid- to late March, as the ground thaws. Sandy soils allow for a quicker thaw and entry into the fields. Sandy soils also allow for quick entry back into the fields following heavy rain. This is important because hardwoods generally provide a smaller window of opportunity to lift in the spring than do most conifers, but that will vary with species. Species like black cherry (*Prunus serotina* Ehrh.) begin to break dormancy in as little as 2 weeks after the ground thaws, while other species like the oaks (*Quercus* spp.) and black walnut (*Juglans nigra* L.) provide about 4 to 5 weeks of opportunity. As individual species reach the point of breaking dormancy, an effort is made to lift all the seedlings of that species. Most hardwood lifting is completed by mid- to late April.

Fall Lifting

When fall lifting occurs, it is usually done in very late October to mid-November, after the seedlings have been exposed to a few frosts or cold temperatures and the leaves have fallen off. Stock does not store well over winter with any leaves still present, especially when lifted wet. Leaves can be removed during the grading process but this is very labor intensive. As long as time and weather conditions allow, it is more cost-effective to let leaves fall naturally.

Outplanting

The outplanting season in southern Wisconsin generally starts in early April and progresses north over the next week or two. Most planting in southern Wisconsin is completed by early May, while continuing later into May in the north. Very little fall reforestation planting is done in Wisconsin due to the risk of frost heaving.

Seedling Preparation for Lifting – Activities and Timing

Undercutting

Hardwood seedlings that are being carried into their second growing season are generally undercut in early May of the second year. This is done for cultural reasons to get better root development and reduce top growth in the second growing season. The seedlings are undercut at a depth of about 8 inches (in) (20 centimeters [cm]) to encourage lateral root development within the 9 in (23 cm) lifting zone depth.

Top Pruning

Top pruning prepares the seedlings for distribution and outplanting. Seedlings are top cut in the fall or in the spring ahead of lifting. Seedlings are typically cut back to between 12 and 16 in (30.5 and 41 cm). Top cutting creates a more balanced seedling and prepares the seedlings for the planting site. Top cutting also allows larger quantities of seedlings to be handled and shipped more economically. Top cutting is avoided when possible for species with an opposite branching pattern such as the maples (*Acer* spp.) and ash (*Fraxinus* spp.) as this can lead to forked trees.

Leaf Removal

A dense layer of leaves can build up in some of the seedling beds, primarily the oaks (*Quercus* spp.). A leaf blower is used ahead of the lifter to blow the leaves out of the beds. This is especially helpful when the soils are wet. Removing the leaves seems to allow the lifter to do a better and faster job of getting the seedlings up on the soil surface, making it much easier for the crew to gather the seedlings.

Lifting

Lifting Equipment

Mechanical lifters are used to harvest the seedlings. We utilize both a power take-off-driven Fobro Super HD and a hydraulic-driven Lundaby Plant Lifter 60, depending on the stock being lifted. White oak (*Quercus alba* L.), bur oak (*Quercus macrocarpa* Michx.), and shagbark hickory (*Carya ovata* [Mill] K. Koch) tend to lift better with the Fobro. Most other hardwoods are more efficiently lifted in our soils with the Lundaby. The lifters are pulled with John Deere model 6330s. These are 85-horsepower tractors with four-wheel drive and infinitely variable hydrostatic transmissions. This allows for exceptional speed control. Equipment is well maintained to reduce breakdowns in the field. Lifters are inspected and greased daily.

Lifting Operations

Once the seedlings are lifted, a 6- to 10-member crew gathers the seedlings into bundles and hands them off to the packer on the wagon. The seedlings are packed into large field crates that sit on wagons alongside the lifting crew. Four crates fit on each wagon and one or two packers are on that wagon. Each lifting crew generally needs two or three wagons to shuttle seedlings to the coolers. Six crates would be better when lifting large hardwoods but a larger wagon would make entry into the field much more difficult. The crates are about 48 in by 45 in by 24 in deep (1.2 meters [m] by 1.1m by 0.6 m). Wet wool or burlap blankets are placed in each crate prior to going to the field and are placed on top of the stock once a crate has been filled. Once the field crates on a wagon are full, they are transported to the distribution building where they are wetted down with water, unloaded with a forklift, and moved into cold storage. Seedlings are packed for distribution in the seedling distribution building. This building was designed to accommodate grading, packing, cold storage, and distribution.

Packing

Material Used

Seedlings are packed into wax-impregnated white boxes that measure 30 in long by 12 in wide by 18 in high (76 cm by 30 cm by 46 cm). The bottom and top flaps are stapled to keep them closed. There is a box-making station where the box is opened up and the bottom is stapled on a pneumatic pedestal stapler. A 2-millimeter plastic liner is placed inside the box and is used to seal the seedlings. When it comes time to close the boxes at the end of the packing lines, there are handheld pneumatic staplers hanging from the ceiling on stretch cords.

Where and how seedlings are packed depends on the type of order. The nursery offers customers ungraded (bulk) and graded (counted) orders. In all cases, the seedlings are misted as they are packed in the boxes to ensure the roots are moist. Hose reels are located above the packing station so water is easily accessible.

Bulk Order Packing

A bulk order consists of 3,000 or more of a single species and age. The number of trees shipped in a bulk order is based on bed-run inventory and may contain 10 percent more or less than the number of seedlings ordered. A determined number of seedlings are lifted from the beds, placed in the large plastic field crates, and transported to the cooler. When the bulk packing crew is ready to pack that species, seedlings are moved out of the cooler, still in the large field crates, to the end of their packing line. The packing line is a roller-type conveyor. The crew takes the entire lift and packs it as evenly as possible into the white seedling boxes. As boxes are being packed, they are placed on wood pallets that are 44 in wide by 60 in deep (1.1 m by 1.5 m). The boxes are stacked on pallets seven boxes per layer and three layers high. The pallet is then placed in the cooler until it is needed to fill bulk orders. Once all the seedlings are packed, the total number of boxes is determined for that lift, along with an estimated number of seedlings per box. This information is then recorded as bulk inventory. To complete a bulk order, the calculated number of boxes is taken from inventory and the customer labels are placed on the side of the boxes.

Grade Order Packing

Grade orders make up the majority of the orders and are typically smaller in size. Once the seedlings have been graded and grouped into bundles of 25 seedlings, the bundle is wrapped with tape. A set quantity of seedlings is then placed into boxes, depending on the size of the seedlings, typically 150 to 500 seedlings per box. The boxes are then stacked 7 boxes per layer and 3 layers high on wood pallets that are 44 by 60 in (1.1 by 1.5 m). The pallets are placed in the cooler until needed in the grade order packing room. Grade orders are filled with a "grocery shopping" method. Pallets of each species are lined up in the room and the packers take the individual orders and go from one species to the next, gathering enough boxes to fill that order. Occasionally, it is necessary to open boxes if the quantity of seedlings ordered cannot be evenly divided by the number per box. In this case, the packer calculates the number of bundles required to complete the quantity needed and repacks those in a new box, often combining them with other species. If they are combined with other species in the same box, one of the bundles is labeled so the customer can identify them. Once an order has been packed for bulk or grade, it is determined if it is a "will call" (customer picking up at the nursery) or if it is being shipped in a refrigerated truck to a central location in each county (by county truck). "Will calls" are placed on a pallet or cart and stored in a designated area of the cooler. Orders shipped on a county truck are placed on the pallets with other orders going to that county. There are seven boxes per layer, but instead of three layers, the boxes are stacked four layers high. The pallet is then shrinkwrapped, labeled for the county, and placed into the cooler until shipped.

Fall Lift Packing

If seedlings are lifted in the fall for fall distribution, the procedures are the same as for spring-lifted stock. When stock is lifted in the fall for spring distribution, however, the procedures are somewhat different. Stock that is lifted in the fall and stored until spring is lifted in relatively dry conditions and stored dry. Leaves are removed during the grading process. There is a much greater occurrence of mold developing during storage when the stock is wet and/or the leaves are still attached at lifting. Instead of packing seedlings into waxed boxes after grading, the bundles are placed back into the large field crates with a plastic liner. After the crate is filled, a dry blanket is placed on top and then covered tightly with a piece of plastic. They are then placed in the cooler set at 25 to 28 °F (-3.8 to -2.2 °C) for storage until spring. The cooler temperature is raised in the spring to between 33 and 36 °F (0.5 to 2.2 °C) and the stock allowed to thaw. Once thawed, the seedlings are then misted as they are being packed into the waxed boxes and placed on pallets just as they would be coming off the grading belt.

Grading Procedures

Seedlings are graded in the packing building in a separate room specifically designed for grading seedlings. The floor is heated and set at about 50 °F (10 °C). This provides some comfort for the workers but is not too warm for the seedlings, given the short amount of time they will spend in this room. The building design incorporates in-floor heat because there is not the warm dry air movement associated with forced air or a unit heater. There are two conveyor belts 30 ft (9 m) long, with tables on each side of the belt. Each table is about 3 by 5 ft (91 by 152 cm). There is enough room for two workers to work at each table. Stools are available for staff to use while grading, although most prefer to stand, especially when working with the larger hardwoods. Seedlings in field crates are brought into the grading room with a forklift and placed alongside the tables, two on each side of the belt. As the graders sort the healthy seedlings that are within acceptable specifications (table 11a.1), the seedlings are sorted into bundles of 25 and placed on the conveyor belt. If the seedlings are being graded in the fall and stored until spring, any leaves that might still remain on the seedlings are also removed. The cull seedlings and other debris are dropped to the floor. Staff are assigned to keep supplies of seedlings on the tables for grading as well as sweep away the cull seedlings and other debris, which is loaded into a dump trailer parked at one end of the conveyor. Two people are stationed at the end of the conveyor. They will take 5 bundles of 5 seedlings to make a bundle of 25, and then, using a large produce tape dispenser, tape the bundles of 25 seedlings. Once the seedling bundle is taped, it is placed on a table at the end of the conveyor belt where the packers can place them in seedling boxes. Bundles of seedlings used to fill larger orders may not always be taped, but instead placed loosely into boxes.

Seedling Storage

Storage Facility Design

There are three independent coolers within the building complex. Cooler 1 is 50 by 60 ft (15 by 18 m) with 13 ½ ft (4 m) of clearance. This cooler is used primarily for storing seedlings that have been packed and are ready to be assigned to a customer or are ready to ship. Cooler 2 is 48 by 53 ft (14.5 by 16 m) with 14 ft (4 m) of clearance. This cooler is primarily used to store the large field crates of seedlings that come in from the field. They are stored there until ready to be graded and packed. This cooler is on the opposite end of the building from cooler 1 and allows for the "flow through" concept to move the stock through the distribution process. Cooler 3 is 24 by 48 ft (7.5 by 14.5 m) with 14 ft (4 m) of clearance, and it is attached to cooler 2. This is a small cooler and is used to handle small batches of miscellaneous stock that might get lost in the two larger coolers. A misting system is installed in each cooler so that stock, mainly in the field crates, can be misted. The coolers are designed to take temperatures below freezing for winter storage. Heaters are also installed in the coolers to prevent the temperature from getting too cold during winter storage.

Temperature

Seedlings are stored in coolers with thermostats set to maintain a temperature between 33 to 36 °F (0.5 to 2.2 °C). Coolers are set to maintain a temperature between 25 to 28 °F (-3.8 to -2.2 °C) during winter storage. Heaters are designed to keep temperatures above 23 °F (-5 °C).

Monitoring

Large probe-type thermometers are used to monitor seedling temperatures in both the field crates and the waxed boxes. Hardwoods typically cool down more quickly than conifers when in a cooler, so they are generally not of much concern, whereas much time is spent monitoring conifers. The cooler temperatures are checked each morning and again at the end of the work day. Small temperature measuring devices called "I-buttons" have been used. These small units are about the

Table 11a.1. Minimum specifications for culling seedlings at Wisconsin State Nurseries.

Species	Age	Caliper (in)	Height (in)	Root Length (in)
Populus tremuloides (Michx.)	1-0	1/8	8	8
Tilia americana (L.)	1-0	1/8	6	8
Betula nigra (L.)	1-0	1/8	8	8
Betula papyrifera (Marsh)	2-0	3/16	10	8
Betula alleghaniensis (Britton)	–	–	–	–
Juglans cinerea (L.)	1-0	1/2	10	8
Prunus serotina (Ehrh.)	1-0	1/8	8	8
Prunus serotina (Ehrh.)	2-0	3/16	10	8
Celtis occidentalis (L.)	1-0	1/8	6	8
Celtis occidentalis (L.)	2-0	3/16	10	8
Carya cordiformis (Wangenh.) K. Koch	2-0	3/16	5	8
Carya ovata (Mill.) K. Koch	3-0	1/4	8	8
Acer saccharum (Marsh.)	2-0	1/8	6	8
Acer saccharum (Marsh.)	3-0	3/16	10	8
Acer rubrum (L.)	2-0	1/8	6	8
Acer saccharinum (L.)	1-0	1/8	28	8
Acer saccharinum (L.)	2-0	3/16	10	8
Quercus macrocarpa (Michx.)	1-0	1/8	6	8
Quercus alba (L.)	2-0	3/16	10	8
Quercus rubra (L.)	1-0	1/8	8	8
Quercus bicolor (Willd.)	2-0	3/16	10	8
Juglans nigra (L.)	1-0	1/4	10	8

in = inches.

size of a quarter and can be placed in a seedling box. They can be programmed to record temperature at many different intervals, which is useful in determining how long it takes to chill seedlings to 34 °F (1 °C) during processing, especially with varying outside temperatures. This information helps to make necessary cooling adjustments.

Structures and Racking

There are no structures or racking in the coolers. The pallet system with shrinkwrap allows for stacking and gives the greatest flexibility for storage.

Maximum Recommended Seedling Storage

Seedling storage time varies by how the seedlings were prepared for storage. With typical spring packing procedures, storage longer than 3 to 6 weeks is undesirable. The earlier in the spring that seedlings are lifted, the longer they can be stored. As seedlings begin to break dormancy in the spring, storage time declines to about 3 weeks. Seedlings packed dry for winter storage may be stored for several months until they are ready to be outplanted in the spring.

Potential Problems During Storage

Not all species store well over winter. There are frequent problems with mold developing in sugar maple (*Acer Saccharum* Marsh.), black cherry, and white oak.

Bareroot Hardwood Seedling Lifting, Packing, and Storage at the Missouri Department of Conservation George O. White State Forest Nursery

11b

G.A. Hoss

Gregory A. Hoss, retired as Forest Nursery Supervisor, George O. White State Forest Nursery, Missouri Department of Conservation

Outline

Facing Page: *Seedling bundles being manifested for shipment in Missouri. (Photo courtesy of Greg Hoss, Missouri Department of Conservation, 2011.)*

Introduction

Nursery Location

The George O. White State Forest Nursery is located in Texas County in south central Missouri. The seedbeds are located along a narrow creek valley with no more than a 1- or 2-percent slope. Average yearly rainfall is about 45 well-distributed inches per year. The nursery typically grows about 4 million hardwood seedlings each year, consisting of about 60 species of native hardwood trees and shrubs, which is around 80 percent of the total nursery production. Because it is centrally located, Missouri grows both what is considered "southern" and "northern" species. Nearly all the hardwoods are grown as a 1-0 seedling, with the exception of a few species grown to a 2-0 seedling.

Labor Source

The nursery uses local labor, and some of the lifting crew have worked at the nursery for many years. No prison labor or contract crews are used. The lifting crew is hired in the fall and employed until the following April. Typically, 16 to 18 seasonal hourly workers are hired for lifting. About 15 to 20 seedling graders are employed soon after the lifting starts each November. They work until grading is finished, usually through the middle to the end of April.

Outplanting Schedule

Most tree and shrub planting in Missouri occurs from February to May, with the majority of seedling demand occurring in March. Every species grown at the nursery should be lifted, graded and ready for shipment by mid-February. Some seedlings are readied for customers for December and January planting, particularly in the Missouri and Mississippi River bottoms as these areas are prone to spring flooding. Often these areas can be planted in the winter months and if not then, it may be June or even July before they can be planted.

Lifting Operations

Timing of Lifting

Seedling lifting begins after November 20 in most years. At least 2 or 3 nights of temperatures below 25 °F (-4 °C) helps ensure that seedlings have hardened off before the lifting operation begins. In some years, it is late November before these temperatures are reached. Experience indicates that some species can be lifted in November and December and other species need to be kept in the seedbeds until needed in the spring. During November and December, lifting operations concentrate on those species that will store well until spring shipping begins. Lifting will continue to mid-April, except during periods of extreme cold, usually in late December into January. During those periods of extreme cold, the lifting crew processes cuttings that are taken from cottonwood (*Populus deltoides* Bartr.) and sandbar willow (*Salix interior* Rowlee) stool beds established in the nursery. The lifting crew cuts down the 1-year old stump sprouts and transports the whips to a cool building. Once inside, the whips are trimmed of all limbs and cut to lengths of 18 inches (in) (46 centimetes [cm]) for cottonwood cuttings and 12 in (30 cm) for willow cuttings, then graded into bundles of 25 cuttings.

It is not uncommon in a Missouri winter to be able to lift nearly every day. Lifting is stopped when the ground is frozen or when morning temperatures fall below 28 °F (-2 °C). Below this temperature, it is simply too cold for field crews to work effectively. Once the temperature rises above 28 °F, the lifting process can begin. At those times when the lifting crew is unable to go out and lift trees, the crew stays inside and assists the grading crew in grading seedlings.

Moisture is the other weather issue affecting lifting operations. Because the nursery is in a creek bottom and the soil is mostly clay (sometimes heavy clay and little sand or gravel), winter rains can keep the soil too wet for operations. The soil is slow to dry out, quick to freeze, and slow to thaw. Lifting after heavy winter rains can become just about impossible, even without freezing temperatures, as equipment cannot get through the seedbeds. Similarly, when there is little rain, the clay soil becomes very dry and blocky, causing the lifter to bring up seedlings and large chunks of soil. It is difficult to remove the seedlings from these large chunks of soil without damaging the roots. In this situation, the irrigation system must be reinstalled to wet those beds to be lifted.

Seedling Preparation

Seedlings are not undercut prior to lifting. Some undercutting was tried in the past, particularly in the heavy-rooted species such as pecan (*Carya illinoensis* Wangenh. K. Koch) and hickory (*Carya* spp.). However, attempting to undercut in the nursery's heavy clay soils tended to pull the seedlings underground instead of cutting them clean. The equipment could not function properly in these heavy soils, and on more than one occasion, the undercutter tool was pulled apart.

The nursery sells a number of hardwood species as an extra-large seedling, and this is a very popular item with customers. These are seedlings that are over 30 or 36 in tall (76 or 91 cm) (depending on species), and the price

Figure 11b.1—An "extra-large" seedling is a popular item with customers. This is a bundle of 25. (Photo courtesy of Greg Hoss, Missouri Department of Conservation, 2011.)

is double that of a regular seedling. Each year nearly all extra-large seedlings are sold.

Top clipping is generally avoided, but must be done under certain circumstances. Currently, the nursery ships about 75 percent of the seedling harvest via United Parcel Service (UPS) or the United States Postal Service (USPS). This can result in getting oversize charges for the tall trees as well as occasional breakage to the tall seedlings. Top clipping is therefore sometimes done to reduce the number of tall trees shipped (but only those species not offered as extra-large). In addition, the nursery ships four or five species with thorns. The UPS and USPS drivers do not like to handle seedling bundles where thorny branches are protruding.

When necessary, seedlings are top clipped to about 22 in (56 cm) tall as this is the maximum cutting height of the mower. It is preferable, but not feasible, to let them grow to 30 in (76 cm). When the trees grow to about 25 in (64 cm) tall, they are clipped back to 22 in (56 cm). This means there may be more than one clipping on a species during the growing season, but every effort is made to cut only new and actively growing wood so that damage to the seedling is minimal. Top clipping is typically done in late July or August, when the trees are actively growing. If field clipping is not feasible for one reason or another, and the seedlings grow to over 30 in tall when mechanical clipping could cause noticeable damage on the stem, seedlings are top clipped by hand during the grading process.

Equipment Preparation

Lundeby tree lifters made in North Dakota by Lundeby Manufacturing are used for lifting. This machine withstands lifting deep-rooted hardwood seedlings in wet clay soil, but not without some modification to the lifters, which are reinforced with additional metal braces to resist heavy soils. Two lifters are kept ready to use throughout the lifting season, usually having both on tractors. The lifter in use is greased daily, and a spare lifting blade is always kept on the nursery during the winter. Tractors with about 90 horsepower, four-wheel drive, and a creeper gear are used for the best lifting operation. Three of the nursery tractors can be used for lifting, so if there are any breakdowns or if two lifters are needed, the equipment to keep lifting is available. If one machine breaks down, little time is lost in getting a second tractor and lifter to the field. This is especially important so that 15 or 20 employees are not standing around waiting for equipment to be fixed. During the off-season, each lifter is thoroughly inspected for any needed repairs or parts replacement.

Prior to the operator entering a seedbed, the depth of the lifter is set by adjusting the four wheels on the Lundeby lifter. The depth is usually set to at least 10 in (25 cm) for hardwoods. The operator enters the bed, lifts several feet of seedlings, gets out and pulls trees to check root length. If the tap root is being severed on the seedlings, the machine is adjusted to dig deeper. It is preferable to cut as little tap root as possible, so often, especially with deep rooted species such as hickory or pecan, the lifter may run as deep as 15 in (38 cm). This does leave a long root system for the customer, but a customer can always prune the root shorter if desired.

Packing

Location, Procedures, and Materials

As seedlings are being lifted from seedbeds, a lifting crew of 15 to 20 employees pick up the seedlings, shake off excess dirt, and put the seedlings into Lewis Bins nested tubs. The lifting crew lifts and tubs every seedling. They are instructed to do no field grading and to get every seedling out of the seedbeds and into the tubs regardless of size. (This is done to eliminate seedlings being left in the seedbeds and resprouting later in the spring.) A tractor and trailer makes continuous runs from the lifting area to the cold storage facility, picking up the tubs of trees and delivering them to cold storage. On cold, wet days, the trailer is filled before it comes back to cold storage, but on windy or warm days, the trailer is constantly delivering trees to cold storage, whether full or not. Every effort is made to have seedlings into cold storage as quickly as possible. Likewise, lifted seedlings are left in the seedbeds when the crew comes in for a break or lunch while lifting on a cold or wet day, but no lifted seedlings should be left on the seedbeds on a windy or warm day.

Once the trailer backs up to the cold storage loading dock, all the tubs are unloaded onto wheeled carts and taken into the cooler. Two workers are in the cooler at all times and with the help of the tractor operator to unload the seedlings and reload the trailer with empty tubs; the turn around time from dock back to field is minimal. The tubs are then dumped onto seedling storage racks and thoroughly watered. Each rack is labeled with species, source (i.e., "north MO" or "south MO") and lifting date. The full racks of seedlings are then stacked in the cooler. Jarke storage racks that can be stacked onto each other are used for stacking. Trees are stored loose on the Jarke racks until they are graded.

Seedling Grading

Every seedling that leaves the nursery has been graded at a seedling grading table by workers inside the packing house. The typical daily goal is to grade about 40,000 trees for a crew of 15 to 20 employees. Care is taken when grading to always rotate seedlings from the cooler to grade from oldest lifted to newest lifted. Trees are graded by height, caliper, and root mass. A height of 12 in (30.5 cm) has been the required minimum for all hardwood seedlings, although flexibility in this minimum criteria is often needed. Some species might fall below this minimum height criteria yet possess good caliper (i.e., greater than 1/2 in or 13 mm) and root development indicating a quality seedling. In these cases, the minimum height requirement is lowered.

Figure 11b.2—*All seedlings processed at the George O. White State Forest Nursery are graded and counted in the packing shed. (Photo courtesy of Greg Hoss, Missouri Department of Conservation, 2011.)*

Similarly, some species or a seedling lot grown at high density may produce seedlings that are well over the minimum height. In this case the minimum height criteria may be raised to ensure that a suitable caliper is obtained. In addition, "special projects" may require a seedling grade different from the standard 12 in (30.5 cm) minimum height. Or, if the sales for a particular species are slow, the minimum standards may be increased so that only the very best seedlings are going out the gate. Proper supervision, observation, and training is the key to make sure the grading process meets the criteria established.

A seedling either makes that grade and goes down the conveyor belt, or it is placed into the cull tub and taken to the compost pile. If there are extra-large seedlings needing to be separated, the grader pulls out the large seedlings and sets these aside to be graded later. The large seedlings are collected, wet down, and either bundled when the regular grade is done, or returned to the cooler to be bundled later. Occasionally seedlings not making the grade are saved to be used for special projects or special requests. Normally seedlings are never regraded for customers. Each seedling makes the selected grade or it does not. This method of grading, while labor-intensive, ensures that if a customer orders 500 trees, the customer gets exactly 500 trees that have been counted, not bulk packaged in the field. There is no guess work to the number of trees a customer is getting. There is also a consistency in size and quality that a customer can count on from year to year.

Each grader looks at every seedling and counts out 5 seedlings that meet the grade and places this bundle of 5 seedlings on the conveyor belt. Another employee picks up 5 bundles of 5 seedlings to make up a standard bundle of 25 seedlings. These bundles are tied together and tagged with a species tag. The tying is done both by hand and with mechanical tying machines. Bundles are placed back onto a Jarke rack and the roots wet down with water mixed with TerraSorb gel, then moved back into the cooler. Seedlings are returned to the cooler after grading as unpackaged bundles of seedlings on Jarke racks. Since these bundles are unpackaged and the roots exposed, they are watered daily until packaging takes place. Unless the seedlings are being sold as extra-large, any seedling top sticking out beyond the edge of the rack is trimmed using an electric hedge trimmer. This gives a clean cut to any long seedling top. The racks of graded trees are labeled by species, source, and date graded.

Packaging and Shipping.

Shipping typically begins the second week of February. Shipping tags are printed weekly for all seedlings to be shipped, delivered, or picked up the following week. A four-person baling crew then packages the seedlings. The bundles of seedlings are now packaged using nursery wrap baling paper, wet sphagnum moss and then banded and labeled. Since all trees come in bundles of 25 and customers can order as few as 25 of each species, often the packages may have 2, 3, 4, or even more species. Contracts with the USPS and UPS allow shipment in open-ended bundles, with trees sticking out the top of the package without paying any excess fees for the open packages. When baling, each method of delivery is kept separate. UPS packages will be processed, manifested, and stacked on racks, then the same will be done with packages being picked up by USPS. Pick-up orders and orders to be delivered will be packed and placed on separate racks according to the customer. All of the packages are then moved back into the coolers, regardless of distribution.

UPS leaves a trailer at the nursery which is filled once or twice a week. When a trailer is picked up, an empty one is left in its place. For USPS orders, carts provided by USPS are used. USPS also comes twice a week with a large trailer truck to pick up filled carts and leave empties. We have been using both carriers for many years and have developed excellent working relations with each. Both UPS and USPS guarantee second-day delivery and rarely is this guarantee not met. USPS is very efficient on small orders going to rural addresses. UPS works best for large orders. Another advantage of having two carriers is that if an issue with one carriers develops, we have another to fill in and ensure seedlings are delivered. The nursery does not currently charge for shipping. The cost to the customer is the same for picking up, shipping, or delivery by a nursery truck.

Many orders are picked up at the nursery. Some customers want to avoid the possibility of damage or delay from UPS- and USPS-shipped seedlings. Some just want their trees in hand and see the nursery operation. Most contractors also prefer to pick up their orders rather than having them shipped to the landowners.

Some orders are delivered by nursery staff. These orders are usually large or multiple orders in the same general location that will fill a big truck or trailer. Delivery is at the discretion of the nursery, not the landowner. Based on the number of packages, delivery location and availability of staff, the nursery decides if it would be more economical to ship or deliver. Customers are allowed to request delivery on a specific date, and the nursery makes every effort to accommodate the request.

Figure 11b.3—*Seedling roots are watered, wrapped with baling paper, and banded in preparation for shipping. Bundles are then returned to the cooler and shipped within a day or two of packaging. (Photo courtesy of Greg Hoss.)*

Storage

Storage Facilities

The primary cold storage building for the George O. White State Forest Nursery is 50 by 250 ft (15 by 76 m). This long, narrow building is divided into 5 bays, each 50 by 50 ft (15 by 15 m). Each bay has its own compressor and temperature control. Additional bays can be turned on when needed as the lifting season progresses. Unused bays can be turned off and shut to save cooling costs as seedlings are shipped in the spring. Each bay will hold 120 Jarke stackable racks. Each row is five double-stacked racks. Space is left between each row for employees to water and find trees.

Every rack is tagged on the upper front right so that each species can be easily identified and located. The cooler manager keeps lists of where every graded and ungraded rack of seedlings is located and this is kept on the forklift, so that any employee can look at this list and find out where a particular species is located within the five bays. Racks are constantly moved around to always keep the oldest graded or ungraded seedlings accessible first.

Coolers are kept at about 34 °F (1 °C) and all trees are wet down each morning. Cooler watering is done by two employees using water hoses. They move in and around all the rows of Jarke racks and thoroughly wet the seedlings. Coolers are watered on late Friday and are not typically watered over the weekend. There is some overhead mist watering, but this does not thoroughly wet the seedlings like hand watering does. Employees not only wet the seedlings, but also wet floors and walls to maintain high humidity.

Storage Problems

There are several potential problems with seedling storage. When seedlings are lifted and brought into the cooler, they are unloaded onto racks, watered, and placed into cold storage. If the seedlings are lifted on a warm day and then stacked tightly on a rack, there can be molding and heating if the seedlings are not soon graded. Seedlings lifted and stacked on warm days are usually graded within a few weeks. This stirs the seedlings and as they are graded, bundled, and put back into the coolers, seedlings that had not cooled properly after lifting now get proper cooling for long-term storage.

A lot of bundles are stacked on a rack during grading. These bundles are watered with a terra-sorb gel mixture as stacked, but as time in cold storage lengthens, bundles in the middle of the rack can dry out, no matter how much surface watering is provided. Again, making sure to ship the oldest graded seedlings first helps keep racks stirred.

Lifting any hardwood seedlings with leaves attached creates many problems. The leaves take up a lot of space on the racks. As they fall off, constant sweeping is required to keep the cooler floors from getting slick. Over time, the wet leaves mold and this creates a slimy mess to deal with and can cause some top dieback in the seedling. Seedlings should only be lifted with leaves still attached if they are going to be shipped out in a very short time after lifting.

Various species get root molds, but this is usually on root tips that were severed during the lifting process. Both aromatic (*Rhus aromatica* L.) and smooth (*Rhus glabra* L.) sumac tend to develop considerable mold on the roots. A thorough wetting eliminates the mold.

Maximum Recommended Storage Times

Over the years, it has been found that some hardwood species can be stored for many months and the customer can still have success in planting and survival. This is not true, however, of all species. Flowering dogwood (*Cornus florida* L.), persimmon (*Diospyros virginiana* L.), Washington hawthorn (*Crataegus phaenopyrum* Ehrh.), sweetgum (*Liquidambar syraciflua* L) and deciduous holly (*Ilex decidua* Walt.) DO NOT store well and outplanting survival may be affected. These species are lifted only as needed. This can cause issues when customers request a particular species that is still in the ground and weather or other factors will not permit lifting operations. Lifting way ahead of shipping, however, is not good for some hardwood species. Lower survival with long-term storage has been observed with the red oak group. Red oaks may be kept in storage for only a few months, but white oak species, particularly swamp white (*Quercus bicolor* Willd.) and bur oak (*Quercus macrocarpa* Michx.), may be cold stored for over six months with still nearly 100% survival. Species such as silver maple (*Acer saccharinum* L.), black walnut (*Juglans nigra* L.), black cherry (*Prunus serotina* Ehrh.), wild plum (*Prunus* spp.), roughleaf (*Cornus drummondii* Meyer) and silky (*Cornus oblique* Raf.) dogwood, Kentucky coffeetree (*Gymnocladus dioicus*, L., K. Koch), bald cypress (*Taxodium distichum* L., Rich.), hackberry (*Celtis occidentalis* L.), serviceberry (*Amelanchier arborea* Michx. f.), hazelnut (*Corylus Americana* Walter), ninebark (*Physocarpus opulifolius* L. Maxim), and others store very well for many months, and these species are the first lifted during December and into January. Pecan, hickories, gray dogwood (*Cornus racemosa* Lam.), tulip poplar (*Liriodendron tulipifera* L.), sycamore (*Platanus occidentalis* L.), river birch (*Betula nigra* L.), and others that store fairly well, along with the red oaks, are lifted as needed or after the species listed above are lifted. Willow oak (*Quercus phellos* L.) and sometimes black oak (*Quercus veluntina* Lam.) seem to never lose their leaves, and these species are not lifted until needed to avoid rotting problems with the leaves. Several species seem to have a problem with hardening off in the seedbeds, particularly tulip poplar and redbud (*Cercis Canadensis* L.). If these species are lifted too early in the lifting season, the tops tend to mold and dieback during storage.

At some point all trees are stored for a long time, sometimes longer than they should be stored. There are customers who do not want their seedlings until late May or even early June. The last of the seedlings are lifted by the first part of April, so every seedling would have 2 or more months of storage before some late orders are shipped.

But, bareroot hardwood seedlings are amazing sometimes. It is usually July before the coolers are shut down and excess seedlings disposed of. It may have been weeks since the last watering, the seedlings have been lifted and stored for months, laying on their sides, stored at 34 °F (1 °C) and yet, even species that do not seem to store well, will be leafing out—without light, without water, and without heat. Some have leafed out and grown several inches, at right angles to the stem, in this environment! It is not clear how well these seedlings would do if outplanted in the summer, but in spite of their final abuses, they are still trying to grow.

Seedling Lifting, Packing, and Storage at the ArborGen Bluff City Nursery

11c

C. Weatherly

Chase Weatherly is production coordinator, ArborGen Inc., Bluff City, AR

Outline

Facing Page: *The hardwood seedling harvesting process at the ArborGen Bluff City Nursery. (Photo courtesy of Chase Weatherly, 2017.)*

Nursery Description

The ArborGen Bluff City Nursery is located in Nevada County in southwest Arkansas, approximately 4 miles south of Bluff City and approximately 3 miles west of White Oak Lake. The nursery has an average elevation of 375 feet (ft) (114 meters [m]) (mean sea level). The dominant soil type falls within the Darden series. The nursery was developed in 1980 and currently grows approximately 40 million bareroot loblolly pine seedlings and over 4 million bareroot hardwood seedlings annually.

Cultural Operations To Improve the Lifting Process

Several cultural practices are used to condition hardwood seedlings for proper lifting and planting, including top pruning, undercutting, lateral pruning, and the use of water stress to condition seedlings for outplanting.

Top Pruning

Top pruning is performed during the months of June to September in order to improve seedling quality. This process slows the top growth of the taller seedlings, allows smaller seedlings to catch up in overall height, and results in a more uniform crop size by the end of the growing season. In addition, it is believed that when seedling stems are cut back, the lower portion of the stems, as well as the root systems, become more robust and produce a higher quality seedling. Care is taken, however, to ensure that top pruning is not too aggressive such that the cut extends into woody tissue, which can damage the seedling and prevent proper growth afterwards. Also, top pruning opposite branched species results in the undesirable characteristic of multiple main stems, while alternate branched species generally maintain the apical dominance of a single stem.

A final seedling height of 18 to 24 inches (in) (46 to 61 centimeters [cm]) will meet most customer seedling specifications. Seedlings that fall outside this range are not necessarily culls, but the target height will generally fall between this upper and lower limit. There are many cases where customers will accept seedlings shorter than 18 in (46 cm), and there are also cases where customers request seedlings taller than 24 in (61 cm). Good communication with customers helps the nursery be prepared for its seedling size requirements.

Top pruning requires a tractor with a high ground clearance so the belly of the tractor passes over the taller seedlings later in the year without damaging the stems. A 6 ft (1.83 m) finishing rotary mower, modified so that it can be leveled out at the desired cutting height in the seedbed is used for top pruning. The PTO shaft / gear box may need to be adjusted to prevent the power take-off (PTO) shaft from pinching or rubbing the frame of the mower due to the height of the mower on the tractor. The three-point hitch brackets on the mower can be adjusted to allow for a higher operational height. The blades of the mower can be altered from the manufacturer specifications by increasing the cutting angle to be more aggressive, as well as extending the edge of the blade further along the shaft. Altering the blade can be extremely helpful in creating a clean cut on the seedling stem. When hardwood seedling stems are cut while top pruning using a dull or improperly angled blade, the top of the stem "shatters" instead of producing a nice smooth cut. This shattering of the stem can cause further tip dieback and can hinder regrowth of new tissue.

Undercutting

Hardwood seedling roots tend to grow deeper than what is desired for proper lifting and outplanting success. Therefore, undercutting is normally done between October and early November with the use of a reciprocating blade machine. The target root length is generally 8 in (20 cm), which meets most customer hardwood specifications although the depth can be modified to meet customer requirements. It is believed that undercutting will create a more fibrous root system, which improves outplanting success. The process of running a reciprocating blade beneath the seedling will also break up the soil around the root system which aids in the lifting process by ensuring a looser soil to pull from.

Undercutting is best performed under wetter conditions so that the soil is able to give way to the blade as it passes through. Too wet and the tractor can create very deep tractor paths and roots could "pull" instead of being cut off by the blade. Too dry and the blades may break prematurely as well as ride up above any hard pans and cut root systems off too short. It is best to test various moisture conditions to determine what works best for specific combinations of soils and equipment. Usually 2 to 4 hours of watering, equaling 1/2 to 1 in of rainfall (13 to 25 mm) the night before undercutting will provide the proper moisture.

As with top pruning, a tractor with high clearance is used to minimize the potential for seedling damage when passing over the stems later in the season, when most seedlings have already reached a height between 18 to 24 in (46 to 61 cm). Reciprocating undercutters have a lot of moving parts that receive tremendous stress during operation, so proper calibration and maintenance is of utmost importance. A spare parts list is kept current so that operations are not shut down due to a lack of parts inventory. Items such as blades, bearings, blade brackets, gear boxes, and rebuild kits for gear boxes are primary items to have in stock. Blades are very sharp, so cut-resistant gloves are available and their use is required for any worker handling the blades.

Lateral Root Pruning

Lateral pruning is normally the last cultural practice completed before lifting season and is done during mid-November to early December. Cutting the lateral roots between drills produces a more compact seedling that lifts easier and helps the tree planters get the entire root system into the planting hole, which is essential for good survival. Lateral root pruning also results in a more fibrous root system. The specific lateral pruner used is made by Silver Mountain Equipment Inc. and has only been modified to lateral prune beds with five drills, which requires six blades. This lateral pruner can be steered from the rear so that the blades stay between the drills. A well-trained and seasoned tractor driver and lateral pruner operator are essential to this operation, as there is little room for error when cutting lateral roots between drills spaced so close together.

As with undercutting, lateral pruning is best done in moist soils, which allows the disc blades to fully penetrate through the root system. The amount of soil moisture necessary depends on the soil type and lateral pruner being used. Heavier soils may require more moisture as compared to sandier soils. The ArborGen Bluff City Nursery will usually require 1 to 2 hours of irrigation the day before lateral pruning a field so that the blades will penetrate to a depth of 8 to 10 in (20 to 25 cm). Care should be taken to ensure the disc blades cut to the depth where the undercutting blade previously passed. This will ensure that lateral roots are fully pruned between drills. Failure to do this could create issues during the lifting process, when longer-than-desired lateral roots intertwine with root systems from adjacent seed drills.

Water Stress Manipulation

Water stress can aid in the development of a more fibrous seedling root system, as well as help condition seedlings for the stresses of outplanting. This practice usually begins in late August and may continue through to lifting. The idea is to manipulate soil moisture so there are periods of wet and dry conditions through the top 10 in (25 cm) of the soil profile. Root systems growing in overly saturated soils tend to be less fibrous, lack adequate mycorrhizal formation, and are often diseased. Later in the growing season (mid-August to early September) and when weather conditions are favorable (warm and dry), soil moisture can be manipulated such that wet periods are followed by extended dry periods, which should trigger seedlings to push their root systems deeper in the soil horizon to look for available moisture.

Considerable knowledge of nursery soil conditions and the use of soil moisture probes and/or sensors at various depths is necessary to correctly manipulate water stress conditioning. The ArborGen Bluff City Nursery installs soil sensors at 3-, 6-, and 10-in (7.5-, 15-, and 25-cm) depth in a soil that represents average drainage conditions. The soil sensor used is a Watermark model 200SS that can be easily installed following the manufacturer's instructions. These sensors measure soil moisture tension in centibars by using electrical resistance. Once it is verified the sensors are working correctly (based on manufacturer instructions) and the seedling crop has reached the target size or is on track to reach target size, irrigation can be manipulated in such a way that the soil is quickly saturated through the soil profile to at least 10-in (25-cm) depth, thus mimicking a heavy rain event. Once the irrigation water has percolated to at least 10 in (25 cm), water is completely shut off and soil moisture monitored using the installed sensors. The process seeks to create very dry soil in the upper 3 in (7.5 cm) of the soil profile and moist soil at 6 to 10 in (15 to 25 cm) of the soil profile. This cycle normally takes 7 to 10 days and then should be repeated. There should be no irrigation other than the initial start to the cycle.

Creating water stress in a seedling crop can be very detrimental to seedlings if done improperly and requires experience, close supervision, and guidance. Soil moisture sensors/probes are critical to fully understanding what is happening in the soil profile, and daily observations are essential. Every nursery field and crop is different, and the above process should be adjusted to fit the site and the species being grown. Oaks and other large seeded species respond well, whereas smaller seeded species tend to need watering more frequently without being harmed. Anyone attempting to use the process of water stress manipulation should establish a protocol and proceed with caution while developing confidence in the process for his or her soil type and species.

Timing of Lifting and Outplanting

The timing of hardwood seedling lifting is determined by the dormancy of the species to be lifted. Seedlings that have not reached an acceptable level of dormancy in the nursery before they are lifted will be at more risk of having poor survival once outplanted. In the same way, seedlings that break dormancy in late winter through early spring can also have poor survival. Historically, the "window" for safely lifting, storing, and shipping hardwood seedlings for outplanting falls between early December and mid-March. This lifting window may vary somewhat based on weather conditions, so it is necessary to determine the level of seedling dormancy. Measuring the number of "chilling hours" has been used by nursery managers for decades to determine the level of crop dormancy. A chilling hour occurs when seedlings have been exposed to 1 hour of temperatures between 32 and 45 °F (0 to 2 °C) after October 1. There are many ways to effectively monitor ambient air temperature. Digital temperature monitors or weather stations can be used to calculate chilling hours. Many of these products have smartphone applications that allow for real-time data monitoring. It becomes safer to lift, store, and ship hardwood seedlings as their exposure to chilling hours increases.

Leaf color and leaf fall can also be used to help determine when hardwood seedlings can be safely lifted. This will vary by species, however, since some hardwood species hold on to their leaves much longer than others. For example, there are lifting seasons where species such as water oak (*Quercus nigra* L) may never lose all their leaves during fall and winter due to unusually mild temperatures. Leaf color changes and leaf fall should, therefore, be used along with other metrics like chilling hours and overall weather conditions. Table 1 provides a guide to help determine which species exhibit early or late leaf fall.

Soil moisture is also an important factor when determining when to begin hardwood seedling lifting. Although nurseries have some form of irrigation system, this is not the case for outplanting sites where droughts can become severe. Great care is needed to properly communicate with customers to monitor soil moisture conditions during times of drought. Customers are contacted weeks ahead of planned lifting dates to get a good understanding of conditions at outplanting sites. Many survival issues can be avoided by ensuring that customers understand the importance of proper site preparation, weather, and soil conditions during planting season, as well as proper seedling handling. When necessary, customers are advised not to plant seedlings on outplanting sites with extreme drought conditions and where seedling survival would be in question.

Lifting Equipment Selection, Preparation, and Maintenance

The general purpose and function of a hardwood seedling lifter is to safely loosen the soil around the root system while also bringing the seedlings to the top of the bed so they can be hand lifted, sorted, and packed (fig. 11c.1). Several hardwood seedling lifter models are available and manufacturers typically have options and accessories for each. Selecting the best model and options for a particular application depends on a number of considerations:

- The total volume of seedlings to be lifted annually, weekly, and daily, which will determine if only one lifter or more should be considered.
- The width of the seedling beds, to match available lifter widths to bed width.
- Seedling height, considering each lifter's maximum clearance measurements and limits
- Tractor type and size; some lifters are rated for certain tractor sizes and others have options of either PTO or hydraulic-motor-driven gears.
- Soil type; some lifters perform better in heavy and/or wet soils while others may not.

After the mechanical lifter has lifted seedlings from the bed, shaken the soil from the roots, and left the seedlings

Table 11c.1*—Time of leaf fall by genus (Williams and Hanks 1994). It is believed there is a relationship between the timing of leaf fall and the onset of dormancy.*

Early Sept. - Oct.	Intermediate Oct. - Nov.	Late Nov. - Dec.
Carya	*2.24*	*Alnus*
Catalpa	*Betula*	*Castaneu*
Cercis	*Celtis*	*Elaeagnus*
Diospyros	*Cornus*	*Quercus*
Fraxinus	*Liquidambar*	
Juglans	*Liriodendron*	
Morus	*Maclura*	
Nyssa	*Plantanus*	
Populus	*Prunus*	
Robinia	*Tilia*	
Robinia	*Ulmus*	

***Figure 11c.1**—Fobro lifter showing the back tine tilt angle and height above bed. (Photo courtesy of Chase Weatherly, 2017.)*

on top of the bed, all further seedling handling, counting, sorting, bagging, and strapping at the ArborGen Bluff City Nursery is accomplished entirely by hand in the field (fig. 11c.2). An important step in this process is to spray the roots of seedlings with a gel slurry. This is accomplished using a trailer that has been altered to house a 500-gallon (gal) (1,892 liter [L]) poly tank with an attached hydraulic Ace pump that can deliver a gel slurry via a 75-ft (23-m) heavy-duty water hose directly to the roots of bundled seedlings laying on top of the bed. This trailer is long enough to hold up to 1,000 empty hardwood seedling bags and up to the same number of 36-in (91-cm) and 48-in (122-cm) plastic zip tics uscd for securing the bags once filled with seedlings (this method does not utilize mechanical strapping machines). Two haul-in wagons hold empty metal seedling racks that are taken to the field so that completely processed seedling bags can be stacked on them and taken to the cooler for storage.

Thorough planning is necessary to ensure all equipment has been properly prepared before lifting begins. Knowing the size and type tractor used for the lifter(s) and haul-in wagons is essential when developing an equipment list for the harvesting process. All tractors need to be inspected to ensure they meet the requirements for the equipment being used and all equipment, such as lifters, haul-in wagons, and strappers need to be inspected and any alterations made to fit any specific requirements. Spare parts for all equipment should be on hand before lifting begins to avoid downtime if spares are not available. A yearly "prelifting" inspection program should be used to inspect all equipment and supplies to ensure they are ready for use, as well as verify spare parts inventories are in place. Consulting owner's manuals and calling other nursery locations can be very helpful. Finally, consideration should also be given to how workers are transported to and from the field. Trucks and/or RTVs should be available as needed to safely transport all workers.

Field Operations

Lifting

All lifting and packing activities at the ArborGen Bluff City Nursery are done in the field so there is no need for packing sheds or process lines. When packed seedling bags are transported from the field, they only need be placed in cold storage to await shipping. With a small crew size (3 to 6 workers), this method can yield anywhere from 10,000 to 20,000 seedlings packed in an 8-hour day. With a larger crew size (21 to 26 workers), this method can yield upwards of 250,000 seedlings in an 8-hour day.

When using either a Lundeby or Fobro style lifter, the tractor operator positions the blade of the lifter so that it is running at a slight angle with the front face of the blade slightly lower than the rear portion of the blade. This will cause the rear tines that help to separate the seedlings from the soil to be tilted upward slightly above the surface of the bed (fig. 11c.1). The more aggressive the angle of the blade in reference to the bed surface, the more the soil will be disrupted, the slower the tractor will need to travel, and the greater the potential for seedlings to clog the lifter instead of sliding over the blade. The less aggressive the blade tilt, the faster the tractor can travel, and soil disruption will be less. Blade tilt adjustments are made so there is adequate soil disruption and seedling separation without a lot of clogging. Once the lifter blade has been set to the desired angle, the depth of the blade is set to minimize the chance of roots being scraped as the blade travels under the bed. With a target root length of 8 in (20 cm) set by the previous undercutting operation, the depth of the lifting blade should be run close to 10 in (25 cm). Tractor speed depends on soil moisture, soil type, and the species being lifted and is generally between 0.5 and 1 miles per hour (0.8 to 1.6 kilometers per hour). Wetter conditions may require slower speeds to help soil separation from seedling roots. Drier conditions may allow for faster speeds. Sandier soils will allow for faster speeds as compared to heavier soils. The lifter operator must constantly check the tractor, lifter, and the quality of lifting so that adjustments can be made as soon as possible.

Packing

Immediately after the seedlings have passed through the lifter frame and once the lifter has moved down the bed far enough to allow for safe access, the crew members should assemble along both sides of the bed in equal numbers so that the seedlings can be hand counted and placed into bundles of either 25 or 50 seedlings. During this process, any culling or grading takes place based on seedling quality standards. The objective is to get the desired number of plantable seedlings into each bundle. If there are relatively few culls (5 percent or less), there is little need for removing the culls from the bundles, which would require additional time. The culls can be left in the bundles as long as the total number of plantable trees are also in the bundle. As the lifter moves along the bed lifting the seedlings out of the bed, the packing crew moves along behind counting and placing seedlings in bundles (fig. 11c.2).

Wet lifting conditions can increase the amount of soil clinging to the root systems. While excess soil on root systems during lifting and packing does not harm the seedlings, it increases the weight of seedling bags and makes them harder to handle. Removal of the excess soil clinging to roots may be accomplished by having the packing crew shake it from the root systems. This activity is time-consuming, particularly in heavier soils and wet conditions. There are no specific guidelines as to whether or not soil removal efforts are worthwhile. The decision is highly dependent upon local conditions and preferences when determining how much time the packing crew should spend shaking seedling bundles to remove excess soil.

Once seedlings have been placed in bundles, the roots are immediately sprayed with a gel slurry mixture using a water hose attached to the gel wagon. The water hose is long enough to reach up and down the bed for at least 50 ft (15.24 m) or more. This will allow a crew member to walk along the bed spraying the bundles as they are placed on top of the bed and before placement into bags. The gel mixture ratio is determined by the manufacture's mixing instructions. Gel mixtures that are too thick will not flow properly through the water hose and will not spread evenly inside the root bundle. The result will be a large portion of dry roots in each bundle. Gel mixtures that are too thin will not deliver enough gel to the roots and the water will simply fall out of the bundle of roots. The result will be a large portion of dry roots in each bundle. Depending on root fibrousness and the amount of soil left on the roots, seedling bundles may need to

Figure 11c.2—*The hardwood seedling harvesting process at the ArborGen Bluff City Nursery, illustrating the sequence of operations performl1c.ed in the field: Lifting, sorting and bundling, gel application, bagging, loading, and transport to cooler. (Photo courtesy of Chase Weatherly, 2017.)*

be turned while being sprayed with the gel mixture to ensure the entire bundle gets adequately sprayed.

A 400- to 500-gallon (1,514- to 1,892-L) tank of gel mixture should be able to deliver enough gel for 150,000 seedlings or more. A large crew of 21 to 26 workers requires at least one refill during a complete day of hardwood lifting. The refilling process takes up to 30 minutes or more, depending on how far the gel wagon needs to travel to get to a water source and how fast the tank can be filled. The gel mixture should not be allowed to freeze, and when not in use, the tank may need to be stored in a building where temperatures do not fall below freezing.

Seedlings are ready to be placed in the seedling bag after the gel mixture has been applied. The two bags used at the ArborGen Bluff City Nursery are:

- 40.5 by 11 by 36 in (103 by 28 by 91 cm), 150 pound (wet strength) 3-ply kraft bags with a water-resistant interior lining. These bags are the most commonly used and can usually hold from 100 to 400 seedlings placed length-wise, rolled, and completely shut using a plastic zip tie.
- 25 by 10 by 36 in (63 by 25 by 91 cm), 150 pound 3-ply kraft with a water-resistant interior lining. These bags are used as needed when seedlings are too tall to fit into the wider bags and when packaging smaller quantities than 100 per bag. These bags will usually hold 100 but can hold 200 seedlings placed root system down and the stems sticking out of the top of the bag. A zip tie is also used to secure the bag.

There are a wide variety of bags and packaging options on the market. Nursery managers need to carefully evaluate these many possibilities when designing a packaging solution that best fits their local requirements.

As indicated, seedlings are either placed root systems down so the stems extend out of the top of the bag or seedlings are placed so they are oriented flat in the bag and the top of the bags are rolled down tight before being strapped shut. When placing the seedlings flat in the bag, bundles of seedlings are alternately placed so that half of the seedlings are pointing one direction and the other half of the seedlings are pointing the opposite direction. This allows for a more uniformly packed bag that stacks, stores and ships more efficiently. Bags will typically hold 100 to 200 seedlings when grown to normal specifications. There are rare occasions when seedlings are so large only 25 to 50 seedlings will fit in a bag. Similarly, small seedlings may be packed at 300, 400, or even 500 seedlings per bag. Plastic zip ties of either 36 or 48 in (91 or 122 cm) length are used to secure the bag. The 36-in (91-cm) long zip ties can be used on smaller diameter bags and the 48-in (122-cm) long zip ties are used on larger diameter bags. Using zip ties instead of poly straps that are applied with strapping machines eliminates the maintenance, adjustment, and repairs associated with those machines.

The bags that have been fully packed and secured with a zip tie are placed back on the seedling bed, where they await loading onto a haul-in wagon. Each bag should be properly labeled with species and seedling number before being loaded onto the haul-in wagon. There may be additional relevant information that could be put on each bag label: customer name, delivery location, lifting date, and any seedling treatments such as pest control applications, etc. All labels have heavy-duty freezer adhesive backing to ensure they do not fall off during transport to the cooler and handling by loading dock personnel and customers. Permanent markers are another option for bag labeling.

Transport

Once seedlings have been fully packed and labeled, they are ready for loading onto seedling racks (industry-standard Jarke style metal stackable racks) and taken to cold storage. A haul-in wagon is driven alongside the bed with workers stacking the bags on seedling racks on the haul-in wagon (fig. 11c.2). One haul-in wagon can hold three to four seedling racks. The seedling racks will have their legs inserted and stretch-wrap will be wrapped around each rack to keep the bags secure during transport to cold storage. Depending on the size of the bags, one rack should hold between 20 and 40 bags. This means that each metal seedling rack can transport 2,000 to 8,000 seedlings, and each haul-in wagon can transport 6,000 to 32,000 seedlings. Two haul-in wagons should keep up with the production of a full crew processing an average of 250,000 to 300,000 seedlings per day. Forklifts unload the full racks as they arrive at the cold storage facility, where each full rack is properly inventoried before going into cold storage. Empty racks are then placed on the haul-in wagons and taken to the field.

Grading

There is no single standard of seedling specifications meeting all State, Federal, and private customer requirements. Each grower should be aware of the needs of its customers as well as general industry standards for seedling size in their market area. All cost-share programs will have a unique set of seedling specifications. In general, the following standards should meet the majority of all hardwood seedling specification requirements:

- Average seedling height 18 to 24 in (46 to 61 cm)
- Average root length 8 to 10 in (20 to 25 cm)
- Average root collar diameter 1/4 to 3/8 in (6 to 9.5 mm)
- Disease and damage-free

Individual species need to be surveyed in August or September for any potential seedling quality and/or specification issues. When possible, customers are notified early of any potential seedling quality issues. This not only helps maintain good customer relations, but also provides time for them to evaluate and determine their minimum acceptable standards or possibly swap species, which is very common in the hardwood seedling market. Some customers have seedling specifications that can only be met by manually grading each seedling. A number of issues must be addressed in these cases. First, production will definitely slow down when field grading and, because the grading is done during field packing, the packing crew must be instructed as to the specifications and what causes a seedling to fall outside the range of acceptability. Prior planning is necessary to determine what should be done with seedlings too small to make the specifications. Will presumed inventory numbers be reduced and how does this affect sales numbers? Should undersized seedlings remain in the field to be later incorporated into the soil? Is there another customer who might be willing to accept the smaller seedling size? These issues need to be addressed in advance.

Seedling Storage

Storage Facilities

A cooler building 90 ft wide by 90 ft long and 20 ft high (27 by 27 by 6 m) with insulated panel walls and roof is used for seedling cold storage at the ArborGen Bluff City Nursery. Large electric insulated doors open to allow for forklift and rack entry and exit. Plastic curtain strips line the inside of each large insulated door to retain the cold air inside. There is adequate space for pedestrian traffic with an emergency exit away from forklift traffic. Seedling storage racks are laid out so that forklifts can safely and easily access all rows. The cooler allows for the storage of 1.2 million to 1.8 million hardwood seedlings. The number of metal seedling racks required to fill the cooler is 300 to 400. Extra racks are in place to meet shipping and satellite storage needs.

The target temperature for hardwood seedling storage is 36 °F (2 °C) and not allowed to fall below freezing. The humidity should be as high as possible, especially when using open-ended bags that allow for the top of the seedlings to extend outside the bag. Air circulation is sufficient to allow for quick cool down during times when the outside air temperature is high or the doors remain open for extended periods of time and warmer seedlings are being lifted and placed into the cooler. Wireless temperature monitors are employed that can be accessed at any time through cell phone applications or websites that download the data. In many cases, alarms can be set to notify the grower when the temperature falls outside a given range or if the humidity falls below a set point.

Storage Time

There are currently no universally accepted set of standards in the forest nursery industry for determining how long hardwood seedlings can be properly stored. Certainly, the personal species-specific experience of individual nursery managers is important. An assessment of seedling dormancy is also important. The ArborGen Bluff City Nursery has specific guidelines that compare the number of chilling hours with the amount of cold storage seedlings can withstand without significant declines in seedling quality.

A general rule that could be safely applied by most nurseries in the Southeastern United States would be the following:

- **Less than 200 chilling hours**

  Seedlings are considered to be very metabolically active. Any seedling lifting should be done with caution and planting should occur within 1 to 3 days.

- **Between 200 and 400 chilling hours**

  Most species can be stored for 1 to 2 weeks before outplanting.

- **Greater than 400 chilling hours**

  Most species can be stored for more than 4 weeks before outplanting.

The above should be taken as a guideline and modified by each nursery location to fit its specific circumstances and experiences. The guideline above also assumes that everything has been done correctly in the lifting and packing process before healthy seedlings have been placed in cold storage. Some species do not store well for long periods of time. Sweetgum (*Liquidambar styraciflua* L.) is one species that does not store as well as most other hardwood species. Growers should communicate with customers to ensure sweetgum is lifted, shipped, and planted in as short a timeframe as possible. When storage is required for sweetgum, reducing the storage times listed in the guideline above by half would be a safe starting point.

Reference

Williams, R.D.; Hanks, S.H. 1976. Hardwood nursery guide (formerly Hardwood nurseryman's guide, revised 1994). Agric. Handb. 473. Washington, DC: U.S. Department of Agriculture, Forest Service. 78 p.

Seedling Lifting, Packing, and Storage at the ArborGen Georgia Nursery

11d

R.E. Cross, Jr.

Robert E. Cross, Jr., retired as Nursery Manager, ArborGen Georgia Nursery, ArborGen Inc., Shellman, GA

Outline

Nursery Description

The Timing of Lifting and Outplanting

- Dormancy
- Hot Planting
- Outplanting Conditions

Seedling Preparation for Harvesting

- Top Pruning
- Undercutting
- Lateral Pruning

Seedling Harvest

- Equipment Preparation
- Harvest Scheduling
- Lifting
- Culling

Storage

- Processing into Storage
- Storage Facilities
- Maximum Recommended Storage Times
- Potential Storage Problems

References

Facing Page: *Field crew lifting hardwoods. (Photo by Robert Cross, Jr.)*

Nursery Description

The ArborGen Georgia Nursery is located in Randolph County, GA. This location is in the southwest corner of Georgia, 30 miles west of Albany, and 30 miles east of Eufaula, AL, or 2 1/2 hours south of Atlanta, and 2 hours north of Tallahassee, FL. The nursery is located at 402 feet (ft) (122 meters [m]) elevation, with deep sandy soils of Lakeland and Troup soil types. The nursery has produced up to approximately 65 million seedlings annually, including 2.5 million hardwoods, which can include more than 50 different species of hardwood seedlings, the majority being in the genus *Quercus*.

The Timing of Lifting and Outplanting

Dormancy

The best time to harvest and outplant hardwood seedlings in the Southeastern United States is when they are most dormant. Typically, this may occur between late December and early March. Fully dormant seedlings are easier to lift and are more resistant to stresses caused by the lifting process. Seedling storability and resistance to adverse outplanting conditions increase as seedlings become more dormant. As a result, dormancy has a direct impact on seedling quality.

The onset of dormancy is almost entirely weather-dependent. Seedlings will exhibit more dormancy as the temperatures drop in the fall. A fairly good indicator of dormancy is the timing of leaf fall (see table 1 in chapter 11c), although some species tend to hang on to their leaves even after several frosts, such as sweetgum (*Liquidambar styraciflua* L.) and the oaks (*Quercus* spp.) (fig.11d.1). Dormancy can also be estimated with the amount of chilling hours received at the nursery. A chilling hour is one hour between 32 and 45 °F (0 and 7 °C). Chilling hours at the ArborGen Georgia nursery are monitored with a Davis Instrument weather station using Vantage Pro software from the first week of October through the first week of January. The minimum for lifting hardwoods is 200 chilling hours. These hours are kept in a spreadsheet for a yearly reference. It is assumed seedlings will become more dormant as chilling hours accumulate, with full dormancy reached at 400 chilling hours.

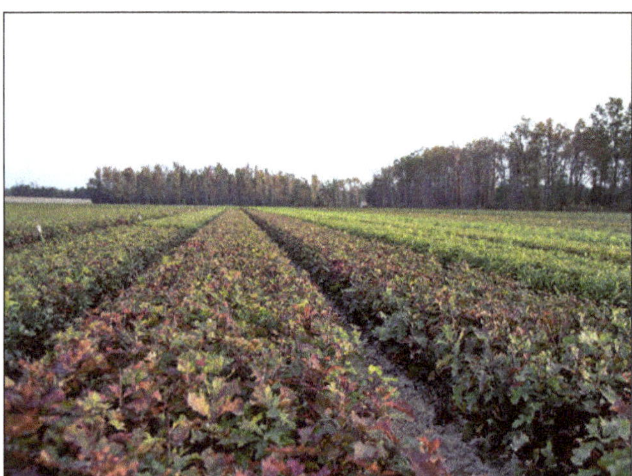

***Figure 11d.1**—Shumard oak in November, 2008. These trees are ready to be lifted. (Photo by R. Cross.)*

"Hot Planting"

Customers sometimes request that seedlings be lifted and outplanted when nondormant. This "hot planting" (less than 100 chilling hours) can begin as early as November 15 in USDA Plant Hardiness Zones 7 and 8, as long as extra attention is given to root handling and moisture retention. Extra root gel (approximately 5 percent) needs to be added to each package during this period of harvesting. (Extra gel should not cause storage problems because the seedlings will not be in storage for an extended period.) The seedlings will need to be replanted in moist soil within 72 hours of harvesting at the nursery. These same "hot planting" precautions regarding seedling handling and outplanting conditions also apply to seedlings lifted after the first week of March, as seedlings may be breaking dormancy by then.

Outplanting Conditions

Another condition that is just as important as dormancy is soil moisture at the outplanting site. A seedling placed in dry soil will have difficulty with survival regardless of dormancy. A nondormant seedling transplanted into dry soil has little to no chance of survival, as root desiccation starts immediately without adequate soil moisture.

The nursery manager has to make a decision as whether to harvest the seedlings requested or delay harvesting until adequate soil moisture is obtained at the planting site. However, if the decision to harvest has already been made by the customer, then other factors need to be addressed. These factors include noting the dry soil conditions, indicating that seedlings be transplanted at 3 to 4 inches (in) (7.5 to 10 centimeters [cm]) deeper than the original ground line in the nursery bed, and suggesting that seedling root systems not be exposed to open air or wind until time of planting. These concerns and factors are not species specific, as dry roots in dry soil results in seedling mortality.

Seedling Preparation for Harvesting

In preparation for harvesting hardwood seedlings, several key objectives must be accomplished to enhance seedling morphology and to ensure outplanting survival and growth. The more species a nursery grows, the more complicated the enhancement process.

Top Pruning

Top pruning is done to produce the desired balance between shoot length and root length. The target is a seeding whose shoot length is, at maximum, three times the root length. If the shoot length is over three times the root length, then unacceptable stress on the seedling root system occurs upon outplanting, as roots will not be able to provide transpiring leaf surfaces with enough moisture to ensure survival. Top pruning helps keep transpirational surfaces in balance with moisture-absorbing surfaces. The timing of top pruning is discretionary, depending on nursery location and temperature patterns. Timing is species dependent, can be started at any time after reaching 18 in (46 cm) of shoot height, and should be completed 2 to 3 weeks before harvesting begins. The objective is to modify the root:shoot ratio and slow growth if needed. The goal is to have seedlings no more than 24 in (61 cm) tall. Oaks and sycamore (*Plantanus occidentalis* L.) respond well to top pruning and may need to be top pruned more than once. Some genera do not respond as well to top pruning, particularly the ashes (*Fraxinus* spp.) and the maples (*Acer* spp.), as their opposite branching pattern results in multiple sprouts when pruned.

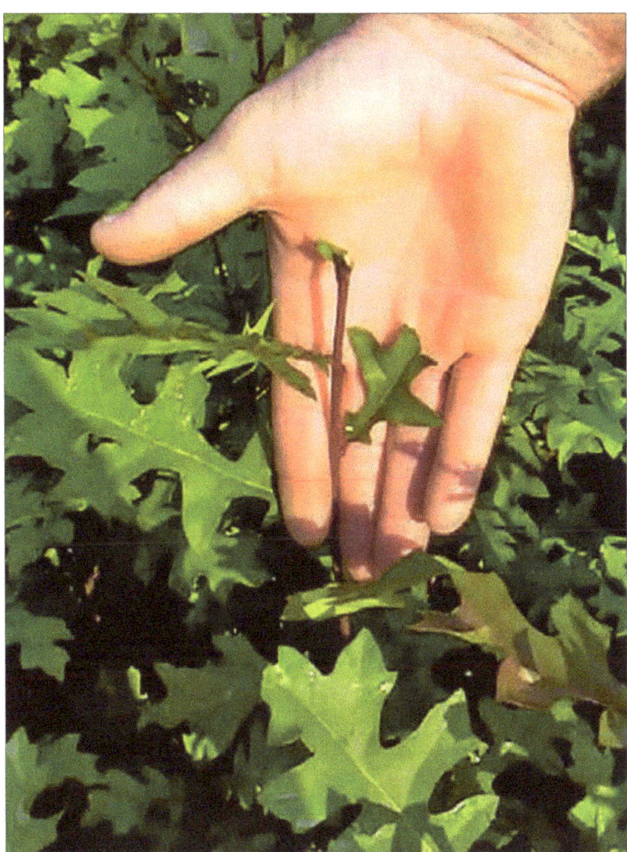

***Figure 11d.3**—Nuttall oak seedling after top-pruning in September, 2005. (Photo by R. Cross.)*

Over the years, top pruning hardwood seedlings has been accomplished using several different methods, including handheld cutters, hedge-type trimmers, rotary mowers, and sickle-type hay mowers. A typical sickle-type mower that is easy to maintain and operate is the Enorossi (fig 11d.2). This is a double-action mower that makes a clean and even cut (fig. 11d.3). A double-action mower cuts in both directions on the cutting bar as the blades reciprocate, thus making a cleaner cut. As with any morphological modification of seedlings, extreme care should be taken to ensure a healthy, vibrant seedling is produced (fig. 11d.4).

***Figure 11d.2**—Nuttall oak being top pruned in September, 2005. (Photo by R. Cross.)*

***Figure 11d.4**—A field of* Quercus *spp after being top-pruned in August, 2008. (Photo by R. Cross.)*

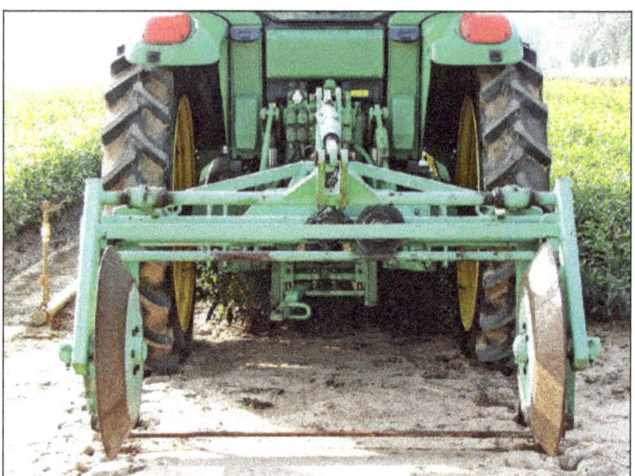

Figure 11d.5—Sawtooth oak being undercut in November, 2007. (Photo by R. Cross.)

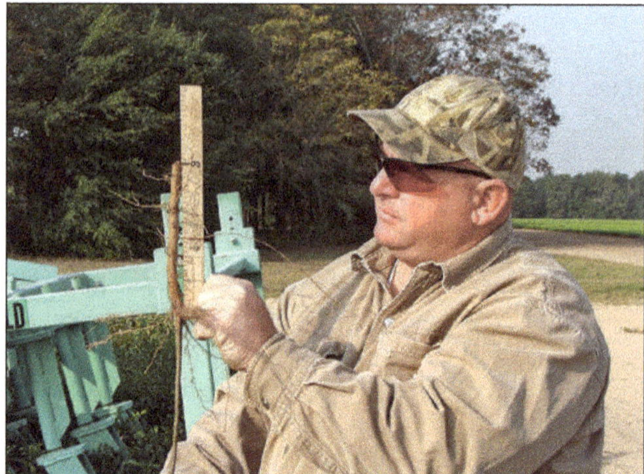

Figure 11d.6—Root system of sawtooth oak after undercut in November, 2007. (Photo by R. Cross.)

Undercutting

The objectives of undercutting are to produce the desired balance between shoot length and root length, enhance the development of fibrous feeder roots, and make transplanting more successful. As indicated earlier, the root length should be one-third that of the shoot length. The goal for a good hardwood root system is to undercut the tap root at 8 in (20 cm). This depth also meets Federal Government guidelines for the Conservation Reserve Program, the Wildlife Reserve Program, and mitigation plantings.

In order to undercut hardwood seedlings that are 2 ft (61 cm) in height, an undercutter with a raised frame is needed to keep from damaging seedlings as they pass through the undercutter body (fig. 11d.5). The Whitfield undercutter has a raised frame with enough clearance for hardwood top passage. This model also has a reciprocating blade that moves side to side. This motion helps make a cleaner cut and assists with movement through the soil.

Typically, undercutting is performed at least 1 month before expected harvest. This timeframe is critical to ensure the cut-off tap root has sufficient time to recover from the effect of undercutting (fig. 11d.6). A high soil moisture content will assist with the firmness of the soil and hold the seedlings and seedling bed in place, resulting in little or no disruption to both. A good soil moisture content for undercutting is 85 percent to 90 percent. As with any morphological adjustment, seedlings should be monitored and irrigation applied if seedlings have been unacceptably stressed.

Lateral Pruning

There are three principal objectives for lateral root pruning. The first objective is to shorten the lateral roots to assist with transplanting and help ensure that all roots are inserted into the planting hole. The second is to promote the development of fibrous feeder roots next to the main tap root. This improves the ratio of root weight to shoot weight and hopefully improves outplanting survival by increasing water absorption into the roots. The third objective is to facilitate lifting. The lateral root trench will sub-divide the bed down the drills so that seedlings can be hand-lifted easily from just the drill in which they were planted (fig. 11d.7). The lateral pruner is inserted between the five drills of hardwoods and the outside bed edges (fig. 11d.8).

Seedling Harvest

Equipment Preparation

Equipment selection depends on the quantity of hardwood seedlings produced, available labor source and supply, soil

Figure 11d.7—Whitfield® lateral pruner. (Photo by R. Cross.)

Figure 11d.8—Whitfield® lateral pruner over sawtooth oak. (Photo by R. Cross.)

types, customer demands, and, to some degree, expected weather conditions. The following equipment is the minimum needed: two tractors, two haul-in wagons to transport seedlings from the field, a lifter (such as a Fobro), a vehicle (preferably a pickup truck), and a radio for communications. Another small but often important item required is a bed map describing the location of each species in the nursery beds.

It is important that equipment used during lifting is in proper working condition prior to operation. Tractors and vehicles should be checked to verify they have completed normal maintenance with oil and filter changes. In the case of cab tractors, the internal filters in the cab for air conditioning and heating systems should be checked and changed if needed. Similarly, tires should be checked for any needed repairs or replacement. It is always a good idea to keep a spare front tractor tire mounted on a rim and ready for replacement. Haul-in trailers used for seeding transport should be checked for wheel bearing greasing or replacement, and a rim-mounted spare tire is very helpful. Trailer frames need to be checked for major cracks or other structure damage, including the front connecting tongue and the handrail and step used for mounting and dismounting the trailer.

The lifter is a major piece of equipment used in the harvest process, and hand harvesting could come to a halt without it. With a sizeable crop of hardwood seedlings, two lifters need to be on site and ready to use, along with a reliable stock of spare parts. Several maintenance items need to be considered with any lifter, including bearings, power take-off (PTO) shafts, PTO joints, gear box, chain with chain repair tool, and spare tire. Lifters are very rugged and can be operated for an entire harvest season with little or no repairs if the proper maintenance is performed, plenty of grease is applied, and little or no water is used during the cleanup process until year end. These lifters tend to be one-person machines, meaning that if the same person operates the lifter every day, there will be fewer maintenance issues during the harvest season.

Harvest Scheduling

As customer requests come in, a daily lifting schedule is prepared of species and the quantities to be harvested. This schedule is given to the hardwood supervisor, who reviews the lifting schedule and prepares the harvest plan. This plan includes labor requirements, bags, bag labels, gel, species location and bed location map, and racks and cooler space required. At this time, the supervisor also determines if the harvest will be picked up, delivered, or shipped, so it can be determined how the lifting schedule will require seedlings to be packaged in the field and at the packing room. The bags for each species are counted, labeled, and placed on a haul-in wagon that is headed to the field.

The footage needed to be lifted for a particular species is determined using the bed location map. This process is facilitated by software that tracks each linear bed foot planted by species. This bed map also has the density listed by species, along with the exact location, total footage, and total seedlings. The supervisor reviews the required quantity of seedlings scheduled for harvest and calculates the footage needed to harvest this amount of seedlings.

Lifting

The first step of the lifting operation is to run the lifter through the species of seedlings scheduled for harvest. The lifter speed is determined by species, soil moisture, and operator experience. Soil moisture plays a major role in the harvesting process, but sometimes the luxury of lifting during ideal soil conditions is not an option. Therefore, proper care and effort should be made to slow down the lifting process so as not to damage the seedlings or cause any undue safety hazards. The lifter has a metal blade that is sharp on the leading edge and, elevated vibrating tines at the rear to loosen the soil and remove as much soil as possible from the seedling root system without causing damage to the seedling roots or tops (fig. 11b.9). The Fobro lifter is a good example of this type of lifter, and it also has enough frame clearance to minimize damage to the seedling shoots and roots.

Figure 11d.9—*Fobro® Lifter. (Photo by R. Cross.)*

There are some safety issues that apply to most lifters:

- The fins on the rear of the lifter become extremely sharp during the lifting season due to soil movement over these fins.
- Extreme caution should be used when removing seedlings or soil from this area.
- A tarp or cover should be placed over these fins when the lifter is not in use.
- Covers for the PTO shaft may have to be made to prevent a hand or arm injury.
- The lifter should be placed on blocks when not in use to prevent erosion of the blade edge.
- Have a radio on hand for communications for the safety of the lifting crew.

Typically, the lifting crew has one person on the lifter tractor, one person on the haul-in wagon, and an even number of crew members on opposite sides of the bed (fig 11d.10). Ideally, the nursery would have a smaller crew of 6 to 8 people harvesting, but on occasion it may be necessary to use as many as 30 crew members to harvest the quantity needed for that particular day's schedule. The members of the lifting crew are separated by 10 to 12 ft (3 to 3.6 m) along the bed to prevent soil or leaf residue from flying onto their fellow workers. This separation also increases production. As the crew progresses down the bed, the crew members maintain this interval, harvesting their section of the bed then moving forward to the head of the lifting line. As the seedlings are harvested, they are culled and counted into bundles of 25 or 50, depending on species or customer request. The seedlings are placed on the ground in these bundled counts (fig. 11d.11). A separate crew of two to four members follows the lifting crew and immediately places the seedlings in paper bags. Bags are kraft paper with a thin, wax-coated liner (fig. 11d.12). Because seedlings have been top pruned, they can be laid horizontally in the bag,

Figure 11d.11—*Field crew lifting sweetgum in January, 2008. (Photo by R. Cross.)*

Figure 11d.10—*Field crew lifting hardwoods. (Photo by R. Cross.)*

Figure 11d.12—*Sweetgum bagged and ready for transport to packing room in January, 2008. (Photo by R. Cross.)*

Table 11d.1—Minimum recommended hardwood seedling size specifications used by the ArborGen Georgia Nursery.

Customer type	Height (in)	Root length (in)	Caliper (in)
Government programs, regardless of species	18-24	8	.25
Nongovernment programs, regardless of species	12-18	6-8	.125

in = inches

allowing for complete bag closure. Most of the seedlings are bagged at 200 per bag, so the crew will put in either 4 or 8 bundles per bag, depending on customer request. Occasionally, a smaller quantity of 25 seedlings is shipped, so these are bagged separately in smaller bags at the same time.

The lifting crew supervisor, who is preferably a company employee, will have the responsibility and accountability to ensure that safety, equipment maintenance, and proper harvesting procedures are followed, and that the correct quantity, species, and seedling specifications meet the customer's request. A contract crew with a foreman is sufficient for the other labor sources.

Culling

Seedlings are culled in the field during lifting operations, removing seedlings that are too small, diseased, or damaged. These culled seedlings are pulled at the same time the other seedlings are lifted and then placed on a haul-in wagon and discarded before the wagon returns to the field. The desired seedling specification is a height of 18 to 24 in (46 to 61 cm), a minimum root collar diameter (RCD) of 1/4 in (6 mm) with a tap root length of 8 in (20 cm). These specifications have to be met for any seedling grown for a Federal Government-subsidized program (table 11d.1). If they are not part of such a program, then seedlings may be grown or selected to meet customer specifications. Some minor species such as dogwood (*Cornus florida* L.), catalpa (*Catalpa bignonioides* Walter), and redbud (*Cercis canadensis* L.) that are often grown for the horticultural industry or game management do not have to meet these specifications.

A company employee can supervise the culling procedure and train contract workers to help with this process. Species-specific culling criteria are communicated to the contract crew involved in the actual lifting process. The culling procedure requires the use of a measuring stick, tape measure, and digital calipers, and is closely monitored to ensure that seedlings meet customer specifications.

Figure 11d.13—Spraying gel on roots inside bag prior to shipment. (Photo by R. Cross.)

Storage

Processing Into Storage

The bags of 200 seedlings lifted in the field are transported on haul-in wagons to the packing room. Further review is done to ensure there are no culls in the bag, correct species labeling is on the bag, and gel is sprayed inside the bag to the root system (fig. 11d.13). The bag is then rolled down as snuggly as possible and double-strapped. The bags of 200 are then counted as they are loaded onto a seedling rack for either storage or shipment. Smaller quantity seedlings, such as 25, 50, or 100, are kept separate and prepared for customer pickup or shipment. The seedling racks are labeled and tagged with species identification and quantity. This information is then entered into a computer using software that tracks the species, number of bags, and bag counts that have been moved into the cooler.

Storage Facilities

The storage facility is designed to maximize the available space. The facility has front and rear doors large enough for forklift entry, as well as a pedestrian door. Clear vinyl strips over the cooler doors help keep cold air inside the cooler and warmer air outside during constant entry and exit of the forklift (fig. 11d.14). Cooler height evenly accommodates seedling storage racks. The cooler is 55 ft long, 34 ft wide, and 18.5 ft high (17 by 10 by 5.5 m) and can store 140 racks. An additional concrete rack storage area is available to accommodate empty racks so cooler space is not consumed with empties. Jarke racks are used for storage of hardwood seedlings. These racks are 44 in high (including the leg), 70 in wide and 45 in deep

Figure 11d.14—Sawtooth tree seedlings in storage on racks. (Photo by R. Cross.)

(1.1 by 1.8 by 1.1 m). They are easily handled with a forklift and can be stacked four high inside the cooler or two high inside a refrigerated van. A temperature and humidity monitor is mounted on the upper wall inside the cooler. This equipment feeds a constant stream of readings to two wireless consoles located in the main office. The readings are real-time with an alarm for unsuitable conditions in the cooler—lower than 90-percent humidity and/or below 34 and above 36 °F (below 1 and above 2 °C).

Maximum Recommended Storage Times

There is no substitute for planting freshly harvested seedlings. These are seedlings that are lifted and replanted within 3 days. This ideal situation rarely occurs, however, and seedling storage is an inevitable and an important part of the seedling handling process. The amount of time seedlings can be stored depends on several factors, including species, cooler storage temperature and humidity control capability, seedling packaging, root coating, and type of storage.

Some species, such as sweetgum, do not respond well to storage and need to be planted within a week of harvest. Other species, such as sycamore, are very resilient when fully dormant and with the proper temperature and humidity control can be stored for 3 months with minimum loss in outplanting survival. Rewatering is not necessary when seedlings are top-pruned and placed horizontally in a closed bag with a good root coating of gel for moisture retention. On the other hand, open-topped bags with the seedling tops exposed (and to some degree the roots) may require that each bag be rewatered after 3 to 4 weeks of storage, depending on cooler temperature and humidity conditions.

The type of storage is critical in determining length of storage. A well-maintained drive-in cooler with forklift access, loading docks, seedling rack storage, and humidity and temperature control provides the best long-term storage capability. Other refrigerated storage types, refrigerated vans for example, require constant monitoring and make long-term storage difficult, if not impossible. Weather conditions often determine the feasible length of nonrefrigerated storage, such as enclosed or open sheds. Seedlings need to be planted within 3 to 5 days when the temperature inside the storage area is between 50 and 70 °F (10 and 21 °C). If temperatures inside the storage area remain above 75 °F (24 °C), seedlings should not be stored more than 24 hours. Seedlings in bags/bundles/boxes cannot be stored for more than a few hours at temperatures above 85 °F (29 °C). Lethal temperatures occur in bag/bundles/boxes at 118 °F (48 °C), but seedlings can be weakened or damaged if temperatures in bags/bundles/boxes remain at 85 °F (29 °C) for very long. The ArborGen Georgia Nursery recommends hardwood seedling storage times and temperatures be similar to those of pine, as specified by the Mississippi Forestry Commission.

Potential Storage Problems

Issues relating to top desiccation, root system dehydration, or diseases are often storage-related discussion topics. All of these are important and relevant, but there are other factors and issues with storage. When producing hardwoods in large quantities (1 million or more), storage capacity is a major issue, as hardwoods take up 6 times more space than pine. Tracking the location, inventory, and date packed of multiple species in a near-capacity storage area can also be a challenge. These problems are compounded when rotating the inventory to ship the longest-stored material first is a priority. Packaging can be another issue when seedlings are stored for an extended time (greater than 4 weeks). The more time seedlings are stored, the more susceptible packaging becomes to the break-down effects of moisture and handling. Some of the best practices for storage include rotating older stock, not over-applying root coating, and using high-quality packing material.

Hardwood seedlings produced in the Southeastern United States are sensitive to freeze damage after lifting. While seedlings may have hardened-off to above-ground freezing temperatures in the nursery, root exposure to below-freezing temperatures after lifting often results in damage to the seedling's root system, resulting in mortality. Seedlings should not be stored where the temperature is 32 °F (0 °C) or less. If temperatures below freezing are expected in the storage area, then temperatures in the storage area and temperatures in the seedling package should be monitored every 2 hours after the temperature goes below 32 °F (0 °C). Seedlings should be moved or covered with a thermal tarp to keep the root systems from freezing.

References

Williams, R.D.; Hanks, S.H. 1976. Hardwood nursery guide (formerly Hardwood nurseryman's guide, revised 1994). Agric. Handb. 473. Washington, DC: U.S. Department of Agriculture, Forest Service. 78 p.

Mississippi Forestry Commission. 2016. Seedling tips and care. http://www.mfc.ms.gov/seedling-tips-care. (January 2017).

Essentials of Nursery Administration

12

K. McNabb, T. Starkey, J.L. Sibley, and D. Bremer

Ken McNabb is W. Kelly Mosley Professor Emeritus, School of Forestry and Wildlife Sciences, Auburn University, Auburn University, Auburn, AL

Tom Starkey is retired from Southern Forest Nursery Management Cooperative, Auburn University, Auburn University, Auburn, AL

Jeff L. Sibley is Barbara and Charles Bohmann Endowed Professor, Department of Horticulture, Auburn University, Auburn University, Auburn, AL

Dan Bremer, is president, AgWorksH2, LLC, Lake Park, GA

Outline

Facing Page: *Reefer units awaiting shipment of nursery seedlings. (Photo by Robert Cross.)*

Introduction

A typical nursery manager is trained in one of the sciences. Whether it be forestry, agronomy, biology, or another field related to natural resources, the manager's education and experience concentrates on the biological side of management. However (and some might say unfortunately), a nursery manager must inevitably deal with a number of administrative issues that have little to do with biology or the growing of plants. Government regulations, whether Federal, State, or local, impact nursery operations in virtually every aspect of management, including personnel, equipment, plant protection, sales, and seedling transportation. No manager can possibly be familiar with all the potential regulations affecting the nursery production business. Managers should, however, have some idea of the scope and reach of the more important regulations universally affecting managers production systems.

The following sections provide a general introduction to key regulatory structures affecting nursery production. This information is in no way intended to substitute for sound legal or expert advice, but rather should be used as a first alert to the many serious issues associated with certain aspects of nursery management. The complexities and potential ramifications of these topics must be given due attention, and any manager is strongly encouraged to seek out, consult, and follow the advice of legally trained individuals familiar with these specific areas.

An Agricultural Enterprise

A forest tree nursery growing hardwoods will qualify as an "agriculture enterprise," a designation that is important for a number of reasons related to taxes, labor management, trucking regulations, and other unique provisions. In States that collect sales tax, most business operations will obtain a sales tax exempt number, which is used to waive sales tax on materials consumed in the supply chain and production process. As an agriculture operation, most States do not require that sales tax be assessed on products grown in the nursery.

The nursery will need to obtain a Federal Employee Identification Number (FEIN). The FEIN is needed to file withholding taxes (Federal and State Income Tax, Medicare, Social Security [FICA], and Federal Unemployment Tax [FUTA]) on employees who are hired directly by the company and not considered as a contract labor. There is a difference between workers hired directly by the company and those that fall under the category of "contract labor" provided to the nursery by an independent contractor. The difference between whether a person is hired as an hourly worker (either permanent or temporary) or as a contract laborer has significantly different tax ramification and may also limit direct supervision of the worker's daily activities. Workers' Compensation Insurance, and other forms of insurance, such as liability, fire, and theft, will also be required by most nurseries. Other permits, licenses, and tax numbers may also be necessary for the business, depending on State or local requirements. Designation as an agricultural enterprise is quite significant to nursery administration for a number of reasons.

Labor

Occupational Safety and Health Act

The Occupational Safety and Health Act of 1970 created the Occupational Safety and Health Administration (OSHA). The Act was intended "to assure safe and healthful working conditions for working men and women by setting and enforcing standards and by providing training, outreach, education, and assistance." Although most workers in the United States are protected by OSHA coverage, it is not universal and may vary by employer type and number of employees. OSHA has prepared standards across virtually all job types, including agriculture, and periodically updates/modifies those standards. The standards can get very specific, such as the need for tractor roll-over bars, or toilet facilities for agricultural workers involved in hand labor activities, labor housing standards, and injury reporting/posting requirements. In addition, OSHA may perform periodic inspections to evaluate standard compliance. OSHA works with States to develop and operate their own job safety programs, and several States in the Eastern United States have these in place.

Fair Labor Standards Act

The FLSA sets the minimum wage across the United States, as well as overtime pay and recordkeeping standards for private sector and government employees, both part-time and full-time. The Act is enforced by the Wage and Hour Division of the U.S. Department of Labor. The Federal law exempts certain types of employees, particularly professional, administrative, and executive employees. "Farmworkers employed by anyone who used no more than 500 man days of farm labor in any calendar quarter of the preceding calendar year" are exempt (DOL 2018a). Like the Federal wage and hour law, State law often exempts particular occupations or industries from the minimum labor standard generally applied to cover employment. Additionally, some State and local governments set minimum wage rates higher than the respective Federal minimum wage. This hourly wage for a State also determines the minimum wage that can be paid to workers considered as contract laborers. Managers should consult the laws of their respective States in determining whether that State's minimum wage applies to a particular employment (DOL 2018b). This information often may be found at the websites maintained by State labor departments. Links to these websites are available at www.dol.gov/whd/contacts/State_of.htm. Overtime, time and one half after 40 hours worked, generally does not apply to "agriculture." However, this exemption can be complex and should be reviewed by management. Records of hours worked and pay records must be maintained for at least 3 years.

Guest Worker Programs

H-2A. Agricultural enterprises may employ foreign nationals brought into the United States through a guest worker program administered jointly by the U.S. Department of Labor (DOL), and the U.S. Citizenship and Immigration Services (USCIS) of the Department of Homeland Security (DHS). "The Immigration and Nationality Act (INA) authorizes the lawful admission of temporary, nonimmigrant workers (H-2A workers) to perform agricultural labor or services of a temporary or seasonal nature" (DOL 2016b). H-2A employers, however, must first show there are not sufficient numbers of U.S. workers who are qualified and available to do the work, nor will the use of guest laborers affect the wages and earnings of U.S. workers.

The hiring and administration of guest workers can be a very complex process. For example, the hourly minimum wage is used as a benchmark for domestic unskilled labor and the adverse effect wage (AEWR) for guest worker programs. Specifically, the AEWR is the hourly wage set by the Government for foreign H-2A workers and corresponding U.S. citizen workers. The AEWR for each State is based on the "prevailing wage" for a similar class of work in a given State (averaging about $10.80 for the Southern States). Therefore, as the minimum wage for domestic workers increases, the AEWR increases as well. Nurseries that utilize contract labor frequently will use workers from the H-2A program. If so, the integrity of such a contractor should be well established, in addition to having documented experience in providing contract labor for nursery operations.

H-2B. The H-2A guest worker program should not be confused with the H-2B program. The former deals specifically with guest workers for agricultural enterprises as defined by the Department of Labor. The latter deals with guest workers for other areas of commerce that may include manufacturing, construction, industrial jobs, and tree planting. For whatever reason, tree planting and other field activities like herbicide spraying, are not considered part of an agricultural enterprise. The regulations covering tree planting, spraying, and other silvicultural operations fall under a different, although related, set of regulations. The Migrant and Seasonal Agricultural Worker Protection Act also applies to this kind of work. In a similar fashion, landscaping work falls under the regulations of the H-2B, while horticultural and forest seedling nursery workers fall under the purview of the H-2A program.

The Migrant and Seasonal Agricultural Worker Protection Act (MSPA). The Department of Labor's Wage and Hour Division is responsible for the administration of the MSPA. The purpose of the MSPA is to safeguard "migrant and seasonal agricultural workers in their interactions with farm labor contractors, agricultural employers, agricultural associations, and providers of migrant housing" (DOL 2016a). The MSPA mandates that farm labor contractors be registered with the Department of Labor before they may begin recruiting, hiring, housing, transporting, and caring for seasonal agricultural workers. It is up to the employer (nursery administration) to verify the registration of individual contractors. The Act also contains a number of specific provisions regarding the interaction between the contractor and the workers in regard to wages, housing, transportation, and other issues. Nurseries and other labor contractors that are subject to the regulations of the MSPA are required to display a poster "explaining the rights and protections for workers required under the MSPA."

Employment Eligibility Verification

The USCIS Form I-9 is used to verify the identity and employment eligibility of individuals working in the United States. It is the employer's responsibility to make sure that a Form I-9 is properly completed and filed for all employees, both citizens and noncitizens alike. Federal law mandates that employers hire only individuals "who may legally work in the United States, either United States citizens, or foreign citizens who have the necessary authorization" (https://www.uscis.gov/e-verify). E-Verify is a web-based Federal program administered by the Department of Homeland Security in partnership with the Social Security Administration and set up to facilitate employment eligibility verification. Currently, 22 States, including 18 from the Eastern United States, require the use of E-Verify for at least some public and/or private employers. Several of these States—Alabama, Georgia, Louisiana, Mississippi, North Carolina, South Carolina, and Tennessee—require E-Verify for most employers. The use of contractors to hire guest workers through the H-2A program may provide a degree of separation between nursery managers and the legal responsibilities associated with hiring guest workers, but the issue is complex and should be thoroughly investigated. The relationship between the nursery owner/manager and the contractor and their respective regulatory responsibilities must be clearly understood by both parties.

Pesticides

The Federal Insecticide, Fungicide, and Rodenticide Act

The Federal Insecticide, Fungicide, and Rodenticide Act (FIFRA) was originally passed in 1947 and has been modified various times since them. It is the overarching law that regulates the use of pesticides in the United States with regulation and enforcement given to the Office of Pesticide Programs (OPP) of the U.S. Environmental Protection Agency (EPA). Although a number of other laws impact pesticide use, such as the Food Quality Protection Act of 1996 and the Worker Protection Standards of 1992, FIFRA provides the basic framework for the registration and use of all pesticides, as well as the monitoring and enforcement of pesticide regulation. The following are some of the key provisions of FIFRA.

1. Any pesticide sold or used in the United States must be registered with the EPA according to criteria and procedures set up by the Agency.
2. The Act establishes the categories of "general use" and "restricted use" pesticides, with general use products available to the general public, while restricted use requires specific knowledge and training.
3. The Act sets the requirements for those engaged in "commercial application" to be certified and qualified as such.
4. "Unlawful acts" and penalties are specified as they relate to pesticide use. The most relevant of these is Section 12 (a) (2) (G) "It shall be unlawful for any person to use any registered pesticide in a manner inconsistent with its labeling."
5. FIFRA also sets up a partnership with the States for implementation of the Act.

It is essential to understand the role and importance of State pesticide authorities for the implementation of FIFRA. Pesticide regulations and even individual product labels may not be easy to interpret or understand. It is essential for pesticide applicators, including nursery managers, to develop a working relationship with their State regulatory authority. State authorities can provide invaluable assistance when seeking a label interpretation for the use of a particular product. In addition, States have the authority through Section 24(c) of FIFRA to "provide registration for additional uses of federally registered pesticides." The assistance of State regulatory authorities using the "24(c)" process has been instrumental in securing the use of certain compounds for nursery management. Finally, nursery managers need to be aware of any training opportunities that State agencies may provide, as well as notices about label or other regulatory changes that may occur.

The Worker Protection Standard

The Worker Protection Standard (WPS) was enacted in 1992 and revised in 2015 with the objective of "reducing the risks of illness or injury to workers and handlers resulting from occupational exposures to pesticides used in the production of agricultural plants on agricultural establishments." The WPS mandates that employers set up protection for two types of employees—agriculture workers and pesticide handlers. It is the responsibility of the employer that "employees are *informed* about exposure to pesticides," that "employees are *protected* from exposures to pesticides," and that employers *mitigate* or "address pesticide exposures that employees may experience." The employer, therefore, carries the burden of meeting the standards of the WPS, which includes posting of application areas, establishment of a Restricted Entry Interval (REI), pesticide safety training for workers and handlers (in a language they can understand), display of the WPS poster, availability of OSHA Safety Data Sheets, and a number of additional requirements. An excellent source of information regarding the WPS is the EPA manual on "How to Comply With the 2015 Revised Worker Protection Standard For Agricultural Pesticides: What Owners and Employers Need To Know," at pesticideresources.org/wps/htc/htcmanual.pdf. State regulatory authorities and the State Cooperative Extension System are excellent sources of information regarding the WPS and are typically involved in setting up training opportunities for workers and/or handlers.

Pesticide Storage Facilities

All nurseries must have proper pesticide storage facilities to protect workers and the environment. The State and Federal regulations regarding pesticide storage facility regulations are variable and constantly evolving. Concerns over contamination of ground water by agricultural chemicals caused by improper storage or mixing have been targeted by Federal and State legislation across the United States (Hawkins and Sumner, 2012). Pesticide storage facilities should be a lock-and-key structure separate from other work stations, with ventilation that operates independent of electrical service. It is very important that the structure have a leak-proof roof, and, where applicable, a possible source of heating and cooling to prevent freezing of liquids, extend the shelf life of pesticides, and maintain readable package labels on the pesticide container. A trap floor or drainage traps to catch and contain spills and rinse water is advisable. Perhaps the most important emphasis is that multi-lingual placards be posted in every area of pesticide storage with "Danger Pesticides" type of warnings. Wash basins, eye-wash stations, and potable water should be available in pesticide storage facilities. To minimize risk of fires (and personal safety), there should be No Smoking signs posted, and pesticides should never be stored in the same area as fertilizers (which may be explosive). In the event of a fire, there should be clear indication of the types of chemicals and the hazards fire-safety personnel will be dealing with (i.e., all fires are not extinguished with water). It is highly recommended that a current inventory be maintained of all the pesticides stored in the facility at any given time. Hawkins and Sumner (2012) have provided detailed information for construction of a pesticide facility. Before construction, or to verify the compliance of an existing facility, check with the appropriate State authority.

Fuel Storage Regulations for Farm and Commercial Operators

Federal regulations apply to farm and commercial operators, construction companies, fuel distributors, and others, for operators with fuel storage exceeding 1,320 total gallons. Total storage includes gasoline, diesel, motor oils, transmission and hydraulic fluids, solvents and paint thinners, kerosene and fuel oils. The regulations require a spill containment basin of 110 percent of the fuel storage. They also include a tank design that prevents draining in an accident (top fill and withdrawal), barriers to prevent damage from vehicles hitting tanks, overflow prevention, alarms, and signage. Also required is a written spill mitigation plan for these facilities. Storage over 10,000 gallons require this plan be written by a licensed professional engineer. A detailed publication of these regulations can be found at the University of Tennessee website (Hawkins, 2010): https://utextension.tennessee.edu/publications/Documents/W250.pdf.

Sales and Marketing

There is much truth in the statement "Anybody can grow a plant, it's selling it that's the challenge." Over time, a reputable nursery will build a customer base generating repeat business. However, for newer nurseries, connecting with those needing quality seedlings can be quite a challenge. Nurseries should establish membership and contact with State/regional forestry/nursery associations that may provide sales contacts. Also, attending and/or exhibiting at regional tradeshows put on by forestry/nursery associations is a strong marketing tool and will possibly increase sales, but more importantly, this will tell others about your nursery and products. Most nurseries prepare a standard, printed price list for postal delivery and one-on-one distribution, and most also have a website for providing online information and pricing for customers.

Shipping

Hardwood seedlings are provided to the customer in two ways: picked up at the nursery by the customer or his agent, or shipped to a location designated by the customer. For customers who request their seedlings be shipped by truck (either refrigerated or nonrefrigerated), a nursery will need to establish contacts with either a trucking broker that handles many independent carriers or a dedicated trucking line. Trucking lines or trucking brokers near a nursery can generally be found online. Most loads of hardwood trees shipped by a nursery will not fill a truck and may require hardwood bundles or boxes be palletized.

For all seedlings leaving the nursery, a shipping ticket should accompany the order and be provided to the person picking up the seedlings with a copy being retained by the nursery.

The shipping ticket should contain certain minimum information:

- Date of shipping
- Customer name
- Address for shipment
- Description of each species of seedlings and quantity of each.

Although this is the minimum information required, providing some additional facts on the shipping ticket may help if there are problems with the seedlings after they leave the nursery.

- How were the seedlings picked up? Were they picked up in a pickup truck? A covered or uncovered trailer? Were they covered with a tarp? Were they picked up in a refrigerated or a nonrefrigerated van?
- Were the seedling bundles or boxes stacked directly on one another or stacked to allow air flow between bundles or boxes?
- What were the weather conditions (including approximate air temperature) when they were picked up?
- If a refrigerated transport was used, what instructions were given to the driver as to the proper temperature to maintain and hours of operation?

Plant Inspection and Certificates

Nurseries growing plant material are subject to annual inspection by the State Agriculture Office or Commissioner of Agriculture and Industries Agency before shipment from the nursery. Each State has regulatory authority to protect the agricultural enterprises of that State from the spread of plant and animal species deemed injurious to its agricultural sector. Federal law, administered by the Animal and Plant Health Inspection Service of the U.S. Department of Agriculture, is responsible for interstate shipment regulations, as well as the import and export of plant materials. The Federal program is administered in partnership with State regulatory authorities. Plant health inspections must be conducted, and phytosanitary certificates issued for the shipment of nursery stock within and into any State, indicating the crop is free of noxious and unwanted pests, such as fire ants, cogon grass, and other unwelcome hitchhikers. In the case of Alabama, for example, nursery stock subject to this inspection "includes all plants, trees, shrubs, vines, cuttings, and grafts, scions and buds grown or kept for or capable of propagation, distribution or sale," and "no inspection certificate shall be issued for the sale, offering for sale or movement of any nursery stock until the stock in question shall have been inspected by the Commissioner and found to be apparently free from seriously injurious plant pests" (ADAI, 2011). Each box, bundle, or package of nursery stock moved from State to State must have a valid official tag bearing a copy of the certificate of inspection and a seal of a State authority from the State of origin conspicuously attached, or an inspection tag of the U.S. Department of Agriculture. Shipments of stock not thus tagged shall be liable to confiscation. It is essential, therefore, that nursery managers work with their State authorities to understand the inspection process, and the requirements necessary for a successful inspection as well as certificate display and recordkeeping. A good source of information may be found on the website of the National Plant Board (http://nationalplantboard.org/), with a current listing of State authorities as well as regulations and other pertinent information.

Recordkeeping

Every nursery is required to maintain certain records. First, of course, are financial records so that taxes can be appropriately filed with the Internal Revenue Service. Pesticide records must be made within 14 days of application and maintained for at least 2 years. The USDA provides helpful guidelines and forms for federally required records: https://www.ams.usda.gov/rules-regulations/pesticide-records. The EPA also requires detailed records be maintained for nurseries that conduct soil fumigation which can be found on the Soil Fumigant Toolbox website: https://www.epa.gov/soil-fumigants. Nurseries should consult their State Department of Agriculture to identify other specific record requirements.

In addition, OSHA requires stringent reporting of death and hospitalization of workers injured in connection to employment. A log of injuries and posting of this log is also required. All employers must keep records of hours worked and pay records of all nonexempt employees. The addition of H2A and H2B greatly increases the recordkeeping requirements and most employers must keep these records for at least 3 years.

References

Alabama Department of Agriculture and Industries 2011. Plant industry administrative code, Chapter 80-10-1. Nursery and nursery stock. http://www.alabamaadministrativecode.State.al.us/docs/agr/80-10-1.pdf.

Department of Homeland Security, U.S. Citizenship and Immigration Services, E-Verify Home page. https://www.uscis.gov/e-verify.

Hawkins, G.L., Sumner, P.E. 2012. Pesticides storage and mixing facilities. Bulletin 1095. http://extension.uga.edu/publications/detail.html?number=B1095.

Hawkins, S.A. 2010.The agricultural producers' comprehensive guide to federal oil pollution prevention regulations. W250 – 11/10. University of Tennessee Institute of Agriculture. https://utextension.tennessee.edu/publications/Documents/W250.pdf.

The National Plant Board. 2018. http://nationalplantboard.org/

U.S. Department of Agriculture. Pesticide record keeping. https://www.ams.usda.gov/rules-regulations/pesticide-records.

U.S. Department of Labor (DOL). 2016a. E-Laws: Employment Law Guide, Wages and Hours Worked: Worker Protections in Agriculture. https://webapps.dol.gov/elaws/elg/mspa.htm.

U.S. Department of Labor (DOL). 2016b. Fact Sheet #26: Section H-2A of the Immigration and Nationality Act (INA). Washington, DC: Wage and Hour Division. https://www.dol.gov/whd/regs/compliance/whdfs26.pdf

U.S. Department of Labor (DOL). 2017. Wage and Hour Division State Labor Offices. Washington, DC: Wage and Hour Division. https://www.dol.gov/whd/contacts/State_of.htm.

U.S. Department of Labor (DOL). 2018a. Handy reference guide to the Fair Labor Standards Act. Washington, DC: Wage and Hour Division. https://www.dol.gov/whd/regs/compliance/wh1282.pdf

U.S. Department of Labor (DOL). 2018b. Minimum wage laws in the states. Washington, DC: Wage and Hour Division, U.S. Department of Labor. https://www.dol.gov/whd/minwage/america.htm.

U.S. Environmental Protection Agency. 2015. How to comply with the 2015 revised worker protection standard for agricultural pesticides: what owners and employers need to know. pesticideresources.org/wps/htc/htcmanual.pdf

U.S. Environmental Protection Agency. 2017. Soil fumigant toolbox. https://www.epa.gov/soil-fumigants.

In accordance with Federal civil rights law and U.S. Department of Agriculture (USDA) civil rights regulations and policies, the USDA, its Agencies, offices, and employees, and institutions participating in or administering USDA programs are prohibited from discriminating based on race, color, national origin, religion, sex, gender identity (including gender expression), sexual orientation, disability, age, marital status, family/parental status, income derived from a public assistance program, political beliefs, or reprisal or retaliation for prior civil rights activity, in any program or activity conducted or funded by USDA (not all bases apply to all programs). Remedies and complaint filing deadlines vary by program or incident.

Persons with disabilities who require alternative means of communication for program information (e.g., Braille, large print, audiotape, American Sign Language, etc.) should contact the responsible Agency or USDA's TARGET Center at (202) 720-2600 (voice and TTY) or contact USDA through the Federal Relay Service at (800) 877-8339. Additionally, program information may be made available in languages other than English.

To file a program discrimination complaint, complete the USDA Program Discrimination Complaint Form, AD-3027, found online at How to File a Program Discrimination Complaint and at any USDA office or write a letter addressed to USDA and provide in the letter all of the information requested in the form. To request a copy of the complaint form, call (866) 632-9992. Submit your completed form or letter to USDA by: (1) mail: U.S. Department of Agriculture, Office of the Assistant Secretary for Civil Rights, 1400 Independence Avenue, SW, Washington, D.C. 20250-9410; (2) fax: (202) 690-7442; or (3) email: program.intake@usda.gov.

USDA is an equal opportunity provider, employer, and lender.

This publication is extensively revised from the *Hardwood Nursery Guide* originally published in 1976 (U. S. Department of Agriculture Forest Service, Agriculture Handbook No. 473).

www.ingramcontent.com/pod-product-compliance
Lightning Source LLC
Chambersburg PA
CBHW042338030426
42335CB00030B/3391

* 9 7 8 1 9 5 1 6 8 2 4 9 1 *